Geisha of Gion

MINEKO IWASAKI

岩崎峰子

With Rande Brown

POCKET
BOOKS

LONDON · SYDNEY · NEW YORK · TOKYO · SINGAPORE · TORONTO

First published in Great Britain by Simon & Schuster UK Ltd, 2002
This edition first published by Pocket, 2003
An imprint of Simon & Schuster UK Ltd
A Viacom Company

5 7 9 10 8 6 4

Simon & Schuster UK Ltd
Africa House
64–78 Kingsway
London WC2B 6AH

www.simonsays.co.uk

Simon & Schuster Australia
Sydney

A CIP catalogue record for this book is available from the British Library

ISBN 0-7434-6900-3 (A-format paperback)
ISBN 0-7434-3059-X (B-format paperback)

Typeset by Palimpsest Book Production Limited,
Polmont, Stirlingshire

Printed and bound in Great Britain by
Bookmarque Ltd, Croydon, Surrey

Mineko Iwasaki, now fifty-three years old, is the mother of one daughter. She lives with her husband in a suburb of Kyoto, Japan.

Rande Brown is an internationally acclaimed translator of books on Japanese culture and philosophy.

Acknowledgements

This work would never have been accomplished without the unfailing patience and support of my husband Jin. From the initial look of surprise on his face when I first told him, many years ago, that I wanted to write a book about my experiences as a *geiko* until today, he has continually encouraged me to fully speak my mind. Through the tears, the laughter, and the squabbles I have treasured his kindness and advice.

I must also thank my daughter Koko for helping me explore questions that I had been carrying around with me for decades. She handed me the keys to unlock the gates of understanding, and for this I am truly grateful.

I would also like to express my deepest gratitude to Rande Brown for her marvellous ability to translate the complexities of the Japanese language and culture into English. It was a great joy to work with her.

Finally, my sincere appreciation goes to Emily Bestler at Atria Books for her skilful guidance in editing and shaping the text. Her insightful questions about traditional Japanese culture brought an invaluable dimension of clarity and sense to the manuscript.

Author's Note

In the country of Japan, an island nation in East Asia, there are special districts, known as *karyukai*, that are dedicated to the enjoyment of aesthetic pleasure. These are the communities where the professionally trained female artists known as *geisha* live and work.

Karyukai means 'the flower and willow world'. Each geisha is like a flower, beautiful in her own way, and like a willow tree, gracious, flexible and strong.

No woman in the 300-year history of the karyukai has ever come forward in public to tell her story. We have been constrained by unwritten rules not to do so, by the robes of tradition and by the sanctity of our exclusive calling.

But I feel it is time to speak out. I want you to know what it is really like to live the life of a geisha, a life filled with extraordinary professional demands and richly glorious rewards. Many say I was the best geisha of my generation; I was certainly the most successful. And yet, it was a life that I found too constricting to continue. And one that I ultimately had to leave.

It is a story that I have long wanted to tell.

My name is Mineko.

This is not the name my father gave me when I was born. It is my professional name, given to me when I was five years old by the head of the family of women who raised me in the geisha tradition. The surname of the family is Iwasaki. By the time I was ten years old, I had been legally adopted as the heir to the name and next in line to own the business and all its holdings.

My career began very early. Events that occurred when I was only three years old and that I will describe in more detail later, convinced me that it was what I was meant to do.

I moved into the Iwasaki geisha house when I was five and began my artistic training when I was six. I adored the dance. It became my passion! I was determined to become the best – and I did so. The dance is what kept me going when the other requirements of the profession felt too heavy to bear – literally. I weigh 90 pounds. A full kimono with hair ornaments can easily weight 40 pounds. It was a lot to carry. I would have been happy just to dance, but the exigencies of the system forced me to debut as an adolescent geisha, a *maiko*, when I was fifteen.

The Iwasaki geisha house was located in the Gion Kobu district of Kyoto, the most famous and traditional karyukai of them all. This is the community in which I spent the entirety of my professional career.

In Gion Kobu we don't refer to ourselves as geisha (meaning *artist*) but use the more specific term geiko, 'woman of art'. One type of geiko, famed throughout the world as the symbol of Kyoto, is the young dancer known as a maiko, or 'woman of dance'. Accordingly, I will use the terms geiko and maiko throughout the rest of this book.

When I was twenty I 'turned my collar', the rite of passage that signals the transformation from maiko to adult geiko. As I matured in the profession, I became increasingly disillusioned with the intransigence of the archaic system and tried to initiate reforms that would increase the educational opportunities, financial independence, and professional rights of the women who worked there. I was so discouraged by my inability to effect change that I finally decided to abdicate my position and retire, which, to the horror of the establishment, I did at the height of my success, when I was thirty years old. I closed down the Iwasaki geisha house, then under my control, packed up the priceless kimono and jewelled ornaments contained within, and left Gion Kobu. I married and am now raising a family.

I lived in the karyukai during the 1960s and 1970s, a time when Japan was undergoing the radical transformation from a post-feudal to a modern society. However, I existed in a world apart, a special realm whose mission and identity depended on preserving the time-honoured traditions of the past. And I was fully committed to doing so.

Maiko and geiko start off their careers living and training in an establishment called an *okiya* – a lodging house, usually translated as 'geisha house'. They follow an extremely rigorous regimen of constant classes and rehearsal, similar in intensity to that of a prima ballerina, concert pianist, or opera singer in the West. The proprietress of the okiya supports the geiko fully in her efforts to become a professional and then helps manage her career once she makes her debut. The young geiko lives in the okiya for a contracted period of time, usually five or seven years, during which time she repays the okiya for its investment. She then becomes independent and moves out on her own, though she continues to maintain an agency relationship with her sponsoring okiya.

The exception to this is a geiko who has been designated as an *atotori*, an heir to the house, its successor. She carries the last name of the okiya, either through birth or adoption, and lives in the okiya throughout her career.

Maiko and geiko perform at very exclusive banquet facilities known as *ochaya*, often translated literally as 'teahouse'. Here we entertain regularly at private parties for select groups of invited patrons. We also appear publicly in a series of annual performance events. The most famous of these is the *Miyako Odori* (*Cherry Dances*). The dance programmes are quite spectacular and draw enthusiastic audiences from all over the world. The Miyako Odori takes place during the month of April in our own special theatre, the Kaburenjo.

There is much mystery and misunderstanding about what it means to be a geisha or, in my case, a geiko. I hope my story will help explain what it is really like and also serve as a record of this unique component of Japan's cultural history.

Please, journey with me now into the extraordinary world of Gion Kobu.

One

I find great irony in my choice of profession.

A first-class geiko is constantly in the glare of spotlights while I spent much of my childhood hiding in a darkened cupboard. A first-class geiko uses all the skills at her command to please her audience, to make every person she comes in contact with feel wonderful while I prefer solitary pursuits. A first-class geiko is an exquisite willow tree who bends to the service of others while I have always been stubborn and contrary by nature, and very, very proud.

While a first-class geiko is adept at creating an atmosphere of relaxation and amusement, I don't particularly enjoy being with other people.

A star geiko is never, ever alone and I always wanted to be by myself.

Odd, isn't it? It's almost as if I was deliberately choosing the most difficult path for myself, one that would force me to face and overcome my personal obstacles.

In fact, if I hadn't entered the karyukai I think I would have become a Buddhist nun. Or a policewoman.

It is difficult to explain why I made the decision to enter the karyukai when I was such a little girl. Why would a small child who adores her parents decide by herself to leave them? Yet I was the one who chose to enter this profession and this workplace, thus betraying my parents.

Let me tell you how it happened, and maybe the reasons will become more transparent in the telling.

Looking back on my life I can see now that the only time I was ever truly happy was when I lived with my parents. I was secure and free, and even though I was very young, I was given my freedom and allowed to do exactly as I pleased. After I left home when I was five, I was never really alone again and spent all my time trying to please other people. All my subsequent joys and triumphs were marred by ambivalence and a dark, even tragic, underside that became part of me.

My parents were very much in love. They were an interesting match. My father came from a family of ancient aristocrats and feudal lords who had fallen on hard times, my mother from a family of pirates turned physicians who were very rich. My father was tall and lean. He was sharp-witted, active and outgoing. He was also very strict. My mother was the opposite. She was short and plump, with a lovely round face and an ample bosom. Where my father was hard, my mother was soft. However, they were both explainers, comforters, peacemakers. His name was

Shigezo Tanakaminamoto – Tanakaminamoto no Shigezo in classical Japanese usage. The Tanakaminamoto line has been in existence for fifty-two generations.

Our lineage was founded by Fujiwara no Kamatari, a man who became a nobleman during his lifetime. The Fujiwara family of aristocrats historically held the position of Regent to the Emperor. During the reign of Emperor Saga, Fujiwara no Motomi was awarded the rank of *daitoku* (the highest rank of court minister as established by Shotoku Taishi). He died in 782. His daughter, Princess Tanaka, married Emperor Saga and gave birth to a prince named Sumeru, who was eighth in the line of imperial succession. As a retainer of the Emperor, he was given the name Tanakaminamoto and became an independent aristocrat.

Minamoto is a name that, to this day, only aristocrats are entitled to use. The family went on to hold various high positions, including Court Geomancer and Official in Charge of Shrines and Temples. The Tanakaminamotos served the Imperial Order for over a thousand years.

Great changes took place in Japan in the middle of the nineteenth century. The military dictatorship that had ruled the country for 650 years was overthrown and Emperor Meiji was installed as the head of the government. The feudal system was dismantled and Japan began to develop into a modern nation state. Led by the Emperor, the aristocrats and intellectuals began a lively debate about the future of the country.

At that time, my great-grandfather, Tanakaminamoto no Sukeyoshi, was also ready for a change. He was tired of the endless factional infighting of the aristocracy and wanted to rid himself of the onerous duties his position demanded.

When the Emperor decided to move the Imperial Capital from Kyoto, where it had been for over a millennium, to Tokyo, he saw his chance. My family's roots ran deep in their home soil, and they didn't want to leave Kyoto. As head of the family, my great-grandfather made the momentous decision to give back his title and join the ranks of the commoners.

Emperor Meiji pressed him to remain in the peerage but he proudly declared that he was a man of the people. The Emperor insisted that he at least retain his name, which he agreed to do. In daily life the family now uses the shortened form of Tanaka.

Though noble in sentiment, my great-grandfather's decision was disastrous for the family's finances. Giving up his title, of course, meant forfeiting the property that went along with it. The family's estates had covered a vast area of north-eastern Kyoto, from Tanaka Shrine in the south to Ichijoji Temple in the north, an area thousands of acres in size.

My great-grandfather and his descendants never recovered from the loss. They were unable to gain a foothold in the modern economy that was propelling the country, and languished in genteel poverty, living off their savings and thriving on their outmoded sense of inherent superiority. Some of them became quite expert in the ceramic arts.

My mother Chie is a member of the Akamatsu family. In olden times, they were legendary pirates who buccaneered the trade routes around the Inland Sea and out towards Korea and China, amassing a fortune in ill-gotten gains that they managed to transform into legitimate wealth by the time my mother came along. The Akamatsu family never served any *Daimyo* (military governor), but themselves had the power and property to govern Western Japan. The family was awarded the name Akamatsu by Emperor Gotoba (1180–1239).

While adventuring in 'foreign commodities' the family gained much knowledge about medicinal herbs and their preparation. They studied the art of healing and eventually rose to become house physicians to the Ikeda clan, the feudal barons of Okayama. My mother inherited these skills from her ancestors and passed her knowledge on to my father.

My parents were both artists. My father graduated from art school and became a professional painter of textiles for high quality kimono and an appraiser of fine porcelain.

My mother loved kimono. One day, while visiting a kimono shop, she happened to run into my father, who fell in love with her on the spot. He pursued her quite relentlessly. Their class differences were such that my mother felt a relationship was impossible. He asked her to marry him three times and she refused. In the end my father got her pregnant with my eldest sister. This forced her hand and they had to get married.

At the time my father was very successful and making a lot of money. His creations attracted the highest prices and he was bringing home a good income every month. But he was giving most of this to his parents, who had little other source of funds. My grandparents lived with their extended family in an enormous home in the Tanaka section of town that was manned by a large staff of servants. By the 1930s the family had gone through most of its savings. Some of the men had tried their hand at civil servant work, but nobody was able to hold on to a job for very long. They simply had no tradition of working for a living. My father was supporting the entire household.

So, even though my father wasn't the oldest son, my grandparents insisted that he and my mother live with them when they got married. Basically, they needed the money.

It was not a happy situation. My grandmother, whose name was Tamiko, was an overbearingly flamboyant character, both autocratic and short-tempered, the exact opposite of my gentle, docile mother. My mother was the one who had been raised like a princess, but my grandmother treated her just like a servant. She was abusive to her from the start and berated her constantly for her common background. There were some notorious criminals within the Akamatsu lineage and my grandmother acted as if my mother was polluted. She didn't think the young woman was nearly good enough for her son.

Grandmother Tamiko's hobby was fencing, and she was a master at wielding the *naginata*, or Japanese halberd. My mother's docility drove the older woman crazy and she started to taunt her by threatening her openly with the curved lance of her weapon. She'd even chase her around the house! It was bizarre and frightening. On one occasion, my grandmother went too far. She repeatedly slashed through my mother's *obi* (kimono sash), severing it from her body. That was the final straw.

My parents already had three children at the time, two girls and a boy. The girls' names were Yaeko and Kikuko. Yaeko was ten and Kikuko was eight. My father was in a quandary because he didn't have enough money to support his parents as well as an independent household. He was discussing his troubles with one of his business associates, a kimono fabric dealer, who suggested that he might try, at least once, to speak to an owner of one of the karyukai establishments.

My father met with the owner of the geiko okiya, Iwasaki, of Gion Kobu, one of the best geiko houses in Japan, and one from Pontocho, another of the geiko districts in Kyoto. He found positions for both Yaeko and Kikuko and was given contract money for their apprenticeships. The girls would be trained in the traditional arts, etiquette, and decorum and fully supported in their careers. After they became fully-fledged geiko they would become independent, all debts would be cancelled, and all the money they earned would be their own. As agent and manager of their careers, the okiyas would continue to receive a percentage of their income.

My father's decision drew the family into a compact with the karyukai that was to affect all of our lives for many years to come. Unfortunately, my sisters were devastated at having to leave the safe haven of my grandparents' house. Yaeko in particular never got over her feelings of abandonment and betrayal. She remains angry and bitter to this day.

My parents then moved with my eldest brother to a house in Yamashina, a suburb of Kyoto. In the ensuing years my mother bore eight more children. In 1939, financially strapped as always, they sent another one of their daughters, my sister Kuniko, to the Iwasaki okiya as an assistant to the owner.

I was born in 1949, when my father was fifty-three and my mother was forty-four. I was the last of my parents' children, born on 2 November, a Scorpio in the Year of the Ox. My parents named me Masako.

As far as I knew, there were only eight of us. I had four older brothers – Seiichiro, Ryozo, Kozo and Fumio, and three older sisters – Yoshiko, Tomiko and Yukiko. I was not aware of the other three girls.

Located on the far side of a canal, on a large piece of land, our house was spacious and rambling. It was surrounded by woods and bamboo groves, and nestled beneath a mountain. One approached it via a concrete footbridge over the canal. There was a large round pond in front of the house bordered by a stand of cosmo bushes. Beyond that was a front yard with fig and pepper trees. Behind the house, our big back garden contained a coop full of chickens, a fish pond laden with carp, a pen for our dog Koro, and my mother's vegetable patch.

The downstairs of the house had a parlour, an altar room, a living room, a room with a hearth for dining, a kitchen, two back rooms, and my father's studio and the bath. There were two more rooms upstairs over the kitchen. My siblings all slept upstairs. I slept with my parents downstairs.

I remember one incident with glee. It was during the rainy season. The hydrangea bush next to the pond was in bloom, the bright blue in harmony with the green of the trees. It was a perfectly still day. Suddenly, big drops of rain began to plop down. I quickly gathered up my toys from under the pepper tree and ran inside the house.

Right after everyone got home it started to pour. The rain was coming down in buckets. In what seemed like minutes, the pond began to overflow its banks and the water started flooding into the house. We all rushed around in a frenzy taking up the *tatami* mats. I found the whole thing very amusing.

After we rescued all of the tatami that we could, we were each given two strawberry sweets as a treat; they had a picture of a strawberry on the wrapper. We were all running around the house, eating our sweeties. A few of the tatami mats were floating on the water. My parents got on them and started using them like rafts, propelling themselves from room to room. They were having more fun than anybody else.

The next day my father gathered us together and said, 'All right, everyone. We've got to clean up the house, inside and out. Seiichiro, you take some helpers and work out at the back, Ryozo, you can clear up the bamboo grove, Kozo, you're in charge of cleaning the tatami, and Fumio, take your baby sister Masako and get instructions from your mother. All right, everyone? Now go out there and do a good job!'

'And you, Dad, what are you going to do?' we all wanted to know.

'Someone has to stay here and man the castle,' he said.

His battle cry energised us but there was one problem. All we had had to eat the night before was those strawberry sweets and we had been too hungry to sleep. We were famished. All of our food had been lost in the flood.

When we complained to my father he said, 'An army can't fight on an empty stomach, so you'd better go out and scour for provisions. Bring them back to the castle and prepare for a siege.'

After receiving their orders, my older brothers and sisters went out and came back with rice and firewood. At that moment, I was very glad to have brothers and sisters, and grateful for the riceball I was given to eat.

Everybody stayed home from school that day and slept like there was no tomorrow.

Another day, I went to feed the chickens and collect the eggs as usual. The mother hen was named Nikki. For some reason, she became angry and chased me back into the house, where she caught up with me and pecked my leg. My father was very annoyed. He picked her up and said, 'I'm going to kill you for this.' He wrung her neck right there and then and hung her dead body under the eaves of the house by her neck. (Usually he hung chickens by their feet.) He left her there until everyone got home from school.

When my brothers and sisters saw her they all thought, Yummy! We're having chicken-in-the-pot tonight. But my father said to them sternly, 'Take a good look at this and learn something from it. This foolish creature took a bite out of our precious Masako, and it ended up dead as a result.

Remember: it is *never* acceptable to hurt other people or cause them pain. *I will not permit it!* Understand?' We all pretended that we did.

That night we had chicken casserole made from the unfortunate Nikki. I couldn't eat a single mouthful.

My father said, 'Masako, you have to forgive Nikki. Most of the time she was a good chicken. You should eat so that Nikki can attain Buddhahood.'

'But my tummy hurts. Why don't you and Mummy help Nikki become Buddha, instead.' Then I said a little prayer.

'That's a good idea. Let's do what Masako says and all eat the chicken so that it can attain Buddhahood.'

Everyone said a prayer for the bird, dug in and thoroughly enjoyed helping Nikki on the path to enlightenment.

Another time, in a rare show of conviviality, I was playing together with everyone else. We went up onto the mountain on the right side of our house, dug a big hole, then took everything out of our kitchen, all the pots and pans and dishes, and dumped them into the hole. Heaven knows why!

We then went to play near my brother's secret fort. We were having a great time when he dared me to climb the pine tree that was there. To my horror, the branch I was on broke and I fell into the pond in front of our house. My father's studio was directly opposite. He must have heard the big splash when I fell, but he didn't overreact. He simply asked calmly, 'What are you doing Masako?'

'I'm in the pond,' I gulped, coughing up water.

'It's too cold to go swimming. What if you catch a chill? I think you'd better get out now.'

'I'll get out in a couple of minutes.' My teeth were chattering.

At that point my mother showed up and took charge. 'Stop teasing her,' she told him, 'and get her out of there this instant!'

My father reluctantly hoisted me up out of the pond, dripping wet, and summarily deposited me in the bathtub.

This should have been the end of it, but then my mother went into the kitchen to make dinner. Of course, since we had removed most of the items there, she found everything gone. She called out to my father, who was taking a bath with me.

'Dear, I'm afraid there's a problem. I won't be able to make dinner. What should I do?'

'What in the world are you talking about?' he said irritably. 'Why can't you make dinner?'

'Because there's nothing here. All of our things have gone missing!'

When I overheard this conversation, I thought I'd better alert everybody to our mother's discovery so I got dressed and started to head out the door. Not quickly enough. My father grabbed me by the collar and held me fast.

Pretty soon everybody came home. (It would have been better if they didn't.) My father prepared to mete out his customary punishment in which he lined them up and hit each one over the head with a bamboo sword. I usually stood by his side while he did it, thinking, I bet *that* hurts. But not this time. That day he yelled at me: 'You too, Masako. You're part of this.' I started whimpering as he lined me up with the others. I remember saying, 'Daddy!' but he ignored me. 'This is also your doing.' He didn't hit me as hard as he hit the others but it was still a great shock. He had never struck me before.

That night, we were sent to bed without any supper. My brothers and sisters cried while they took their baths. My brother complained that he was so hungry, he floated in the bathtub like a balloon.

My parents' involvement in aesthetic pursuits meant that our house was always full of beautiful objects: quartz crystals that glittered in the sunshine, fragrant pine and bamboo decorations that we hung up for the New Year, exotic-looking tools and implements my mother used for preparing herbal medicines, shiny musical instruments like my father's bamboo *shakuhachi* flute and my mother's one-stringed *koto*, and a collection of fine handcrafted ceramicware. The house also boasted its own bathtub, the old-fashioned kind that looked like an enormous iron soup kettle.

My father was the ruler of this little kingdom. He had his studio at home, and he worked there with a few of his many apprentices. My mother had learned the traditional method of Japanese tie-dyeing known as *roketsuzome* from my father and became a professional in the field. My parents were also known for their herbal remedies. People were constantly coming over to ask them to concoct something for them.

My mother did not have a strong constitution. She

suffered from malaria and it had weakened her heart. Yet she still had the fortitude and perseverance to give birth to eleven children.

When I couldn't be with one of my parents I preferred my own company to anyone else's. I didn't even like to play with my sisters. I loved silence and couldn't stand all the noise that the other children made. When they came home from school I would go and hide or find some other way to ignore them.

I spent a lot of time hiding. Japanese houses are small and sparsely furnished by Western standards, but they have enormous cupboards. That is because we store many household items in them when not in use, such as our bedding. Whenever I was upset or uncomfortable about something, or I wanted to concentrate or just relax, I would head into the cupboard.

My parents understood my need to be alone and never forced me to play with the older ones. Of course they kept an eye on me, but they always let me have my own space.

Yet I do remember wonderful times when the family was all together. My favourite occasions were the beautiful moonlit nights when my parents would perform duets, he on the shakuhachi and she on the koto. We would gather round to listen to them play. I had no idea how soon these idyllic interludes were going to end.

But soon they did.

Two

I can identify the exact moment when things began to change.

It was a cold winter afternoon. I had just turned three. My parents had a visitor – a very old woman. I was shy in front of strangers and hid in the cupboard as soon as she stepped into the entranceway. I sat in the dark listening to their conversation. There was something oddly compelling about this woman, and I was fascinated by the way she talked.

The visitor's name was Madam Oima. She was the proprietress of the Iwasaki okiya in Gion Kobu and had come to ask if my sister Tomiko might be interested in becoming a geiko. Tomiko had visited the Iwasaki okiya a number of times, and Madam Oima could see her potential.

Tomiko was the most delicate and refined of my sisters. She loved kimono, and traditional music, and fine ceramics, and was always asking my parents questions about these things. She was fourteen at the time. I didn't understand everything they were talking about but I gathered that this lady was offering Tomiko a job.

Unbeknownst to me at that time, the Iwasaki okiya was in severe financial straits. All I knew was that my parents were treating our visitor with a marked degree of respect and that she projected the greatest air of authority of anyone I had ever met. I could feel the regard in which my parents held her.

Pulled by her voice, I slid open the cupboard door and peeked out to see who the voice was coming from. The lady noticed the movement and said, '*Chie-san*, who is in there?'

My mother laughed. 'That's my youngest, Masako.'

When I heard my name I came out into the room.

The lady looked at me for a second. Her body was very still but I saw her eyes widen. 'Oh, my goodness,' she said. 'What black hair and black eyes! And such tiny red lips! What an exquisite child!'

My father introduced us.

Madam Oima kept looking at me but addressed my father. 'You know, Mr Tanaka, I have been looking for an *atotori* (one who comes after, or successor) for a very long time and I have the oddest sensation that I may have just found her.'

I had no idea what she was talking about. I didn't know what an atotori was or why she needed one. But I felt the energy in her body change. It is said that a person who has the eyes to see can penetrate to the core of a person's character, no matter how old that person might be.

'I'm serious,' she said. 'Masako is a magnificent little girl.

I've been in this business a long time and I can tell she is a treasure. Please consider the possibility of enrolling her in the Iwasaki okiya as well. Really – I think she could have a wonderful future there. I know she's still a baby, but won't you think about allowing her to train for a career?'

Training to become a geiko in Gion Kobu is a closed system. It is organised in a way that only girls living in an okiya in Gion Kobu are able to study all the requisite disciplines with the accredited schools and teachers, and are able to meet the demands of the gruelling schedule. You cannot become a geiko while living on the outside.

My father was clearly nonplussed by this unexpected turn of events and didn't answer her right away. Finally he said, 'We will discuss your offer to Tomiko with her in depth and we will encourage her to accept your proposal, although the ultimate decision is up to her. We will get back to you as soon as she has made up her mind. But about Masako – I'm terribly sorry, but I can't even consider it. I simply won't give up another one of my daughters.' If Tomiko agreed to join the Iwasaki okiya he would, in a real sense, have already given up four of his seven girls.

Let me explain what I mean by give up. When a young girl leaves to join an okiya it is as if she is going to fulltime boarding school. In most cases she will still go home to visit her parents when she has time off from school, and they are free to visit her whenever they like. That is the usual scenario. However, when a girl is chosen to be the successor to a house and its name, she is adopted by the proprietress as her legal heir. In that case she takes the name of the okiya family and effectively leaves her birth family for good.

When she came to see us, Madam Oima was eighty years old and deeply concerned about the fact that she had not yet secured a proper successor. None of the women presently under her management were qualified, and she couldn't die without finding someone. The Iwasaki okiya owned millions of dollars' worth of property (real estate, kimono, priceless art and ornaments) and supported a staff of over twenty people. She was responsible for ensuring that the business continued. To guarantee its future, she needed an heir.

Madam Oima visited us many times that year to discuss Tomiko's enrolment. But she was campaigning to win me over as well.

My parents never discussed any of this in front of me, but I imagine they explained it all to Tomiko. Madam Oima was the woman to whom they had entrusted my oldest sister Yaeko all those years ago. Madam Oima had appointed Yaeko her atotori and raised her to be a geiko. But Yaeko had deserted Gion Kobu without fulfilling her obligations. This was a great embarrassment to my parents. They hoped Tomiko's tenure would help make up for Yaeko's defection.

There was no way for Tomiko to become the next atotori, however. At fourteen, she was considered too old. Ideally, atotori are groomed from the time they are little girls.

Nobody told me she was leaving. I suppose my parents thought I was too young to understand what was going on so they didn't try to explain it to me. All I knew was that

Tomiko left school one day, went away for the holidays the next, and never came home. These days, under modern law, a girl must complete her secondary-school education before she is allowed to enter geiko training school.

I was sorry that Tomiko had gone. She was my favourite sister, cleverer than the rest and more sensible, too.

Tomiko's move didn't curtail Madam Oima's visits, however. Despite my father's protests, she continued to pursue the matter. She kept coming back to visit and each time she did so, she asked for me again, month after month. And, month after month, my father continued, albeit politely, to refuse her.

Madam Oima used every argument she could to convince him that I would have a brilliant career with her and that he and my mother shouldn't stand in my way. She begged my father to reconsider. I specifically remember her telling him, 'The Iwasaki is by far the best okiya in the Gion, and we can provide Masako with greater opportunities than she will find anywhere else.'

Eventually Madam Oima's persistence began to wear down my father's resolve. I sensed the shift in his position.

One day I was cuddled up in my father's lap while the two of them were talking. She brought the subject up yet again, and my father laughed. 'Very well, Madam Iwasaki, it's still too soon but someday, I promise, I will bring her along to visit you. You never know, it's up to her, maybe she'll like it.' I think he said that just to put an end to her pestering.

At this point, I decided it was time for Madam Oima

to go home. I knew people usually went to the bathroom before they left the house so I turned to her and said, 'Pee.' She thought I was asking, rather than commanding, and enquired graciously if I wanted her to take me to the lavatory. I nodded, got off my father's lap, and took her hand. When we got there I said, 'There,' and marched back into the parlour.

Madam Oima came back a few moments later.

'Thank you for taking such good care of me,' she said to me.

'Go home,' I said stoutly.

'Yes, I should be going. Mr Tanaka, I'll take my leave. I think we made some real progress here today.' And with that, she left.

Although I didn't spend many years under my parents' roof, during the short time I was with them, they taught me lessons that were to serve me in good stead for the rest of my life. My father especially did everything he could to teach me the value of independence and responsibility. Above all, he instilled within me a deep sense of pride.

My father had two favourite sayings. One was a kind of proverb that says a samurai must keep to a higher standard than the common man. Even if he has nothing to eat, he pretends that he has plenty, meaning that a samurai never lets go of his pride. But he also used it to mean that a warrior never betrays weakness in the face of adversity. His other expression was 'hokori o motsu'. Hold on to your pride. Live with dignity, no matter what the circumstance.

He repeated these aphorisms so often and with such conviction that we accepted them as gospel.

Everyone says I was a strange little girl. My parents told me that I almost never cried, even as an infant. They were worried that maybe I was hard of hearing or had something wrong with my voice or was even somewhat retarded. My father would sometimes put his mouth up to my ear and speak loudly or wake me up on purpose when I was deeply asleep, to test me. I'd look startled but I still didn't cry.

As I got older they realised that I was fine, just inordinately quiet. I loved to daydream. I remember wanting to know the names of all the flowers and birds and mountains and rivers. I believed that if I asked them, they would tell me what they were called. I didn't want other people to spoil it by giving me the information. I believed that if I looked at something long enough it would talk to me. I still do.

One time my mother and I were looking at a lot of white and peach-coloured cosmos that were blooming on the other side of the pond outside our house. I asked her, 'What's the name of this flower?'

'Cosmos,' she answered.

'Hmm, cosmos. And what is this little one called?'

'That's a cosmos too,' she answered.

'What do you mean? How can two different flowers have the same name?'

My mother looked perplexed. 'Well, the name of the family of flowers is cosmos. It is the kind of flower it is.'

'But we have a family of people living in our house and they each have their own name. That means each of these flowers should have its own name too. So I want you to give each of them a name, just like you gave names to us. That way none of them will feel bad.'

My mother went over to where my father was working. 'Masako just said the oddest thing. She wants me to give a name to each one of the cosmos flowers.'

My father said to me, 'We don't need any more children, so we don't have to give them names.'

The thought that we didn't need any more children made me feel lonely.

I especially remember one beautiful May afternoon. There was a soft green breeze blowing down from the mountains to the east. The irises were in full bloom and it was perfectly quiet. My mother and I were relaxing on the front verandah. I was sitting on her lap and we were basking in the sunshine. She said to me, 'What a lovely day it is today!' I distinctly remember saying to her, 'I am so happy.'

This is the last truly blissful memory I have of my childhood.

I looked up. There was a woman crossing over the footbridge, approaching the house. She was somehow indistinct, like a mirage.

Every muscle in my mother's body tensed. Her heart began to race and she broke out in a sweat. Her smell changed. She shrunk back into herself, as though she were recoiling in terror. Her arms hugged me tighter in an instinctive gesture of protection. I sensed the danger she felt.

I watched the woman walk towards us. Suddenly I felt time stop. It was as if she was walking towards us in slow motion. I remember exactly what she was wearing. It was a dark kimono belted with an obi that had a beige, brown and black geometric pattern on it.

A sudden chill went through me and I ran inside the house to hide in the cupboard.

I couldn't believe what followed next. My father came into the room and this woman began to speak to my parents with pure hatred in her voice. They tried to answer her but she kept interrupting them, becoming increasingly strident and aggressive. Her voice got louder and louder. I didn't understand most of what she was saying but I knew that she was using a lot of bad words and very rude language. I had never heard anyone use that tone of voice before. She was like some kind of demon. Her harangue seemed to go on for hours. I didn't know who she was and couldn't imagine what my parents could have done to make her act like that. At last she left.

Afterwards, a dark cloud descended on the house. I had never seen my parents so upset. It was creepy. Dinner that night was strained. We couldn't taste our food. I was very, very scared. I crept over into my mother's lap and snuggled my face into her side.

My brothers and sisters went to bed right after dinner. As always, I stayed nestled into my mother while my parents relaxed around the table, waiting for my father to announce that it was time for us to go to bed. They hardly spoke. It got later and later and my father didn't move. Finally, I fell asleep in my mother's arms. I awoke with them and Koro the dog in their futon the next morning.

The horrible woman showed up again a little while later. This time she brought two boys with her. She left them with us and went away. All I knew about them was that they were her sons.

The older one was named Mamoru. He was a brat and I didn't like him very much. He was three years older than me, the same age as one of my brothers, and the two of them hit it off. The younger one was named Masayuki. He was only ten months older than I was. He was nice and we became friends.

The boys' mother came to visit them about once a month. She brought toys and sweets for her sons but never anything for us, even though we were children too. It made me remember my father's saying about the samurai. I couldn't stand the sight of her. There was something rapacious and cold about her eyes. When she came I would hide in the cupboard and put my hands over my ears. I wouldn't come out until she had left.

Three

My father was planning a visit to Madam Oima and asked me if I wanted to come along. I loved going on outings with him so I said yes. He assured me that we were just going for a visit and we could leave anytime that I wanted to.

I was still scared to walk over the footbridge in front of our house and my father had to pick me up and carry me. We walked to the tram stop and boarded the one bound for Sanjo Keihan Station.

My world at the time was still very small. There weren't any other houses on our side of the bridge and I didn't have any playmates. So I was wide-eyed at all the sights of the big city, at the number of houses that lined the streets of Gion Kobu and all the people that were about. It was exciting and a little bit scary. I was already on edge by the time we arrived.

The Iwasaki okiya was located on Shinbashi Street, three doors east of Hanamikoji Street, built in the elegant architectural style typical of the Kyoto karyukai. It was a deep and narrow building with transom windows overlooking the street. I thought it looked forbidding.

We entered through the *genkan* (entrance vestibule) and stepped up into the reception room.

The place was filled with women, all wearing informal kimono. I felt shy, but Madam Oima invited us in with a broad smile on her face. She was effusive in her greetings and hospitality.

Tomiko then appeared, wearing an elaborate hairdo. To my astonishment, she looked like a bride.

Then a woman came into the room attired in Western-style dress.

My father said gently, 'Masako, this is your older sister.'

'My name is Kuniko,' she told me, and smiled.

I was dumbstruck.

And then, who should walk into the room but that really nasty woman, the one I couldn't stand, the mother of the boys who were living in our house.

I started tugging on the sleeve of my father's kimono and said, 'I want to go home.' I couldn't deal with this situation.

When we got outside, my tears started to fall, slowly and steadily, and I didn't stop crying until we reached Sanjo Keihan Station. I know that's where we were because I remember seeing the little school there with the turrets on top.

We boarded the train home and I retreated into my customary silence. My father seemed to understand what

I was feeling. He didn't try to talk to me about what had happened but just put a comforting arm around my shoulder.

The minute we got home and I saw my mother I burst into tears and flung myself hysterically into her arms. After a while I extricated myself from her lap and went inside the cupboard.

My parents left me alone and I ended up spending the night buried in the dark.

The next day I came out of the cupboard but I was still very upset from my trip to the Iwasaki okiya. What I had seen of the karyukai was so different from everything I knew. My small world was beginning to shatter. I was confused and scared, and spent most of the time hugging myself, staring off into space.

About two weeks later I resumed my normal routine. I did my daily chores and went back to 'work'. When I was too big to sit in my father's lap, he had taken an orange crate, turned it into a desk for me, and put it next to his. I spent hours happily occupied by his side.

Madam Oima chose to pay us a visit on that very day. The mere sight of her sent me into a panic and I fled right back in the cupboard. It was worse than usual this time. I was so scared of going outside that I wouldn't even go out to play under the pepper tree on the other side of the pond. I clung to my parents constantly and refused to leave their sides.

But still, Madam Oima kept coming and asking for me.

This went on for a few months. My father was worried about me and tried to come up with a way to lure me back out into the world. Eventually, he hit upon a plan. One day he said to me: 'I have to make a kimono delivery in town. Would you like to come with me?' He knew how much I loved to go out with him. I was still wary of what might happen but, even though I was suspicious, I said that I would go.

He took me to a kimono fabric shop somewhere on Muromachi Street. When we walked in through the door the proprietor greeted my father with great deference. My father told me that he had some business to discuss and asked me to wait for him in the store.

The salespeople entertained me by showing me the different items that were for sale. I was fascinated by the variety and richness of the kimono and obi, and could see, clearly and in spite of my age, that my father's kimono were the most beautiful ones in the store.

I couldn't wait to tell my mother everything that had happened and, when we got home, I launched into a long-winded description of each kimono I had seen. My parents had never heard me talk for such a long stretch before and were amazed by the amount of detail I had retained. And about kimono, of all things! I made a big point of telling my mother how proud I was that my father's kimono were the best ones in the store.

My father said, 'Masako, it makes me very happy that you liked the kimono so much. I have something I need to talk to Madam Oima about. Would you come with me when I go to see her? If we get there and you don't like it, we can turn right around and come home, I promise.'

I was still vaguely disturbed at the thought of going, but I have an almost morbid compulsion to conquer whatever scares me, and I believe this trait was already evident when I was three. Thus I agreed to make the journey.

We went soon after. I was quiet but not as upset as I had been the first time. I hardly remembered any details of the house from my first visit, but the second time I went I was calm enough to pay attention to my surroundings.

We entered the house through the old-fashioned genkan that had a floor of tamped earth instead of wood. The genkan led directly into a tatami room, or reception area. There was a lovely screen at the rear of this room that hid the inner chambers of the house from view. In front of the screen was a flower arrangement. On the right side of the entranceway a tall shoe cupboard stood from floor to ceiling. Beyond that was a cupboard filled with dishes and braziers and chopsticks and other tableware. There was a wooden fridge, the old-fashioned kind that was cooled by blocks of ice.

The genkan also opened on to a corridor that ran the entire length of the house, a long earthen passageway. There was a scullery on the right side, complete with cooking stoves. The rest of the rooms were off to the left of the corridor, marching one behind the other. The first was a reception room, or parlour. Beyond that was the dining room, where the geiko family gathered to eat and relax. It had an rectangular brazier in the corner and a stairway leading up to the first floor. The sliding doors of the dining room were open, revealing a formal living room behind that contained a large standing altar. Outside the altar room was an enclosed garden.

Madam Oima invited us into the dining room. I saw a young maiko. She was wearing ordinary clothes and her face wasn't painted, but she still had traces of white make-up on her neck. We sat down across from Madam Oima at the rectangular brazier. She sat with her back facing the garden, while we visitors were treated to the view. My father bowed and paid his respects.

Our hostess kept smiling at me as she spoke with my father. 'I am happy to report that Tomiko's lessons are going well. She seems to have a natural ear and is learning to play the *shamisen* beautifully. Her teachers and I are extremely pleased with her progress.'

I heard a rustling sound coming from the earthen-floored passageway, stuck my head out to investigate and found a dog lying there.

'What's your name?' I asked him. The only response I got was a bark.

'Oh,' Madam Oima said. 'That's John.'

'Big John would be a better name for him,' I piped up.

'Well then, in that case I think we should go ahead and call him Big John,' she answered.

Just then another lady appeared. She was beautiful but had a nasty look on her face. Madam Oima called her Masako, the same name as me, but I gave her a nickname in my head: I called her Sour Puss. Madam Oima told my father that this was the geiko who was going to be Tomiko's 'Older Sister'.

'I think the name John is fine by itself,' she said in a snotty tone of voice.

'But Miss Masako thinks that Big John is a better name,' countered Madam Oima, 'and if that is what she thinks, then that is what we are going to call him. Listen, everyone. From now on I want you all to call the dog Big John.'

I remember this conversation verbatim because I was so impressed by Madam Oima's power. She could change the name of a dog, just like that. And everybody had to listen to her and do what she said. Even Sour Puss.

I immediately bonded with Big John. Madam Oima said that Tomiko and I could take him out for a walk. Tomiko told me where Big John came from. She said that some dog had had an illicit affair with a collie that belonged to a famous pickle-maker in the neighbourhood and that Big John was the result.

Someone stopped us on the street.

'Who is that beautiful little girl? Is she an Iwasaki?' the woman asked.

'No, she's just my baby sister,' Tomiko answered.

Then a few minutes later somebody else said, 'What an adorable Iwasaki!' and my sister said again, 'No, she's just my baby sister.'

This kept happening. My sister was getting very annoyed, and it was making me uncomfortable so I asked Tomiko if we could go back. Before she could answer yes Big John turned on his own and started heading for home.

Big John was a great dog. He was exceptionally intelligent

and lived until the venerable age of eighteen. I always had the feeling that he could understand me.

We returned to the Iwasaki okiya and I said to my father, 'It's time to go home, Daddy. I'm leaving.' I blurted out a polite, 'Bye,' to everyone else and, stroking Big John, proceeded to bounce out of the door. My father said a proper goodbye and followed after me.

He took my hand as we walked to the tram station. I had no idea what my father and Madam Oima had been talking about while Tomiko and I were out, but I could tell that my father was agitated and upset. I began to suspect that something was really wrong.

As soon as we got home I went straight into the cupboard and hid. I overheard my parents talking. My father said, 'You know, Chie, I just don't think I can do it. I don't think I can bear to let her go.' My mother said sombrely, 'I don't think I can either.'

After that I began to spend even more time in the darkened cupboard, my quiet womb within the bustle of family life.

That April, my oldest brother Seiichiro got a job with the national railway. The night he brought home his first pay-cheque we had *sukiyaki* to celebrate, and everyone gathered around the table to share in the feast. My father made me come out of my hiding-place and sit up to dinner.

My father was in the habit of making a little speech each night before we ate. He would recount the important events of the day and congratulate us on our achievements, such as a good mark at school or a birthday.

I was sitting in his lap when he proceeded to congratulate my brother on his independence.

'Today your brother Seiichiro begins to contribute to the household expenses. He is now an adult. I hope the rest of you children learn from his good example. When you become self-supporting, I want you to think of other people beside yourselves and contribute to their welfare and wellbeing. Do you understand what I'm saying?'

We answered in unison, 'Yes, we understand. Congratulations, Seiichiro.'

My father said, 'Very good,' and then proceeded to eat. I couldn't reach the sukiyaki from where I was sitting on his lap and I said, 'Daddy, what about me?' 'Oops, I was forgetting about Masako,' he said, and started to feed me from the sukiyaki pot.

My parents were in a good mood. As I chewed first one piece of beef and then another, I started to think about how happy they were and the more I thought, the quieter I got and the less I wanted to eat. Would it be better if I went to the Iwasaki okiya? I asked myself. How was I going to do it? How was I going to get there? I had to think of a plan.

One of my favourite outings was our annual cherry blossom viewing excursion, so I asked my parents, 'Can we go and see the cherry blossoms? And then can we visit the Iwasaki okiya?' There was no logical connection. We always picnicked under the trees that lined the banks of the canal, literally steps from our front door. But I knew the cherry blossoms would never look the same from the other side of the canal.

My father responded immediately. 'Chie, let's make a plan to see the cherry blossoms.'

'It's a lovely idea,' my mother answered. 'I'll plan a picnic lunch.'

'But right after we look at the cherry blossoms, can we visit the Iwasaki okiya?'

They knew how stubborn I was, once I got hold of an idea. My father tried to distract me.

'I think we should go to the Miyako Odori after we look at the cherry blossoms. Don't you think that's a better idea, Chie?' he asked my mother.

I interrupted before she could answer.

'I'm going to the Iwasaki okiya after we look at the cherry blossoms. I'm not going to see the Miyako Odori!'

'What are you saying, Masako?' asked my father. 'Tell me why you want to go to the Iwasaki okiya.'

'Because if we go there,' I stated, 'then that lady will stop being horrible to you and Mum. I want to go right away.'

'Hold on there a minute, Masako. The situation between that lady and Madam Oima and us has nothing to do with you. You are too little to understand what is going on, but we owe Madam Oima an enormous debt of gratitude. And your sister Tomiko has gone to the Iwasaki okiya to uphold our honour. You don't have to worry about it. It is something that we grown-ups have to take care of by ourselves.'

My father finally agreed to let me spend one night at the Iwasaki okiya. I wanted to take my favourite blanket and pillow. My mother gathered them together and packed while I sat on the front step and stared at the bridge.

It was time to go. My mother came outside to see us off. When we got to the bridge my father leaned down to pick me up and carry me as always but I said, 'No, I'm going to do it myself.'

I had never walked over the footbridge by myself. I was too afraid.

There is a canal that runs under that bridge. And in the canal is cold, clear water, a stream that comes down from Lake Biwa in the north. The water rushes through the canal as it flows towards the Nanzenji aqueduct. It courses through the aqueduct, past the miles of cherry trees lining the banks, and then drops down into the main waterway of Kyoto. It continues past the zoo and the Heian Shrine, runs along Cold Spring Avenue, and finally empties into the Kamogawa River, where it streams towards Osaka and out to the open sea.

I'll never forget walking over the bridge by myself for the first time. The contrast between the white concrete, the hand-knitted red dress my mother had made me and my red canvas shoes is burned into my memory.

Four

It was early afternoon when we got to the Iwasaki okiya. My father left soon afterwards and I sat quietly in the parlour, not saying anything but only watching and observing, riveted by the details. I did look around until I saw where the cupboard was so I had a place to escape to if necessary. But other than that I just sat very still, staring at everything around me. When people asked me something, I answered them politely, but I kept saying I was fine just where I was.

In the late afternoon Madam Oima took my hand and we went to another house. We opened the door to the entranceway and went inside. Madam Oima bowed low to a lady I had never met before. She introduced her as Madam Sakaguchi and told me I was to call her 'Mother'. Madam Oima laughed and said Mother Sakaguchi was her boss.

The woman was very friendly and we immediately hit it off.

After we returned from our visit to the Sakaguchi okiya,

it was time for dinner. This meal was served differently in the okiya from at my house. Instead of sitting around a table, everyone ate off individual trays that were arranged in a U-shape around the oblong brazier. As a guest, I assumed that I would sit next to Madam Oima. I went to do so just as Sour Puss herself came into the room and made to sit in the same place.

'That is my seat,' I piped up.

The woman was about to protest when Madam Oima said, with a big smile, 'Yes, child, that's right. Take your seat.'

I sat down next to the brazier.

Sour Puss sat down in a huff next to me and snatched up her chopsticks, beginning to eat without saying the customary grace of *itadakimasu*, which means 'I receive this food with humble gratitude.' It acknowledges the efforts of the farmers and other providers in bringing the food to the table. Madam Oima was the head of the household so no one was supposed to eat anything before she said these words and picked up her chopsticks. It was an unthinkable breach of etiquette.

'It's rude to eat before Madam Oima has said itadakimasu and taken the first bite of food,' I reprimanded her. 'You have terrible manners.'

Madam Oima interjected, 'Listen to what the child says. She has a lot to teach you.' Then she turned to the rest of the women sitting around the long brazier and said, 'Please don't any of you speak to Miss Masako unless she speaks to you first.' I couldn't believe my hostess was putting me ahead of all these fancy grown-ups.

'Well, aren't we the little princess?' hissed my rival in a stage whisper that I was obviously intended to hear.

It made me feel bad so I said, 'I can't eat this.'

Madam Oima said, 'Why? What's wrong with it?'

'I can't eat if I'm sitting next to this horrid old lady.' I stood up quietly, found Big John, and took him for a walk.

When I got back, my older sister Kuniko asked me if I wanted to eat a nice rice ball or take a bath.

'I won't eat anyone's rice balls except Mummy's and I won't take a bath with anyone but Daddy,' I answered. Then I lapsed into silence and didn't speak again for the rest of the night.

At bedtime, Kuniko wrapped me up in my favourite blanket, which was turquoise and had white tulips on it, and laid me down beside her on the futon. I still couldn't sleep without nursing, so she let me suckle her breast until I drifted off.

My father came to get me the next morning. There is an unwritten rule in the okiya that visitors are not allowed in before ten o'clock, but he turned up very early, at six-thirty.

I was thrilled to see him. I said, 'Bye, everyone,' and was out of the door like a flash. Madam Oima called after me, 'Please come again, very soon.'

'Yes, I will,' I called back.

I was annoyed at myself for answering like that because it was not what I meant to say; in fact, it was the exact opposite of what I felt. I meant to say I was *never* coming back, but I couldn't get the words out of my mouth.

My mother was so happy to see me when I got home that I thought she was going to cry. However, I didn't even wait around long enough for her to hug me, but made straight for the safety of the cupboard.

Eventually my mother tempted me out of the darkness with my favourite food, *onigiri*, a sort of rice sandwich with seaweed on the outside and a savoury treat on the inside. Pickled plums and bits of salmon are popular fillings, but my favourite was dried bonito flakes. That's the kind my mother made for me that day. Dried bonito fish is a staple of Japanese cuisine, by the way. The flakes are widely used as the basis for soup stock and to flavour other dishes.

They were delicious.

This was the beginning of my move to the Iwasaki okiya. It began with that one night. A while later I went for two nights. And then I started to visit for days at a time. The days stretched into weeks. And finally, a few months after I turned five, I moved in for good.

Five

It is difficult to express in contemporary terms the prominence, almost the sanctity, of the okiya owner and her successor within the hierarchy of Gion Kobu. The okiya owner is the queen of the realm, the atotori is the heir apparent, and the other members of the okiya are like the royal court, bound to accept the dictates of the reigning queen without argument or question. The future queen is treated with the same degree of deference.

Though not yet official, Madam Oima acted as though I were her atotori from the moment I moved into the household. She made everyone treat me as such. The other members of the okiya were there to serve me and cater to my every need. They used honorific language when they addressed me, weren't allowed to speak to me unless I spoke first, and basically had to follow my commands. I imagine that some of them were jealous of me but it was so much in everyone's best interest to please Madam Oima that I was never aware of any negative reaction to my arrival. It all seemed perfectly natural to me.

Madam Oima asked me to call her 'Auntie', which I was happy to do. I continued to sit next to her, in the place of honour, for all meals. I was always given the choicest bit of whatever food we were having, and was always served first.

Soon after I moved in, tailors began arriving to take my measurements. A few days later I had a new set of clothes, Western-style coats and dresses and Japanese kimono and obi. I didn't wear anything that wasn't handmade until I became an adult. I wore kimono around the neighbourhood, but often put on a dress to go to the Kabuki Theatre, the sumo matches, or the amusement park.

Auntie Oima spent hours playing with me and thought up endless ways to keep me amused. She let me look at the geiko's kimono whenever I wanted. If my hands were very clean she let me touch the rich embroidery, let me trace the patterns of autumn scenes and rolling waves with my fingers.

She set up a desk for me in the genkan so I could do my homework. This is where I drew my pictures and practised writing my letters, just like I had when I lived with my father.

Another nice thing we did together was to convert a stone basin in the courtyard garden into a home for gold fish. This became quite an undertaking, and we planned every aspect of it together. We found wonderful rocks and duckweed to give the fish a place to hide, and bought colourful pebbles, an ornate bridge, and a sculpture of a heron to create a fairytale environment for my pets.

One day Auntie Oima and I were outside in the garden cleaning the fish basin, which was one of my favourite things to do because I didn't have to talk to anyone else when I was doing it. I would have cleaned it every day but she wouldn't let me. She told me that the fish couldn't live in the water if it was too clear. We had to let the water stand so that the algae had time to grow. While I worked, I asked her something that had been bothering me.

'Auntie, you don't let many people speak to me, just you and Old Sour Puss. But that Yaeko lady talks to me too, whenever she wants to. And why are her sons living at my house?'

'Oh, Mine-chan, I thought you knew. Yaeko is your parents' first daughter. She is your oldest sister. Your mother and father are the boys' grandparents.'

I felt as if I was going to faint. 'That's not true! You're a liar!' I shouted. I was really upset. 'An old person like you shouldn't tell lies, because soon you are going to go to the *Enma* (the King of Hell) and he's going to rip your tongue out for not telling the truth!' I burst out crying.

Auntie Oima said as calmly and kindly as she could, 'I'm sorry, my child, but I'm afraid it's true. I didn't realise no one had told you.'

I had known there must be some reason why Yaeko kept turning up in my world, but this was worse than I had imagined. If she was my sister, then those boys were my nephews! Ugh!

'You don't have to worry about her,' Auntie Oima comforted me. 'I'll protect you.'

I wanted to believe her, but I still got a bad feeling in my stomach whenever Yaeko was around.

When I first arrived at the okiya, I stayed constantly by Auntie's side. After a few weeks, as I started to feel more at home, I began to explore my new surroundings. I decided to use the cupboard in the dining room, under the staircase, for my hideaway. This was the cupboard where Kuniko stored her bedding. I inhaled her scent whenever I nestled into the quilts. She smelled like my mother.

I journeyed up the stairs, I found a cupboard there that I also liked and decided to use it as an alternative. There were four big rooms on the first floor, and lots of dressing tables with containers of make-up for the maiko and geiko. Not particularly interesting.

I went to check out the guesthouse next. This was a great find. The main room there was the 'best' room in the okiya, reserved for important visitors. It was airy, spacious and immaculate. I was the only person in the household who was allowed to spend time there. In a sense, I was the only person living in the house who was a 'guest'.

Behind the guesthouse was a formal garden, the same size as the central garden off the altar room. I sat on the verandah for hours at a time, hypnotised by the tranquil beauty of the rocks and moss.

The bathhouse was located on the other side of the garden. It had a big modern bathtub made of fragrant *hinoki* (white cedarwood). Auntie Oima or Kuniko bathed me every night. I remember the smell of the garden air drifting into the steamy bathhouse from the window high in the wall.

Most nights I slept with Auntie Oima in the altar room; she let me suckle her breast until I fell asleep. Sometimes, when the night was especially warm or the moon particularly bright, we slept in the guesthouse instead.

Other times I slept with Kuniko in the dining room. In traditional Japanese houses, the sparsely furnished tatami rooms are used for a variety of purposes. Living rooms often serve as bedrooms as well. Kuniko was the apprentice housekeeper, and thus given the important position of keeping watch over the kitchen and hearth, the heart of the house. Accordingly, she would simply move the low tables out of the way and lay her futon down on the tatami at night. Kuniko was twenty-one when I moved into the okiya. I felt safest cuddled into her warm plumpness. She adored children and took care of me as if I were her own.

I continued waking up at six o'clock in the morning as I had with my father. Everybody in the okiya had to stay up late so no one was awake at that hour, not even the maids. Most of the time I stayed curled up in my futon and read one of the picture books that my father brought me. But sometimes I would put on my slippers and wander around.

That's when I found out where everybody slept.

The two maids moved the screen partition back and slept on the tatami in the genkan. Everybody else slept upstairs. Sour Puss had one of the middle rooms all to herself. Kuniko explained to me that that was because she was an Iwasaki. The other geiko and maiko slept together in the big front room. That's where Tomiko was. There was one other large room but no one used it for sleeping. That is where everyone got dressed.

One of the women didn't sleep in the okiya, even though she always seemed to be in the house. Her name was Taji. Everyone called her Aba, 'Little Mother'. She oversaw the meals and the clothes and the shopping and the cleaning. Aba was married to Auntie Oima's brother and lived somewhere else.

I was trying to work out the hierarchy of the household. It was very different from my own family set-up. My father cooked, my mother rested, my parents treated us all the same. I thought everyone in a family was equal. But not here.

There were two groups. Auntie Oima, Sour Puss, the geiko and maiko and I were in the first one. Aba, Kuniko, the apprentices and the maids were in the other. The first group had more power and more privileges than the second one. This disturbed me because Kuniko, whom I loved, wasn't in my group, and people whom I disliked, such as Yaeko, were.

The second group wore different clothes, used different toilets, and waited until we had finished eating before they began. They ate different food from us, too, and were relegated to sit at the edge of the dining room near the kitchen. And yet they were the ones whom I actually saw working all the time.

One day I saw a whole grilled fish sitting on Kuniko's plate. It still had its head and tail on and it looked delicious. I had never seen anything like it before. Even when I lived with my parents, we only ate fish that had been filleted – a legacy of my father's aristocratic upbringing.

'Aba, what is that?'

'It's called a dried sardine.'

'Can I have some?'

'No, my dear, sardines are not your kind of food. You wouldn't like it.'

Sardines were considered peasant fare, and I was only served the best types of fish: sole, turbot, conger eel. But a fish with a head and a tail! Now that seemed special.

'I want to eat what Kuniko is eating!' I wasn't much of a whiner, but this time I made an exception.

'That food isn't suitable for an atotori to eat,' Aba repeated.

'I don't care, it's what I want. I want to eat what other people are eating, and I want all of us to eat together.'

The next thing I knew there was a table in the dining room and, from then on, we ate our meals together, like we had at my house.

One day Auntie Oima announced that she was changing my name to Mineko. I was horrified. I knew she had the power to do this to a dog but I never imagined she would do it to me. My daddy had given me the name Masako and I didn't think anyone else had the right to change it. I told her she couldn't.

Patiently, she explained that Sour Puss's name was

Masako too, and that it would be confusing if we both had the same name. I still refused, but she wouldn't give way.

Soon after that, Auntie Oima started to call me Mineko and insisted that everyone else do the same. I wouldn't answer to it. If anyone called me Mineko I would ignore them or turn on my heels and storm into the cupboard. I was determined not to give in.

Finally, my father was sent for, to help negotiate the situation. He did his best to reason with me. 'I'll take you home if that's what you want, Masako. You don't have to put up with this. If you want to stay here, you can always pretend that they are calling you Masako when they say Mineko. But that won't be much fun. So maybe you'd better come home with me.'

While he was trying to reason with me, Sour Puss put in her pennies' worth. 'I certainly don't have any desire to adopt you, you may be sure,' she said sniffily. 'But if Auntie Oima makes you our successor I'll have no choice.'

'What does she mean, Daddy? When was I adopted? I don't belong to them, do I? Don't I belong to you?' I hadn't understood that being the atotori meant I would have to be adopted.

'Of course you do, Masako. You are still my little girl. Your last name is still Tanaka, not Iwasaki.' He tried to comfort me and then turned to Auntie Oima. 'You know, I think it might be better if I took her home for a little while.'

Auntie Oima became frantic. 'Wait a minute, Mr Tanaka! Please don't go, I beg of you! You know how much I adore her. Please don't take her away. She means so much to me. Just think about what you are doing, and try to explain the importance of the situation to Masako. I'm sure she will listen to you. Please, Mr Tanaka. *Please!*'

My father remained firm. 'I'm sorry, Auntie Oima. My daughter is a child who makes up her own mind about things. I'm not going to force her to do anything she doesn't want to do. I know this is a big opportunity, but it's my job to see that she is happy. Maybe we shouldn't rush into this. Let me think about it again.'

This was the one time I almost wavered in my resolve. But as soon as I heard his words I was overcome with guilt. Oh no, here I go again, I thought. I'm being a selfish baby. The problems are going to start all over again and it will be all my fault.

As my father stood up to leave, I told him hastily, 'Never mind, Daddy, I didn't mean it. It's all right. They can call me Mineko, really. I don't care. I'll stay right where I am.'

'You don't have to say that, Masako,' he said gently. 'Come, let's go home.'

'No, I'm going to stay here.'

When I first came to live in the Iwasaki okiya it wasn't clear to me whether Auntie Oima was going to make me into a geiko like most of the other women in the house or not. I knew she wanted me to be her atotori, but she herself wasn't a geiko so that didn't seem to be a requirement of the position.

She did talk to me often about dancing. I understood by that time that all the geiko who were dancers had begun their careers as maiko. And Auntie Oima kept telling me stories about legendary maiko of the past. I wasn't particularly interested in becoming a maiko but I really wanted to dance, not to show off to others but just because it looked like so much fun. I wanted to dance for myself.

Auntie Oima promised me that I could start taking lessons on 6-6-6: 6 June after my fifth birthday – counted as my sixth birthday in the old system, when the year you were born was considered your first. 6-6-6. In my imagination this became a magical day.

As my first day of classes drew near, Auntie Oima told me that we had to decide on who was going to be my Older Sister.

The female society of Gion Kobu is organised along the lines of nominal kinship, with seniority determined by status. Thus, regardless of age, the owners of the okiya and ochaya are referred to as mothers or aunts, while the maiko and geiko are called 'Older Sister' by anyone who has begun active service after they have. In addition, every maiko and geiko is assigned a senior sponsor who is known as her particular *onesan*, or Older Sister.

The senior geiko acts as a role model and mentor to the junior one. She oversees her artistic progress and mediates any conflicts that arise between the novice and her teachers or peers. She helps her Younger Sister prepare for her debut and accompanies her on her first professional engagements. The Onesan guides the younger woman through the intricacies of banquet room etiquette and introduces her to important customers and other people who can advance her career.

One day I overheard Auntie Oima, Mother Sakaguchi, and Sour Puss talking about my Onesan. Mother Sakaguchi mentioned Satoharu.

If it could only be her!

Satoharu was a famous geiko from the Tamaki okiya who was one of the Sakaguchi family 'Sisters'. She was a willowy, graceful beauty who was very sweet and nice to me. I still remember her exquisite dancing in *Chikubushima* (*Chikubu Island*) and *Ogurikyokubamonogatari* (*Tale of the Chestnut Horse*). I wanted to be just like her.

Then Sour Puss mentioned the dreaded Yaeko. 'But isn't Yaeko the natural choice? After all, she really *is* Mineko's older sister and belongs to our own okiya. Though we have had some problems with her in the past, I think it will work out quite well.' My heart sank.

Mother Sakaguchi countered: 'I think Yaeko's minuses outweigh her pluses. Why saddle Mineko with the taint of Yaeko's defection and divorce? Our little girl deserves better than that. Besides, the other geiko don't like Yaeko and she might end up causing Mineko more harm than good. What's wrong with Satoharu? I think she would make an excellent choice.'

As with the rest of Japanese society, personal relationships are often the key to success and Mother Sakaguchi wanted me attached to a geiko who would elevate my status within the community.

Please, everybody, listen to her, I prayed from the security of the cupboard.

But Sour Puss stood firm. 'I'm afraid that won't be possible,' she bridled. 'I don't think I could work that closely with Satoharu. I find her stuck-up and difficult. I think we would be better off going with Yaeko.'

Mother Sakaguchi tried to reason with her but the other woman had made up her mind.

I've often wondered why Masako chose the tainted Yaeko over the resplendent Satoharu. It must have had to do with issues of control. I think she felt that Yaeko would have to listen to her in ways that Satoharu never would.

And so, much to my disappointment, it was decided that Yaeko was going to be my Older Sister. It seemed there was nothing I could do to get away from her.

My mother and father visited me often at the Iwasaki okiya. My father brought me picture books and my favourite foods. Mother would bring me a hand-knitted sweater or dress. But I began to dread their visits, because their presence in the house always set off one of Yaeko's rages. She would scream that my parents were baby-sellers and throw things around the kitchen. It was terrifying to me, and made all of my efforts to protect them seem useless.

I was five years old and still subject to magical thinking. I really believed that I was the only one who could protect my parents from this madwoman. I started to ignore them when they did visit, hoping that would make them stay away. Looking back on it now, as a mother, I can only imagine how agonising my aloofness must have been for them.

Gradually, I started to find a place for myself in the Iwasaki okiya and on the streets of Gion Kobu. There were many children in the post-war neighbourhood and I made my first friends. All the surrounding adults, knowing who I was and who I might become, showered me with treats and attention. I began to feel very safe and secure under the umbrella of the Iwasaki name. I was becoming one of them.

Six

A untie Oima was a great storyteller.
   I spent many cold winter nights huddled with her
around the brazier, roasting nuts and drinking tea. Or we
would while away a summer evening fanning ourselves on
stools in the garden.

She told me how Gion Kobu came to be.

'In olden times there was an entertainment district near
the Imperial Palace, on Imadegawa Street near the river. It
was called the "willow world". In the late sixteenth century
a powerful General unified the country. His name was
Hideyoshi Toyotomi. Hideyoshi was very strict and wanted
people to work hard, so he moved the willow world away
from the palace and out of the city altogether.'

'Where did he put it?'

'He moved it south to the town of Fushimi. But people
naturally want to enjoy themselves, so a new section of
town arose to take its place.' She looked at me. 'Guess
where that was?'

'Here?'

'Clever girl! Pilgrims have been coming to Yasaka Shrine for thousands of years, to view its legendary cherry blossoms in the spring and maple leaves in the autumn. During the seventeenth century, taverns known as *mizukakejaya* opened near the Shrine for the refreshment of the visitors. These became the ochaya of today, and Gion Kobu grew up around them.'

Yasaka Shrine lies nestled in the foothills of the Higashiyama Mountains, the chain that flanks the eastern border of Kyoto. The Gion Kobu, to the west of the Shrine, is about one square mile in size. The district is crisscrossed by a neat grid of lanes. *Hanamikoji* (Cherry Blossom Viewing Path) runs through the centre of the district from north to south, and Shinmonzen Street divides it east to west. An ancient canal, bearing clear water from the eastern mountains, meanders diagonally through the neighbourhood. Shinbashi Street, on which the okiya was located, leads up to the precincts of the Shrine.

Auntie Oima told me about herself.

'I was born here, not long after Admiral Perry came to Japan. If Captain Morgan had seen me first, I bet he would have married me instead of Oyuki.'

This made us scream with laughter. Oyuki was one of the most famous geiko of all time. She had a patron named George Morgan who was an American millionaire. He ended up marrying her, they moved to Paris, and she became a legend.

'You were never as beautiful as Oyuki!' we protested.

'I was *more* beautiful!' Auntie Oima teased back. 'Oyuki was funny-looking. She had a big nose but, you know, foreigners like that kind of thing.'

There was no way we were going to believe her.

'I became a *naikai* and worked my way up to manageress of Chimoto, the famous restaurant south of Pontocho. I dreamed of owning my own establishment some day.'

Naikai are the women who oversee and serve the banquets at the ochaya and exclusive restaurants. Being a naikai is a skilled occupation in and of itself.

'And I lived here too,' Aba chimed in. 'That was before I married Uncle. We were one of the busiest establishments in Gion Kobu. You never saw such coming and going. It was a grand time.'

'We had four geiko and two maiko,' Auntie Oima added. 'One of our geiko was the biggest star in Gion Kobu. Her name was Yoneyu. She was one of the greatest geiko of them all. I hope you are going to be like her. Mineko, Mother Sakaguchi's family owned a big okiya back then,' she told me. 'My mother, Yuki Iwasaki, was associated with them, which is why the Iwasaki okiya is a branch of the Sakaguchi okiya. That's also why I always ask Mother Sakaguchi to help me decide things and why I call her Mother, even if I am ten years older than she is!' They both laughed.

Over time, the bits and pieces of the story came together into a coherent whole.

Yoneyu had a brilliant career. She was the highest earning geiko in pre-war Japan, ensuring that the Iwasaki okiya was one of the most successful houses. A classic beauty, men fell all over her. One of her sponsors was a very important Baron who kept her on a generous retainer so that she would be available to entertain him and his guests whenever he so desired.

This sort of arrangement is not unusual. Having a principal geiko at your beck and call is a major status symbol in Japanese society, and the 1930s were a time of flourishing abundance for Gion Kobu. The district attracted guests from all over, men from the highest ranks of the business world and the aristocracy. They competed with each other to help support the most popular geiko. It is somewhat similar to the patronage of say, the opera, but instead of being on the board of the opera house a man would choose to support his favorite diva. And in the same way that a patron of the opera does not expect sexual favours from the diva, the Baron supported Yoneyu solely because of the artistic perfection that she embodied and the lustre that she lent to his reputation.

However, I don't want to give the wrong impression. You can't put talented, beautiful, elegant women together with rich and powerful men and expect nothing to happen. Romantic entanglements happen all the time, some leading to marriage and others to heartache. I met the love of my life, for example, while I was working. Sour Puss, on the other hand, was constantly falling in love with customers who ended up breaking her heart.

Yoneyu herself had a long-term relationship with a wealthy and powerful man named Seisuke Nagano, the heir to a major kimono concern. It was not uncommon in pre-war Japan for successful men to have extra-marital affairs. Marriages were arranged for the purpose of continuing bloodlines, not for pleasure, and men of means often had mistresses.

Yoneyu became pregnant with Seisuke's child, and when she gave birth to a baby girl at home in the okiya on 24 January, 1923, the household met the news with great joy. A girl child was a treasure. She could be raised in the okiya and, if talented, might become a great geiko herself. She might even become an atotori. Boys, however, presented a problem. Okiya were only for women. The mother of a boy child had to move out of the okiya and live separately or give him up to foster care.

'What was Yoneyu's baby's name?' I asked.

'Her name was Masako,' Auntie Oima winked.

'You mean *Sour Puss*?' I was incredulous when she first told me this part of the story.

Even though Auntie Oima didn't have a daughter, I somehow assumed that my rival was her granddaughter.

'Yes, Mineko, Sour Puss as you call her *is* Yoneyu's daughter. She and I aren't related by blood.'

At the time that Masako was born, Auntie Oima, as Yuki's natural daughter, was in line to inherit the business. She had no children of her own and so had adopted Yoneyu as her daughter to ensure uninterrupted succession. Yoneyu was an ideal candidate for successor. She was versed in all the accomplishments of a complete geiko and was in a position to train those who came after her. She had established a large base of patrons to introduce to the geiko under her care, which would enable her to sustain and grow the business.

Maintaining an unbroken line of succession is one of the chief responsibilities of the owner of an okiya. Auntie Oima and Yoneyu had their eyes out for someone who could be next in line. Thus they were thrilled with Masako's arrival. They prayed that she would have the qualities and develop the qualifications required of an atotori.

Masako began to study *jiuta* (a classical form of Japanese music and singing) when she was three and showed a great deal of promise. When she was six she began classes in tea ceremony, calligraphy and *koto* (Japanese lute). But as she grew it became evident that she had a difficult personality. She was blunt to the point of sarcasm and not particularly friendly.

Auntie Oima confided in me later that Masako suffered terribly from the fact that she was an illegitimate child. Seisuke visited her regularly while she was growing up but he was not in a position to publicly acknowledge his paternity. She felt great shame at this, and her embarrassment only intensified her inherently melancholic nature.

Eventually Auntie Oima and Yoneyu came to the reluctant realisation that Masako was not atotori material and that, in fact, she wouldn't make a very good geiko either. They encouraged her to get married and live the life of an ordinary householder instead. Accordingly, when Masako left school she was sent to a temple finishing school to study the wifely arts. But she hated it and came home three days later. She decided to live at home until her elders found her a husband.

I don't mean to imply that a geiko can't be married. Some of the most successful geiko I knew were married and lived independently from their okiya. I was in awe of one geiko in particular, a tall, willowy woman named Ren, for the way she skilfully balanced the demands of an active career with those of a husband. But most of us found the idea too daunting and waited until we retired to get married. Others enjoyed their independence so much they never gave it up.

In 1943, when Masako was twenty, she was betrothed to a man named Chojiro Kanai. He went off to war. She stayed home and worked on her trousseau. Unfortunately, the wedding never took place. Chojiro was killed in action.

Once they passed over Masako, the family had to find someone else to be Yoneyu's successor. This is when Auntie Oima was introduced to my father by a mutual acquaintance and agreed to bring Yaeko into the Iwasaki okiya. It was 1935. Yaeko was ten years old.

In those days, Yaeko was an adorable child, outgoing and funny, and as beautiful as the Mona Lisa. Auntie Oima and Yoneyu decided to groom her to be the atotori. Because of Yoneyu's enormous success, they were in a position to make a huge investment in Yaeko's career, which they did. They brought her out as a maiko in 1938, when she was thirteen years old, under the name Yaechiyo. Before the war, girls didn't have to complete their secondary education before they became maiko. Some debuted as early as eight or nine. The two women spent three years planning Yaeko's spectacular debut into the karyukai.

Decades later, people were still talking about the magnificence of Yaeko's wardrobe. They ordered her kimono from the very best shops in Kyoto, such as Eriman. One could have built a house from the cost of one of her ensembles, and she had many. No expense was spared to provide her with the best hair ornaments and other accoutrements of a maiko's costume. Auntie Oima told me again and again how extraordinary it was. She said that Yaeko's wardrobe was a direct testimonial to the wealth and power of the Iwasaki patrons.

To mark the occasion, Yoneyu's Baron presented the thirteen-year-old Yaechiyo with a ruby the size of a peach pit. It was not a lavish gift for Gion Kobu, where patrons are generous and extravagant gifts are customary. But despite all this, Yaeko was not happy. In fact, she was miserable. She felt betrayed by our parents and hated having to work. She later told me that she felt as if she had fallen from heaven into hell.

According to Yaeko, life with Grandmother Tomiko had been bliss. My grandmother adored her and the two of them were always together. Yaeko sat in her lap while she reigned imperiously over her fifty-odd servants and assorted family members. Occasionally my grandmother would get up and shout, 'Look at this, Yaeko!' and chase my mother around with her lance. Apparently, Yaeko found this very amusing.

Yaeko says that when she was little she didn't even know

that our mother and father were her parents. She thought they were just members of my grandparents' staff and called out, 'Hey, you!' to them when she wanted something.

So it came as a terrible shock to her when she suddenly found herself living in the Iwasaki okiya, having to follow a strict regimen of lessons and protocol. She had no sympathy for the fact that what had been heaven for her was hell for my mother. And, of course, she was too young to understand their financial situation. Her anger coalesced into a burning sense of victimisation that she has carried her whole life.

I'm sure her distress was real, but I have to add that Yaeko was by no means the only daughter of the aristocracy to find herself in this predicament. Many noble families became impoverished after the Meiji Restoration and found a livelihood for their girls in the karyukai. Here was a place where they could practise the dance and tea ceremony they had learned at home, wear the quality of kimono they were used to, become financially independent, and have a chance at making a decent marriage.

Not Yaeko. She just felt cheated.

My eldest sister hid her seething resentment behind a carefully sculpted mask of flippant seductiveness. She got away with doing as little as she could and taking as much as she could get.

When she was sixteen Yaeko fell in love with one of her customers, a young man named Seizo Uehara who regularly accompanied his father to Gion Kobu. The Ueharas were from Nara where they owned a large hat company. The relationship seemed to improve her temper and, as Seizo was single, didn't pose a problem for anyone.

At first Auntie Oima and Yoneyu were satisfied with Yaeko's progress. Yoneyu was the top ranked geiko in the Gion Kobu (thus all of Japan) and Yaeko soon became number two. Yoneyu and Yaechiyo became household names throughout the country. The fortunes of the Iwasaki okiya looked bright.

But there was a problem. It soon became evident that Yaeko wasn't serious about her career. Frankly, it is possible for a maiko, especially one as stunning as Yaeko, to glide for a while on her magnificent costumes and childlike charisma, but her career can't blossom unless she capitalises on her talent. Yaeko was lazy and undisciplined. She got bored easily and didn't see things through. She hated lessons and barely paid attention during rehearsals. Her dancing wasn't getting any better. Auntie Oima told me it was making her very nervous.

They had invested so much in Yaeko, and now they were losing confidence in her as the right successor. But Yoneyu felt she had no choice. Masako was out of the running.

So, almost by default, she adopted Yaeko into the family.

And then things started to fall apart.

A year after Yaeko became a maiko, in 1939, Auntie Oima's mother Auntie Yuki died. Auntie Oima became head of the Iwasaki family. Yoneyu was still in active service and not ready to retire so Auntie Oima had to put her dreams of owning a restaurant on hold and take over the Iwasaki okiya.

That is about the time that my sister Kuniko joined the household. Kuniko was my parents' third eldest daughter and was in primary school at the time. She had a warm and nurturing personality but, unfortunately, had two flaws that prevented her from becoming a maiko. The first was her terrible eyesight: she couldn't see well enough to navigate the world without glasses. The second problem was that she had inherited my mother's physique and was short and fat. So between her eyesight and her amplitude the powers-that-be decided it would be best if she trained as a support person rather than any kind of geiko. She was sent to school and began her apprenticeship with Aba as an assistant.

On 8 December 1941, Japan entered World War Two. The war lasted for four long years during which time Gion Kobu, along with the rest of the country, suffered severe hardship. In its effort to focus the nation's resources and attention on the war effort, the government closed down the Gion Kobu for business in 1943. Many geiko went home to their families. Those that were left were conscripted to work in a munitions factory.

The Iwasaki okiya didn't own any kimono made from indigo dyed cloth (like that worn by labourers) so they made work clothes out of their old geiko costumes. They must have looked strange to people from outside the karyukai. Work clothes were ordinarily made out of cotton, never from flimsy silk. As Auntie Oima told me years later, 'Even though it was wartime, those of us who lived in Gion Kobu competed with each other over who had the most beautiful silk work clothes. We attached collars to our necklines, and braided our hair neatly in two long braids, and wore sharp white headbands. We still wanted to feel feminine. We became famous for lining up, heads held high, to go to work in the factory.'

Auntie Oima divided the okiya's possessions into three lots and sent each one to a different place for safekeeping.

Yoneyu, Masako, Yaeko and Kuniko, the core of the family, were the only people Auntie Oima allowed to remain in the okiya. She sent the remaining maiko and geiko back to their parents. The city ran out of food. Auntie Oima and Kuniko told me that they were afraid they were going to starve. They subsisted on a meagre diet of scavenged roots and a thin gruel made from water, salt, and a bit of grain.

Yaeko's boyfriend Seizo became an officer and was stationed in Japan throughout the war, during which time they continued their relationship. In 1944 she announced that she was leaving to marry him. She had not yet repaid the money the Iwasaki okiya had invested in her career but Auntie Oima didn't want to fight with her. She decided to absorb the loss and graciously let Yaeko out of her contract. This sort of breach is not unheard of but is in very bad form. She just turned her back and walked away.

Because Yaeko was legally a member of the Iwasaki family, Auntie Oima treated her like a daughter and sent her off with a proper dowry. It consisted of jewellery, including the ruby the Baron had given her, and two large dressing chests filled with valuable kimono and obi. Thus Yaeko moved to Osaka and began her new life.

In December of that same year the Iwasaki okiya suffered another blow when Yoneyu died unexpectedly of kidney disease. She was only fifty-two. Auntie Oima was left without a successor and Masako, then twenty-two, was left without a mother.

Both of the Iwasaki okiya's stars had gone out.

When the war ended on 15 August, 1945, the Iwasaki okiya was at an all-time low. There were only three women living in the spacious house: aging Auntie Oima, depressed Masako, and chubby Kuniko. That was it. Auntie Oima told me she was at her wits' end and considered closing down the okiya altogether.

But then things began to look up. The American Occupation Forces ordered Gion Kobu to reopen and the karyukai slowly came back to life. The Americans then requisitioned part of the Koburenjo Theatre as a dance hall. The military officers started to patronise the ochaya. A few of the geiko and maiko who had left the okiya during the war asked if they could return, including Koyuki, the Iwasaki geiko with the largest following. Aba too, resumed work there. The Iwasaki okiya was back in business.

I asked Auntie Oima if people had difficulty welcoming the Americans into the ochaya after we had just lost the war to them. She said it wasn't that cut and dried. Of course there was some resentment, but in general the officers were kind. Most people were happy just to have the business. And the ability to serve all honoured guests equally, without discrimination, is deeply ingrained in the psyche of the karyukai. However, she did tell me a story that seemed to portray her true feelings.

One night Koyuki was summoned to appear at a banquet for General MacArthur at the Ichirikitei. He was so taken with the kimono she was wearing that he asked if he could have it to take back to the United States with him.

The owner of Ichirikitei transmitted the request to Auntie Oima, who made the following retort: 'Our kimono are our lives. He can take the kimono if he wants, but he'll have to take me with it. He may occupy my country, but he will never occupy my soul!'

The owner of Ichirikitei conveyed the response to the General, and he never asked for the kimono again. Whenever Auntie Oima told me this story she lifted her chin up in the air and beamed. Her sense of pride was one of the things I loved about her.

I still own that kimono. It is stored safely away in a chest in my house.

The Iwasaki okiya struggled forward, along with the rest of Japan, for the next few years.

Masako was still waiting for her fiancé to come home from the war. The government did not notify Chojiro's family of his death until 1947. When Masako heard the news, she was devastated. Hugging her marriage quilt to her chest, she cried for days. Now she was truly alone, with no future prospects and nowhere to go.

After long consultations with Auntie Oima, Masako decided to become a geiko. She debuted as a *jikata* (musician) geiko in 1949, when she was twenty-six, under the name of Fumichiyo.

Even though she was quite beautiful, Fumichiyo was not skilful at charming customers. She lacked the playful artifice and sense of humour that a successful geiko needs. Being a geiko is not simply a matter of mastering one's art form. One must also have passion and enthusiasm for the profession, which requires a profound commitment, an enormous amount of work, an unflappable countenance and the presence of mind to stay calm in the midst of disaster.

None of this describes Masako. But, feeling she had no other choice, she persevered. And then she met with more misfortune. Soon after she began working, she came down with tuberculosis and had to stop for over a year. She went back to work in the early 1950s but her desultory efforts did little to improve the overall economy of the household.

Kuniko had now reached the marriageable age of eighteen. Enquiries were made and arrangements discussed, but she refused to consider any offers. It was her duty, she believed, to continue living in the Iwasaki okiya to uphold our family's honour in the light of Yaeko's defection. As things turned out, Kuniko worked in the Iwasaki okiya for the next thirty years. She remained single her entire life.

At this point, the Iwasaki okiya was barely making ends meet. The house owned a magnificent collection of costumes and retained a full staff trained to dress geiko in them, but there weren't enough geiko to put them on. The few who were there were not enough to carry the whole operation.

Auntie Oima needed to find fresh talent if the Iwasaki okiya was to survive. That is what led her to come and speak to my parents about Tomiko in the winter of 1952.

What's more, with Yoneyu dead and Yaeko gone, she had to find a successor.

Seven

A untie Oima never expected to see Yaeko again and was
totally unprepared when she reappeared at the Iwasaki
okiya, unbidden, soon after Tomiko had moved in.

She was coming back to work, she announced. Her
marriage had turned out to be a disaster and she had filed
for divorce. Seizo, it seemed, was an inveterate womaniser.
He had also got involved in some shady business deals and
lost all of their money, after which he abandoned Yaeko
with two small boys and a mountain of debt for which she
was legally responsible. Yaeko decided that reclaiming her
position in the Iwasaki okiya would solve all her problems.
She wanted Auntie Oima to pay off her debts. In return,
she would pay her back by working again as a geiko.

Had Yaeko lost her mind? Auntie Oima demanded. What
she was proposing was out of the question, for reasons
almost too numerous to name. First of all, her last name
was no longer Iwasaki; it was Uehara. As she was no longer
a member of the family, she could not be the atotori. But

even when her divorce became final, Auntie Oima would not want to reinstate her. Yaeko had shown by her own actions that she didn't deserve the mantle; she was just too selfish and irresponsible.

Secondly, when a geiko retires her career is deemed over. Yaeko would have to be entirely relaunched. It costs a small fortune to outfit a geiko and Yaeko no longer owned any costumes. If anything, she owed the Iwasaki okiya money, not the other way around. Besides, all Auntie Oima's cash reserves were being used to prepare for Tomiko's debut. She had nothing left over to pay off Yaeko's debts. In any event, Yaeko had turned her back on the okiya in a time of need and Auntie Oima had not forgiven her.

The list went on and on. Yaeko hadn't been a very good geiko when she was actively in service, so she surely wasn't going to be any better now. She hadn't taken a dance class in seven years. People didn't like her. And what about her sons? They certainly couldn't live with Yaeko in the Iwasaki okiya. The whole idea was repugnant to Auntie Oima. It was a complete breach of protocol. To the old lady, this was the most distressing thing of all.

Citing all of these reasons in vigorous detail, Auntie Oima told Yaeko no. She suggested that she either go to her in-laws for help because Yaeko and the children were actually their responsibility now, or find a job in an ochaya or restaurant, for which her training made her well-qualified.

During this rather heated exchange, Auntie Oima let slip that Tomiko was now in her care and that she was very much hoping I too would come and live with her and be her successor.

Now, Yaeko hadn't been in touch with my parents in years and didn't even know that I existed. Auntie Oima's words sent her into a fury. Not only was she being usurped by a pretender to the throne, but the pretender was another issue from her loathsome parents. She stormed out of the Iwasaki okiya and caught the next tram.

Yaeko was very cunning, and in the short ride to Yamashina she assessed her options. She now saw that it would be impossible for her to inherit the Iwasaki okiya. But she also knew that the only collateral she had against her debts was her future earnings, and that being a geiko was the quickest way for her to earn money. She had to make Auntie Oima take her back.

Now, what had the old lady said? She said she really wanted Masako to join the Iwasaki okiya.

Yaeko could read Auntie Oima like a book and she knew the system. She knew how much Auntie Oima needed me.

Maybe I can use the little brat as a bargaining chip to buy my way back in, she must have thought. And what else? Oh yes, the boys. No problem. My parents can take care of them. They owe me.

She was wearing a dark kimono belted with an obi that had a beige, brown and black geometric pattern on it. That was the day I had nestled in my mother's lap and watched her walk over the bridge and approach the house, bringing a dark cloud with her.

My parents were powerless in the face of her vehemence and their own guilt. She accused them of making babies in order to sell them. They agreed to take in her two sons.

Yaeko went back to Auntie Oima and told her she was now free to move back in and begin work. And she promised Auntie Oima that she would deliver me on a silver platter.

Auntie Oima was confused. She was willing to sponsor Yaeko if it would help bring me to her. Yaeko was lazy but she had been a big star. A tarnished star might be better than nothing. She went to talk it over with Mother Sakaguchi.

'I want to meet the child,' Mother Sakaguchi said. 'The one you fell in love with. I trust your instincts, and I think we should do what we can to bring her into the Iwasaki okiya. Let's give in for the time being and turn the tables on Yaeko so she ends up helping us. Besides, she was very popular in her day and will bring a certain amount of income and respect back to the house.'

'What about her debts? I don't have the money to cover them right now.'

'I'll tell you what I'll do. Let me pay the debt instead of you – but let's keep it between ourselves. Yaeko is not to know. She must be under your control as much as possible and I don't want any attitude from her. You can return the money to me when she pays it back to you. Agreed?'

'I humbly accept your generous offer.' Auntie Oima bowed all the way to the tatami. 'I will do everything in my power to introduce you to Masako as soon as possible.'

Yaeko was thrilled that her scheme seemed to be working. She moved back into the Iwasaki okiya and made preparations to return to work. But she didn't have any-thing to wear. The Iwasaki okiya's spare kimono were in reserve for Tomiko. Yaeko had the gall to prance out to the cupboard, where the kimono were stored, pull out a few of the best and announce, 'These will do. I'll wear these.'

Auntie Oima told me she was struck dumb by this deed. It's difficult for me to adequately express the importance of kimono in a geiko's life or to convey just how shocking Yaeko's behaviour was. Kimono, the costumes of our profession, are sacred to us. They are the emblems of our calling. Made from some of the finest and most expensive textiles in the world, kimono embody beauty as we understand it. Each kimono is a one-of-a-kind work of art that its owner has taken an active role in creating.

In general, we can tell a lot about a person from the quality of the kimono that he or she is wearing: financial status, sense of style, family background, personality. There may be little variation in the cut of a kimono but there is a tremendous variety in the colours and patterns of the materials used to make them.

There is an art, too, to matching the choice of kimono to the situation in which it is worn. Seasonal appropriateness is paramount. The canons of traditional Japanese taste divide the year into twenty-eight seasons, each of which has its own symbols. Ideally, the colours and patterns on the kimono and obi (sash) reflect the exact season – nightingales in late March, for example, or chrysanthemums in early November.

Yaeko's casual appropriation of Tomiko's kimono was a violation. It was almost as though Yaeko had assaulted Tomiko or invaded the deepest recesses of her privacy. But Auntie Oima was powerless to stop her. I hadn't yet arrived.

Yaeko went to my parents and announced that she had promised me to the Iwasaki okiya. They told her over and over again that she had no right to make that decision, but Yaeko refused to listen.

In the midst of this drama, I decided to go and live with Auntie Oima in the Iwasaki okiya. I made the decision independently, of my own free will.

Looking back on it now, I am surprised and a little impressed at how determined and resolute I was at such a young age.

Eight

On 6 June, 1954, I woke up early in the morning, just as I had when I lived with my parents. Crows were cawing overhead. There were new green leaves on the maple tree in the garden.

No one was stirring, not even the maids. I pulled out one of my books, a present from my father. I had read it to myself so many times that I could recite the words by heart.

In Japan there is a long-held custom that children destined for professional artistic careers officially begin formal training in their discipline on 6 June of the year they turn six (6-6-6). However, many children who wish to pursue a traditional art form begin lessons as early as three.

This early training is particularly characteristic of Japan's two great theatrical traditions, Noh and Kabuki. Noh drama, developed in the fourteenth century, is based on the ancient court dances that were performed as offerings to the gods. It is aristocratic, stately and lyrical. Kabuki theatre, developed two hundred years later as entertainment for the common people, is more lively than Noh and can be likened to Western opera.

Both Noh and Kabuki are performed exclusively by men. The sons of the lead actors begin training as children. Many grow up to succeed their fathers. A number of famous contemporary performers can trace their lineages back ten generations or more.

On my first day, I woke at dawn and impatiently waited until it was safe to awaken Auntie Oima. Finally the neighbourhood 'alarm clock' went off. There was a grocery store across from the okiya on Shinbashi Street. The old lady of the shop sneezed three times every morning. Very loudly. At exactly 7.30. I depended on her for years!

I nudged Auntie Oima awake. 'Can we go yet?'

'Not yet, Mineko. But there is something we have to take care of first.'

She brought out a small tin bucket. Inside the bucket were brushes, a little broom, a feather duster, tiny floor cloths, and a miniature container of scouring powder. She had thought of everything.

We went into the altar room to say our morning prayers. Afterwards, she tucked up my long sleeves with a *tasuki* string so I could work and stuck the feather duster in the back of my obi. Then she took me to the lavatory and taught me the proper way to clean a toilet.

Since this is the first responsibility that a person gives to his or her successor, handing me the toilet brush was like passing me the baton. Auntie Oima's work was now done. Mine had only just begun.

The Iwasaki okiya had three lavatories, which was quite extravagant at the time. There were two downstairs, one for geiko and guests, and one for the servants. The third one upstairs was for the residents. All three had adjoining sinks and I was responsible for keeping those spotless as well.

The task suited me perfectly. It was work I could do all by myself, and I didn't have to talk to anyone while I was doing it. It also made me feel very grown-up and productive. I was very proud of myself when I finished.

Kuniko made me a special breakfast for my big day. We finished eating at about nine o'clock. After that, Auntie Oima dressed me in a new practise kimono of red and green stripes against a white background and a red summer obi for my first meeting with my teacher. She gave me a colourfully printed silk bag containing a fan, a *tenugui*, or towel, a fresh pair of *tabi* socks wrapped in silk covers that she had sewn herself, a toy and a snack.

Mistress Kazama was the name of the dance teacher who trained the Sakaguchi family. I had met her many times at Mother Sakaguchi's house, knew she had taught both Yaeko and Satoharu, and assumed that she was going to be my teacher as well. Instead, Auntie Oima told me that we were getting ready to go to the house of the *Iemoto* (grandmistress), the Kyomai Inoueryu Iemoto, Yachiyo Inoue IV. The Iemoto was going to be my teacher.

Once everyone had finished dressing in formal attire, we set off. Auntie Oima led the way, followed by Sour Puss,

Yaeko and myself. Kuniko was in the rear, carrying my little pack. We went to Mother Sakaguchi's house and she and Mistress Kazama joined our tidy procession. It was only a few minutes' walk to the Iemoto's studio, located in her home on Shinmonzen Street.

We arrived at the studio and were ushered into a waiting room near one of the rehearsal rooms. The atmosphere of the rehearsal room was very quiet and very tense. I was suddenly startled by a loud sound. It was the distinctive noise that a closed fan makes when it is hit against a hard surface.

I was watching the lesson when the teacher reprimanded one of the students by slapping her on the arm with her fan. I bolted at the noise, instinctively looking for somewhere to hide. I soon lost my way, and got stranded in front of the bathroom. After a few moments of panic, Kuniko found me and ushered me back to the others.

We entered the studio. Mother Sakaguchi had me sit down next to her before the Iemoto in the formal posture of respect and bowed deeply. 'Ms Aiko' (her real name), 'please allow me to introduce you to this precious child. She is one of our treasures, and we pray that you will take extraordinary care of her. Her name is Mineko Iwasaki.'

The Iemoto bowed in return. 'I will do my best. And so shall we begin?'

My heart was beating fast. I had no idea what I was supposed to do and stood there, frozen to the spot. The Iemoto came over to me and said kindly, 'Mine-chan, please sit down on your heels. Straighten your back and put your hands in your lap. Very good. Now, the first thing we do is learn how to hold our *maiohgi* (dancing fan). Here. Let me show you.'

A dancer's fan is slightly larger than an ordinary one, with bamboo spines about twelve inches long. The maiohgi is kept tucked inside the left side of the obi with the top facing upwards.

'Pull your maiohgi out of your obi with your right hand, and place it on your left palm as if you were holding a bowl of rice. Then slide your hand along the body of the maiohgi to the nib, and hold the end with your right hand as though you were holding a bowl of rice. Holding the maiohgi with your right hand, lean forward and place it on the floor in front of your knees, like so and, keeping your back perfectly straight, bow, saying "*Onegaishimasu*." (Please honour my humble request to be taught.) Is that clear?'

'Yes.'

'Not yes. *Yes*.' She used the Gion pronunciation *hei* instead of the *hae* that I had been taught. 'Now you try it.'

'Yes.'

'*Yes*.'

'Yes.' I was concentrating so hard on placing my maiohgi properly that I forgot to request teaching.

'What about "*Onegaishimasu*"?'

'Yes.'

She smiled indulgently. 'All right then. Now stand up and we'll try a few steps.'

'Yes.'

'You don't have to answer yes every time I say something.'

'Uh-huh,' I nodded.

'And you don't have to keep nodding your head. Now follow me. Put your arms like this, and your hands like that, and point your eyes over there.'

And that is how it began. I was dancing.

Traditional Japanese dance looks very different from its Western counterparts. It is done in white cotton tabi socks rather than special shoes. The movements, unlike ballet, for instance, are slow and focus on one's relationship to the ground rather than the sky. Like ballet, however, the movements require highly trained muscles to perform and are taught as fixed patterns (*kata*) that are strung together to form an individual piece.

The Inoue School is considered the best school of traditional dance in Japan. The Inoue Iemoto is therefore the most powerful person in the traditional dance world. She is the standard by which all other dancers are judged.

After an appropriate interval Mother Sakaguchi said, 'Ms Aiko, that should be enough of a lesson for today. Thank you so much for your kindness and consideration.'

It seemed like a very long time to me.

The Iemoto turned in my direction. 'Good, Mine-chan. The dance we have been learning is called *Kadomatsu*. This is all we will do today.'

Kadomatsu is the first dance taught in the Inoue School to children who are beginning their lessons. The *kadomatsu* is a decoration made out of pine branches that we display in our homes as part of the New Year celebration. They are festive and have a wonderful smell. I associated them with happy times.

'Yes,' I said.

'After you say "*yes*", you should sit down and say "thank you".'

'Yes,' I said again.

'And then, before you leave the studio, you should say thank you one more time and then say goodbye and then make your final bow. Do you understand?'

'Yes, I understand. Goodbye,' I said and returned gratefully to the secure side of Mother Sakaguchi, who was grinning with delight.

It took awhile before I connected understanding and doing, and even longer before I became comfortable with the geiko dialect. The version of the Kyoto dialect I learned at home was the dialect of the aristocracy. It was even slower and softer than the variation spoken in the Gion Kobu.

Mother Sakaguchi patted me on the head. 'That was wonderful, Mineko. You did such a good job. What a clever child you are!' Auntie Oima's smile was barely hidden by her raised hand.

I had no idea what I had done to receive such praise but was glad that they both seemed so happy.

Nine

The Iwasaki okiya was one street south of Shinmonzen on Shinbashi Street, three houses east of Hanamikoji. Mother Sakaguchi lived on the other side of Hanamikoji, six houses to the west of us. The Iemoto's dance studio was north-west on Shinmonzen Street, the Kaburenjo Theatre a short stroll to the south. When I was a child I walked everywhere.

Elegant storefronts line the streets of the Gion, providing the services that the local geisha industry requires. Besides the hundreds of okiya and ochaya, there are florists and gourmet shops, art galleries and fabric stores, hair ornament and fan emporiums. The neighbourhood is dense and compact.

My life became much busier after 6-6-6. I began to take calligraphy lessons from a wonderful man named Uncle Hori who lived two houses down, and *koto*, singing, and *shamisen* lessons from his daughter, who was a master of a form of *jiuta* important to the Inoue School. The koto and shamisen are both stringed instruments that came to Japan from China.

The koto is a large thirteen-stringed lute that rests on the floor when played. The shamisen is a smaller three-stringed instrument that is played like a viola. It is used to accompany most of our dances.

Besides taking daily lessons, I also cleaned the toilets every morning, and went to dance class every afternoon.

Now that I was a big girl I had to act like the atotori. I wasn't allowed to shout or use rude language or do anything that was unbefitting to a successor. Auntie Oima started to make me use the dialect of Gion Kobu, which I had been fervently resisting. Now she corrected me all the time. I was forbidden to play rough games or run around. People cautioned me constantly against hurting myself or breaking something, especially a leg or a hand, because it would impair my beauty and my dancing.

Auntie Oima became serious about teaching me how to be her successor. Until then I had played beside her as she went about her tasks. Now she started explaining to me what she was doing. As I began to understand what was going on, I could participate in the daily routine of the Iwasaki okiya in a more conscious way.

My days began early. I still woke up before the rest of the household, and now I had a job to do. While I was working on the toilets, Kuniko got up to start breakfast and the maids appeared to begin their morning chores.

The maids cleaned the Iwasaki okiya from the outside inwards. First, they swept the street outside and then the path from the gate to the entranceway. They sprinkled water on the path and placed a fresh cone of salt next to the entrance of the house to purify it. Next they cleaned the genkan and turned everyone's sandals around so that the shoes were facing the door, ready to be worn into the outside world. Inside the house, the maids tidied up the rooms and put away the items we had used the night before. Everything was back in place before Auntie Oima arose.

Finally they prepared the Buddhist altar for Auntie Oima's morning prayers. They dusted the statues, cleaned out the incense burner, disposed of the previous day's offerings, and put new candles in the holders. They did the same for the Shinto shrine that sat on a raised shelf in the corner of the room.

People who live in Gion Kobu tend to be very devout. Our livelihood is fully vested in the religious and spiritual values on which traditional Japanese culture rests. Practically speaking, our daily lives are closely interwoven with the ceremonies and festivals that punctuate the Japanese year and we reproduce them as faithfully as possible.

Every morning, upon arising and washing her face, Auntie Oima went into the altar room and said her morning prayers. I tried to finish cleaning in time to say them with her. This is still the first thing I do in the morning.

Then, in the short time remaining before breakfast, Auntie Oima and I gave Big John a thorough petting. By this time the apprentices were up and they would help the maids finish their morning chores. Cleaning is considered a vital part of the training process in all traditional Japanese disciplines and is a required practice for any novice. It is accorded spiritual significance. Purifying an unclean place is believed to purify the mind.

After the house was in order, the maiko and geiko began to wake up. They worked late every night and were always the last ones to rise. Their income was supporting the rest of us, so they no longer had to do any housework.

Aba arrived and we had breakfast. Then everyone went her separate way. The maiko and the geiko went to the Nyokoba for lessons or to the rehearsal hall if they were training for a performance. A child is not considered a professional until she enters the Nyokoba, the special school where we train to be geiko, after leaving school early at the age of thirteen. Then the maids would get busy with their remaining duties: airing the bedding, washing the laundry, cooking, shopping. Until I began school the following year, I 'helped' Auntie Oima with the morning's business.

Auntie Oima and Aba spent the morning sorting out the schedules for all the maiko and geiko under their management. They reviewed the tallies of the previous night's appointments, made notes of income due and income received, organised requests for appearances and accepted as many engagements as the geiko's schedules would allow. Auntie Oima decided which costumes each maiko and geiko would wear that evening and Aba had to see to the coordination and disposition of the ensembles.

Auntie Oima's desk was in the dining room on the other side of her seat at the brazier. There was a separate ledger for each geiko in which she kept a running account of each woman's activities, including which outfits were worn to entertain which clients. Auntie Oima also noted any specific expenditure made on a woman's behalf, such as the purchase of a new kimono or obi. Fees for food and lessons were fixed and deducted on a monthly basis.

Most tradesmen came in the morning. Men were allowed in the Iwasaki okiya after 10 a.m., when most of the inhabitants had left. The iceman brought in the ice for the refrigerator. Kimono salesmen, caterers, bill collectors and others were greeted in the genkan. There was a bench they could sit on while conducting business. Male relatives, like my father, were allowed to come in as far as the dining room. Only priests and children were allowed deeper entry. Not even Aba's husband, Auntie Oima's younger brother, was free to come and go at his own will.

This is why the whole notion of 'geisha houses' being dens of ill-repute is so ridiculous. Men are barely allowed inside these bastions of feminine society, let alone permitted to frolic with the inhabitants after they arrive.

When the evening's schedule was set, Auntie Oima got dressed to go out. Every day she visited people to whom the Iwasaki okiya owed a debt of gratitude: the owners of the ochaya and restaurants where her geiko had performed the night before, the dance and music teachers who taught them, the mothers of allied okiya, the local artisans and craftsmen who dressed us. It took the efforts of many people to present one maiko or geiko.

This informal visiting back and forth is pivotal to the social structure of Gion Kobu. It is how the interpersonal relationships upon which the system depends are cultivated

As an infant, with my father, mother, brother, and sisters.

The concrete bridge over the canal in front of my house.
This is the same canal in which Masayuki drowned.

Aged six.

In the Gion, 1956, aged seven.

Playing a poison mushroom, aged eight (right).

Kuniko, aged thirty.

Butterfly role, aged ten.

Auntie Oima (left), Aba (centre), Aba's husband (right).

Yaeko (left), Mother Sakaguchi (right).

As a minarai, in front of the doll display that distracted me
in the ozashiki.

and maintained. Auntie Oima began to take me with her on her daily round of calls as soon as I moved in. She knew that the connections she was seeding in those meetings would serve me for the rest of my professional career, or my life, if I chose to spend it in the Gion as she had.

Most of the household gathered back at the Iwasaki okiya for lunch. We ate traditional Japanese fare (rice and fish and vegetables) and only ate Western food like steak and ice cream when we were taken out to a trendy restaurant for a treat. Lunch was the main meal of the day, since geiko can't eat a heavy meal before performing in the evening.

Maiko and geiko are not allowed to eat at a private banquet, no matter how sumptuous the delicacies displayed before them. They are there to entertain the guests – to give, not to take. An exception to this rule is when a geiko is invited to join a customer for a meal in a restaurant.

After lunch Auntie Oima or Kuniko handed out the assignments for that evening to the assembled geiko. Then each woman 'got to work' researching the people she would be entertaining that evening. If one of her customers was a politician she studied the legislature he was sponsoring; if one was an actress she read an article about her in a magazine; if one was a singer she listened to his records. Or read his or her novel. Or studied the country where the guest came from. We used all the resources at our disposal to do this. I spent many an afternoon, especially when I was a maiko, in bookstores, libraries and museums. Younger girls turned to their Older Sisters for advice and information.

Besides doing research, the geiko had to pay their courtesy calls in the afternoon, in order to remain on good terms with the owners of the ochaya and the senior maiko and geiko. If any member of the community was sick or injured, protocol demanded that they call on her promptly to voice their concern.

Kuniko took me to my dance lesson mid-afternoon.

In late afternoon the maiko and geiko returned to the Iwasaki okiya to dress, and the doors of the Iwasaki okiya were closed to outsiders for the rest of the day. The maiko and geiko took baths, arranged their hair, and applied their highly stylised make-up. Then the dressers would arrive to help them into their costumes. All of our dressers came from the Suehiroya.

Most dressers are men, and they are the one exception to the no-men-in-the-inner-apartments-of-the-okiya rule. They were allowed up to the main dressing room on the first floor. Being a dresser is a highly skilled profession, one that takes years to master. A good dresser is critical to a geiko's success. Balance is essential. When I debuted as a maiko, for example, I weighed 79 pounds. My kimono weighted 44. I had to balance the whole costume on 6-inch high wooden sandals. If one thing was out of place it could have spelled disaster.

Kimono are always worn with either wooden or leather sandals. *Okobo*, 6-inch high clog-like wooden sandals, are a distinctive part of a maiko's outfit. The height of the sandal is a counterbalance to the dangling ends of the maiko's long obi. Okobo are difficult to walk in, but the mincing gait they ensure is thought to add to the maiko's allure.

Maiko and geiko always wear white tabi socks. The big toe of the tabi is separated, like a mitten, so that the toes can grip the sandal easily. We wear socks one size smaller than our shoe size, which lends a neat and dainty appearance to the foot.

The *otokoshi* (dresser) I was given when I was fifteen was the male heir to the house of Suehiroya, an establishment that had been taking care of the Iwasaki okiya for many years. He dressed me every day for the fifteen years of my career, except for the two or three times that he was too sick to serve. He knew all of my physical idiosyncrasies, like a displaced vertebra I had received in a fall that made it painful for me to walk when my kimono and numerous accoutrements were not fitted correctly.

The whole point of the geiko enterprise is perfection, and the dresser's job is to ensure that perfection. If anything is missing, slightly out of place, or seasonally inappropriate, the dresser is the person who ultimately bears the blame.

The relationship goes far beyond the external. Because of their intimate access to the internal workings of the system, the dressers have become the standard brokers of various relationships within the karyukai such as the Elder/Younger Sister pairings. They serve as escorts in appropriate situations. And lastly, they are our friends. One's dresser often becomes one's confidant, a person one turns to for brotherly advice and counsel.

As the women completed their preparations and runners arrived with last-minute requests for appearances, the maids prepared the entranceway for the maiko and geiko's departure. They swept it thoroughly again, sprinkled it with water, and replaced the pile of salt next to the entry hall with a fresh one. In the early evening the maiko and geiko, resplendent in their magnificent attire, left for their appointments.

The house quietened down after they left. The trainees and staff ate dinner, while I practised the dance I had learned that day, the *koto* piece I was working on, and my calligraphy. After I started school I also had to do my homework. Tomiko practised the shamisen and singing. She still had to squeeze in courtesy calls to the ochaya, to pay respects to the older maiko and geiko who would be guiding her later on, and to curry favour with the managers of the teahouses where she would be working.

There were over 150 ochaya in Gion Kobu when I lived there. These elegant, beautifully appointed establishments were busy every night of the week, preparing and serving the constant round of private parties and dinners scheduled by their select roster of customers. A geiko might attend parties at as many as three or four different establishments in an evening, entailing a great deal of coming and going.

In September 1965, a party line system was installed in the Gion that linked all the okiya and ochaya. It had its own phones. They were beige and they were free. Often the house phone would ring while the apprentices were doing their homework. It was one of the maiko or geiko, calling from an ochaya, asking us to bring her something she needed for her next engagement, like a fresh pair of tabi socks or a maiohgi to replace one she had given away as a gift. No matter how sleepy they were, this was a very important part of the apprentices' day. It was the only way they got to see how a working ochaya actually functioned. And it allowed the people in the ochaya and around Gion Kobu to become familiar with the faces of the Iwasaki apprentices.

I went to sleep at a reasonable hour, but it was well after midnight by the time the geiko and maiko returned home from work. After changing out of their work clothes, they might take a bath, have a snack, and relax for a while before going to bed. The two maids who slept in the genkan woke up one after the other to take care of the geiko as they drifted in. They never lay down to uninterrupted sleep until well after two o'clock in the morning.

Ten

D ance class was the high point of my day. I couldn't wait to get there and always dragged on Kuniko's sleeve to make her hurry.

Walking into the studio was walking into another world. I was in love with the whispering of kimono sleeves, the lilting melodies of the strings, the formality, the grace, and the precision.

The genkan was flanked by a wall of wooden cubbyholes. I liked one box in particular and always hoped it would be empty so that I could put my *geta* (traditional wooden sandals) there. It was on the second to the top row, a little to the left. I decided that was my place and was out of sorts when it wasn't available.

Upstairs in the rehearsal rooms, I got ready for my lesson. First I took my maiohgi out of its case with my right hand and tucked it into the left side of my obi. With my hands positioned flat on my thighs, fingers pointed inwards, I glided soundlessly over to the *fusuma* (Japanese sliding door).

The tube-like fit of the kimono dictates a distinctive way of walking, cultivated in all well-bred women, exaggerated in the dancer. Knees slightly bent, toes come off the ground in a silent pigeon-toed shuffle that prevents the front fold of the kimono from opening and indecorously revealing a glimpse of ankle or leg. The upper half of the body is held still.

This is how we are taught to open a (Japanese sliding) door and enter the room.

Sit down in front of the door resting buttocks on heels; bring the right hand up chest high and place the fingertips of your open palm on the edge of the doorframe or in the hollow, if there is one. Push the door open a few inches, being careful not to let the hand cross the midline of the body. Bring the left hand up from the thigh and place it in front of the right. Continuing to rest the right hand lightly on the back of the left wrist, slide the door across the body, creating an opening just wide enough to pass through. Stand up and enter room. Pivot, and sit down facing the open door. Use the right fingertips to close the door to just left of midline, then, using the left hand supported by the right, close all the way. Stand up, pivot, and go to sit before the teacher. Take the maiohgi out of your obi with your right hand and place it horizontally on the floor and bow.

Placing the maiohgi between oneself and the teacher is a highly ritualistic act, indicating that one is leaving the ordinary world behind and is ready to enter the realm of the teacher's expertise. By bowing, we declare that we are prepared to receive what the teacher is about to impart.

Knowledge passes from dance teacher into the student

through the process of *mane*. This word is often translated as 'imitation', but learning to dance is more a process of total identification than one of simple copying. We repeat the movements of our teachers until we can duplicate them exactly – until, in a sense, we have absorbed the teacher's mastery into ourselves. Artistic technique must be fully integrated into the cells of our bodies if we are to use it to express what is in our hearts, and this takes many years of practice.

The Inoue School has hundreds of dances in its repertoire, from simple to more complex, but they are all composed of a fixed set of *kata*, or forms. We learn the dances before the forms as opposed to, say, ballet. And we learn the dances by watching. Once we have learned the forms, however, the teacher will introduce a new dance as a series of kata.

Kabuki, with which you may be familiar, uses an enormous repertoire of movements, postures, mannerisms, gestures, and facial expressions to portray the kaleidoscopic range of human emotion. The Inoue style, in contrast, condenses complex emotions into simple, delicate movements, punctuated with dramatic pauses.

I had the great privilege of studying with the Iemoto every day. After giving me verbal instructions, she played the shamisen and I performed the piece. She corrected me. I went off to practise on my own. When I could dance a piece to her satisfaction she gave me another. Thus we all learned at our own pace.

There were three other instructors who taught in the Iemoto's studio, all of whom were accomplished students of hers. Their names were Teacher Kazuko, Teacher Masae, and Teacher Kazue. We referred to the Iemoto as 'Big Mistress' and the others as 'Little Mistress'. Mistress Kazuko was the granddaughter of Inoue Yachiyo III, the previous Iemoto.

Sometimes we had group lessons and sometimes I took a class with another teacher. I sat in the studios for hours at a time and watched intently as other dancers had their lessons. Kuniko had to tear me out of there when it was time to go home. And then I practised for hours in the living room.

The Inoue School is, without question, the most important institution in Gion Kobu, and the Iemoto, therefore, the most powerful person. Yet Inoue Yachiyo IV wielded her authority gently, and, although she was strict, I was never scared of her. The only time I ever felt intimidated was when I actually had to perform with her on stage.

The Iemoto was remarkably unattractive. She was very short, quite plump, and had a face like an orang-utan. Yet she became exquisitely lovely when she danced. I remember thinking that this transformation, which I witnessed thousands of times, was an eloquent statement of the style's ability to evoke and express beauty.

The Iemoto's given name was Aiko Okamoto. She was born in Gion Kobu and began studying dance when she was four years old. Her first teacher soon recognised the child's ability and brought her to Inoue headquarters. The previous Iemoto, Inoue Yachiyo III, was suitably impressed with Aiko's talent and invited her to join the main studio.

There are two separate curricula in the school. One is to

train professional dancers (maiko and geiko) and the other is to train professional dance teachers. There is another set of classes for women who want to study on an amateur basis. Aiko was recruited for the teacher division.

She fulfilled her early promise and grew into a masterful dancer. At twenty-five she married Kuroemon Katayama, Inoue Yachiyo III's grandson. Kuroemon is the Iemoto of the Kansai branch of the Kanze School of Noh Theatre. The couple had three sons and lived in the house on Shinmonzen Street where I had my lessons.

In the mid-1940s Aiko was chosen to succeed Inoue Yachiyo III and given the name Inoue Yachiyo IV. (Mother Sakaguchi was on the board of regents that confirmed her selection.) She led the school until May 2000, when she retired in favour of the current Iemoto, her granddaughter, Inoue Yachiyo V.

The Inoue School of Dance was founded by a woman named Sato Inoue around 1800. She was a lady-in-waiting in the inner apartments of the Imperial Palace, an instructor to the noble house of Konoe, who taught the various forms of dance practised in court ritual.

In 1869, when the Imperial Capital was moved to Tokyo, Kyoto was no longer the political centre of Japan. However, it has continued to be the heart of the cultural and religious life of the country.

The governor of the time, Nobuatsu Hase, and the councillor Masanao Makimura enlisted Jiroemon Sugiura, the ninth-generation proprietor of Ichirikitei, the most famous ochaya in Gion Kobu, in his campaign to promote the city. Together they decided to make the dances of the Gion the centrepiece of the festivities and they approached the head of the Inoue School for advice and direction. Haruko Katayama, the third Iemoto of the school, put together a dance programme that featured the talented maiko and geiko who were her students.

The performances were so successful that the governor, Sugiura, and Inoue decided to make them an annual event called the *Miyako Odori*. In Japanese this term means 'dances of the capital' but outside Japan it is commonly referred to as the *Cherry Dance*, taking place as it does in the spring.

Other karyukai have more than one school of dance, but Gion Kobu only has the Inoue School. The Grand Master of the Inoue School is the ultimate arbiter of taste within the community, as well as the dance itself. The maiko may be our most potent symbol, but it is the Iemoto who decides what that symbol will be. Many of the other occupations in the Gion Kobu, from musical accompanist to fan-maker to stage-hand at the Kaburenjo Theatre, take their cues from the artistic direction of the head of the Inoue School. The Iemoto is the only person who is allowed to make any changes to the standard repertoire of the school or choreograph new dances.

When word spread throughout the area that I was taking lessons from the Iemoto, a buzz of expectation began to form around me that kept growing until it peaked at the time of my debut ten years later.

People talk to each other all the time in Gion Kobu. It is a bit like a small village where everyone knows everyone else's business. I am by nature very private, and this is one of the things I found distasteful about living there. But, the fact is, people were talking about me. I may have been only five years old but I was already establishing quite a reputation.

I was making rapid progress in my dance lessons. It ordinarily takes a student a week to ten days to memorise a new dance, but it took me, on average, three. I was galloping through the repertoire. It's true that I was very driven and practised more than the other girls, but it did seem as if I was blessed with a good deal of natural ability. In any event, dancing was an apt vehicle for my determination and my pride. I still missed my parents terribly and the dance became an outlet for my pent-up emotional energy.

I performed in public for the first time later that summer, when the Iemoto's non-professional students put on an annual recital called the *Bentenkai*. The name of the piece was *Shinobu Uri* (*Selling Ferns*). There were six of us dancing and I was in the middle. At one point in the performance, all the other girls held their arms in a parallel position and I had mine pointed over my head in a triangle. From the wings, Big Mistress stage-whispered, 'Keep it up, Mineko.' I thought she meant, 'Keep going,' so I continued, moving my arms into the next position. Meanwhile, all the other girls brought their arms up into triangles above their heads.

When we left the stage, I immediately turned on the other girls. 'Don't you know that we are students of the Iemoto! We are not supposed to make mistakes!'

'Whatever are you talking about, Mineko? You were the one who messed it up!'

'Don't try to blame me for your mistakes!' I shot back. It never crossed my mind that I was in the wrong.

When we got backstage I overheard Big Mistress talking to Mother Sakaguchi in measured tones: 'Please don't be upset. There's no need to punish anyone.' I assumed she was talking about the other girls.

I looked around. Everyone had left. 'Where did everybody go?' I asked Kuniko, bewildered.

'They went home,' my sister told me.

'Why?'

'Because you made a mistake and then yelled at them,' she shrugged.

'I didn't make a mistake! They did.'

'No, Mineko, you're wrong. Now listen to me. Didn't you hear Big Mistress talking to Mother Sakaguchi? Didn't you hear her tell her not to scold you?'

'No, YOU'RE WRONG. She was talking about the other girls. Not me. She wasn't talking about me.'

'Mineko! Stop being a stubborn little girl.' Kuniko rarely raised her voice. When she did I paid attention. 'You did a very bad thing and you have to go and apologise to Big Mistress. This is very important.'

I was still sure I hadn't done anything wrong, but I heeded the warning in Kuniko's voice. I went to Big Mistress's room simply to pay my respects and thank her for the performance.

Before I could say anything, she said, 'Mineko, I don't want you to worry about what happened. It's all right really.'

'You mean, umm . . .'

'That mistake you made — please just forget about it.'

That's when I got it. I *had* made a mistake. Her kindness only intensified my shame. I bowed and left the room.

Kuniko came up behind me. 'Don't get upset, Mine-chan,' she soothed, 'as long as you understand and do better next time. Let's put it behind us and go out to eat that custard.' She had promised to take us all out to Pruniet's for custard pudding after the recital.

'No. I don't want it any more.'

Big Mistress came up to us. 'Mine-chan, haven't you gone home yet?'

'Big Mistress, I can't go home.'

'Of course you can. Now, off you go.'

'I can't.'

'Yes, yes. Didn't you hear me? There's nothing to worry about.'

'Yes.' Big Mistress's word was absolute.

'Come on, let's go home,' Kuniko sighed. 'Or maybe we should go and visit Mother Sakaguchi for a while.'

Mother Sakaguchi already knew I had made a mistake. So that might be all right. I nodded.

At Mother Sakaguchi's house, she came out to greet us. 'How nice to see you,' she told us warmly. 'What a good job you did today, Mineko!'

'No, I didn't,' I mumbled. 'I was terrible.'

'You were? Why?'

'I made a mistake.'

'A mistake? Where? I didn't see any mistakes. I thought you danced beautifully.'

'Mother, can I stay here with you?'

'Of course. But first you have to go home and tell Auntie Oima where you are so she doesn't worry.'

I dragged my feet the whole way.

Auntie Oima was waiting for me in front of the brazier. Her face lit up when she saw me. 'You've been gone such a long time! Did you stop at Pruniet's for a treat? Was it yummy?'

Kuniko answered for me. 'We stopped in at Mother Sakaguchi's for a visit.'

'How nice of you! I'm sure that made her very happy.'

The kinder everyone was to me, the worse I felt inside. I was furious at myself and filled with self-loathing.

I headed into the cupboard.

The next day Kuniko took me to the little shrine at the foot of Tatsumi Bridge where I always met up with the other girls on the way to the studio. They were all there. I went up to each one and bowed. 'I am sorry that I made a mistake yesterday. Please forgive me.'

They were pretty nice about it.

The day after any public performance we are required to pay a formal visit to our teacher to say thank you. Accordingly, we went straight to Big Mistress's room when we got to the studio. I hid behind the other girls.

After we had bowed in unison and said our thanks, the Iemoto complimented us on our performance the day before. 'You did a lovely job. Please keep up the good work in the future. Practise hard!'

'Thank you, Teacher,' everyone said. 'We will.'

Everyone except me, that is. I was pretending to be invisible.

Big Mistress dismissed us and, just as I was about to heave a sigh of relief, she looked directly at me and said, 'Mineko, now I don't want you to worry about what happened yesterday.'

I was flooded with shame again and ran out into the waiting arms of Kuniko.

It may sound as if Big Mistress was trying to comfort me, but she wasn't. She wasn't that kind of teacher. She was sending me a message, loud and clear. She was telling me that it was not permissible to make mistakes. Not if I wanted to become a great dancer.

Eleven

I started school when I was six, a year after I began dance lessons. Because the school was in Gion Kobu many of the pupils came from families who were directly involved in the karyukai.

Kuniko was busy helping Aba in the mornings so one of our two maids, either Kaachan or Suzu-chan, took me to school. It only a short distance north of the Iwasaki okiya, off Hanamikoji.

This was the time of day I did my 'shopping'. It was simple, really. I went into a shop and picked out what I wanted or needed. The maid said, 'It's for the Iwasakis of Shinbashi,' and the shopkeeper handed me the item. A pencil. An eraser. A ribbon for my hair.

I didn't know what money was. For years I believed that all you had to do to get something was to ask for it. And if you said, 'It's for the Iwasakis of Shinbashi,' you could get anything at all.

By now I was becoming used to the fact that I was sort

of an Iwasaki. But then, that first year of school, Sour Puss showed up on Parents' Day instead of my mother and father. She wore a light purple kimono with a sharkskin pattern and a fancy black *haori* (a jacket-like garment worn over kimono). She had on heavy make-up and a strong perfume. Every time she fluttered her fan a cloud of scent wafted into the room. It was very upsetting.

The next day my classmates called me 'Little Miss Geiko' and said that I was adopted. I got angry because it wasn't true.

The next time there was a parents' function at school, Sour Puss was busy and Kuniko came in her place. That made me much happier.

I liked going to school. I liked learning things. But I was painfully shy and kept mostly to myself. The teachers went out of their way to play with me. Even the Principal tried to coax me out of my shell.

There was one little girl I liked. Her name was Hikari, or Sunbeam. She was extraordinary-looking. Her hair was golden blonde. I thought she was very lovely. Hikari didn't have any friends either. I approached her and we began to play together. We spent hours whispering and giggling under the ginko tree in the playground. I would have given anything for hair like hers.

Most days I tore out of school as soon as the bell rang, anxious to get to my dance lesson. I had the maid tidy up my desk for me and ran home ahead of her. But once in a while the dance teachers were busy with something else and we had an afternoon off.

One time when I wasn't busy Hikari-chan invited me to go to her house after school. I was supposed to go straight home but decided to accompany her instead.

Kaachan came to pick me up that day. She was a tattletale who had a habit of stealing things. Bother, I thought. I suppose I'll just have to trust her. 'Kaachan,' I said, 'there's something I have to do. Please go and have a cup of tea and I'll meet you back here in an hour. And promise me you won't tell Auntie Oima. Understand?'

Hikari-chan lived alone with her mother in a skinny little terraced house surrounded by neighbours. How terribly convenient, I remember thinking, to have everything and everyone so close by. Hikari's mother was gentle and warm. She served us an after-school snack. I didn't usually eat snacks. My older brothers and sisters were always scrambling to get whatever there was, so I never ate anything. In this case I made an exception.

The time flew and soon I had to leave.

I went back to Kaachan and she took me home. As soon as we arrived, it was obvious that news of my whereabouts had preceded me.

Auntie Oima was ready to explode. 'I forbid you to go there again,' she yelled. 'Do you understand, young lady? Never, ever again!'

Confused by her anger, I tried to explain. I told her all about Hikari-chan, and how sweet her mother was, and how they lived with all these nice people, and what a good time I had when I was there. But she refused to listen to anything I had to say. It was my first encounter with prejudice, and I honestly didn't understand it.

In Japan there is a group of people called the *burakumin*. They are considered unclean and inferior, somewhat like the Untouchables in India. In olden times this group took care of the dead and handled other 'polluted' substances like beef and leather. They were the undertakers, the butchers, the shoemakers. The burakumin are no longer as segregated as they once were, but were still largely confined to ghettos when I was growing up.

I had unwittingly walked over a line. Not only was Hikari-chan an outcast, but she was also a half-breed, fathered out of wedlock by an American GI. It was all too much for Auntie Oima, who couldn't contain her fear that I would be contaminated by association. Keeping my reputation unsullied was one of her major preoccupations. Hence the hysteria generated by my innocent 'transgression'.

I was very frustrated and took my anger out on poor Kaachan for tattling. I'm afraid I made her life miserable for a while. But then I started to feel sorry for her. She came from a poor family and had lots of brothers and sisters. I caught her pilfering small items from the house to send to them. Instead of telling on her, I gave her little presents so she wouldn't have to steal.

Hikari-chan and her mother moved away soon after this incident. I often wondered what became of her.

But life was too full for me to dwell on anything for very long. When I was seven I became self-conscious of the fact that I was a 'very busy person'. I always had somewhere to go, something to do, someone to see. I always felt I needed to finish whatever I was doing as quickly as possible and trained myself to be incisive and efficient. I was in an eternal rush.

My longest sprint of the day came between the end of school and the beginning of dance class. I got out of school at 2.30 p.m. Dance lessons started at 3 p.m. and I wanted to be the first one there, by 2.45 p.m. if possible. So I raced back to the okiya. Kuniko had my dance clothes ready and she changed me from Western dress into kimono. Then I bolted out of the door. Kuniko, carrying my dance bag, trailed behind me.

By this time I had grown very attached to Kuniko and was as protective of her as she was of me. I hated it when people treated her like an inferior. Yaeko was the worst offender. She called our sister ugly names like 'pumpkin face' and 'mountain monkey'. This infuriated me, but I had no idea how to combat it.

It was Kuniko's responsibility to take me to dance class and bring me home. She never missed a day, no matter how busy she was at the okiya. I had devised a whole sequence of daily rituals that I performed on my way to and from dancing school, and she patiently endured my routine. There were three things I had to do on my way to class.

First I had to take a piece of molasses candy to Mother Sakaguchi's house. (I thought up this idea by myself and put it into action.) Mother Sakaguchi gave me a snack in exchange. I put the snack in my bag for later.

Next I had to stop at the shrine and say a prayer.

Third I had to run and pet Dragon, the big white dog who lived in the florist shop.

Then I could go to my class. At the end of it, Kuniko was always waiting to take me back to the okiya. I enjoyed the route home immensely.

First we went to the florist shop and I fed the snack that Mother Sakaguchi had given me to Dragon. Then I looked around the store. I loved the flowers because they reminded me of my mother. The girl in the shop let me pick one out in exchange for bringing a treat to Dragon. I thanked her and took the flower to the owner of the take-away gourmet shop down the street. In return, she cut two slices of *dashimaki*, a sweet omelette made in the shape of a swiss roll, and gave them to me to take home.

Dashimaki was Auntie Oima's favourite snack. When I proudly handed her the package, she always grinned with delight and acted surprised. Every single day. Then she burst into song. There is a song she sang whenever she was happy, a famous jingle that goes, '*Su-isu-isu-daradattasurasurasuisuisui!*' To fool me, she would sing, '*Su-isu-isu-dara*R*attasurasurasuisuisui!*' and I had to correct her before she would eat the dashimaki. Then I would sit down and tell her everything I had done that day.

The first time I had to go to Family Court was when I was eight years old. Sour Puss took me. My mother and father were there. Before I could be adopted, the court had to ascertain that I wanted to become an Iwasaki of my own free will.

I was completely torn and unable to make a decision. The whole thing was so stressful that I was violently sick in front of everybody in the courtroom. You see, I wasn't yet ready to leave my parents.

The judge said, 'This child is obviously too young to know what she wants to do. We have to wait until she is old enough to know her own mind.'

Sour Puss took me home to the okiya.

Twelve

M y life began to revolve around going to Shinmonzen and I tried to spend as much time in the school as possible. With each passing day I became more passionate about the dance and increasingly determined to become a truly great dancer.

One day I arrived at Shinmonzen and heard Big Mistress speaking to someone in her studio. I was disappointed because I liked to have the first lesson. When I entered the room I saw that the woman, though older, was stunning. There was something about the way she carried herself. I was immediately intrigued.

Big Mistress told me to join in the lesson. The older woman bowed and welcomed me. Big Mistress taught us a dance entitled *Ebony Hair*. We practised it quite a few times. The woman was an exquisite dancer. At first I felt quite self-conscious dancing with her but soon got lost in the flow of the movements.

Big Mistress criticised my work, as always. 'That's too

slow, Mine-chan. Pick up the tempo. Your arms are sloppy. Make them tighter.' But she didn't say one word to the other woman.

After we had finished, Big Mistress introduced me to the guest. Her name was Han Takehara.

Madam Takehara was considered one of the greatest dancers of her generation. A master in a number of different schools, she penetrated to the core of the medium by pioneering an innovative style of her own. I was privileged to have danced beside her.

From the time I was little I loved to observe accomplished dancers and sought the opportunity to study with them whenever possible. This was one of the reasons I spent so much time at Shinmonzen, because dancers came from all over Japan to study with the Iemoto. Some of the women I met in those early years are now the Iemoto of their own schools. Of course, I also spent countless hours observing Inoue teachers and students at their lessons.

A few months after my first (flawed) recital, I was chosen to dance a child's role in the *Onshukai Dances* that took place that autumn. This was the first time I appeared on a public stage. I danced in the *Miyako Odori* the following spring, and continued to enact children's roles until I was eleven. Being on stage was a great education, because I got to feel and experience the dancers up close.

Unbeknownst to me, Auntie Oima invited my parents to attend every one of my performances and, as far as I know, they always came. My eyesight was so poor that I couldn't pick out individuals in the audience, but somehow I always knew they were there. Like little children everywhere, my heart crowed out to them, 'Look at me, Mum and Dad! Look at me dance! Aren't I getting good?'

We have school on Saturdays in Japan, so Sunday was my only day off. Instead of sleeping in, I got up early and ran over to Shinmonzen, because it was so much fun for me to check out what the Iemoto and the Little Mistresses did in the morning. Some days I got there at 6 a.m.! (I said my prayers and cleaned the toilets after I got back from the studio.) Children's classes started at eight o'clock on Sundays, so I had plenty of time to follow the Little Mistresses and watch what they were doing.

The first thing Big Mistress did was say her prayers, just like Auntie Oima. While she was in the altar room, the Little Mistresses cleaned the school. They wiped down the wood surfaces of the stage and the long corridors with rags and scrubbed the toilets. I was impressed. Even though they were my teachers they had to follow the same routine as I did, because they were still disciples of Big Mistress.

Big Mistress and the Little Mistresses then ate breakfast together. Then Big Mistress gave lessons to the Little Mistresses and I got to watch. This was the highlight of my week.

I also enjoyed the summers, which in Kyoto are hot and humid. As part of my training, every summer day I had to sit behind Big Mistress and cool her with a big round paper fan. I loved the job. It was a perfect chance to watch her giving lessons, uninterrupted, for long stretches of time. The other girls didn't like to do it much, but I was able to sit there for hours. Eventually Big Mistress would make me take a break. The other girls did paper/scissors/rock to decide who got the next turn. Ten minutes later I was back fanning again.

Along with the dance, I was working hard on my music. When I was ten years old I put away the koto and began to study the shamisen, a stringed instrument that has a square body and a long neck and is played with a plectrum. Shamisen music is the customary accompaniment to Kyoto-style dance, including the Inoue School. Studying the music helped me understand the subtle rhythms of the movement.

There are two words that mean dance in Japanese. One is *mai* and the other is *odori*.

Mai is considered sanctified movement, and is derived from the sacred dances of Shrine maidens that have been performed since ancient times as offerings to the gods. It can only be performed by people who are specifically trained and authorised to do so. Odori, on the other hand, is dance that celebrates the vicissitudes of human life; that commemorates joyous occasions and solemnises sad ones. It is the kind of dance commonly seen during Japanese festivals, and can be performed by anyone.

There are only three forms of dance that are termed mai: *mikomai*, dances of the Shinto Shrine maidens, *bugaku*, dances of the Imperial Court, and *Noh mai*, dances of the Noh drama. Kyoto-style dance is mai, not odori. The Inoue School is specifically associated with *Noh mai* and is stylistically similar.

By the time I was ten I was aware of these distinctions. I was proud that I was a dancer of mai and a member of the Inoue School. I was perhaps a little too proud. I became a real stickler for detail.

One cold winter day I arrived freezing at the studio and went to the *hibachi* to warm up. There was a teenage girl in the room whom I had never seen before. I could tell by her hairstyle and what she was wearing that she was a *shikomisan*. This is the term used for someone who is in the first stage of apprenticeship to become a geiko, specifically one who is under contract to an okiya. I, for example, was never called a shikomisan because I was an atotori.

The shikomisan was sitting in the coldest part of the room, near the door.

'Come and sit next to the fire,' I urged her. 'What's your name?'

'Tazuko Mekuta.'

'I'll call you Meku-chan.'

I thought she was probably five or six years older than me, but in the Inoue School seniority is determined by date of matriculation, not biological age. So she was in fact my 'junior'.

I took off my tabi. 'Meku-chan, my little toe itches.' I stuck out my foot and she respectfully stroked it.

Meku-chan was sweet and gentle and had the most striking eyes. She reminded me of my older sister Yukiko. I instantly fell in love.

Unfortunately, she didn't attend the school for very long. I missed her and was hoping to find another friend like her, so I was excited, later that winter, when I went to the hibachi and saw a new girl about Meku-chan's age sitting there. But this girl was already nestled up to the brazier and ignored me when I came into the room. She didn't even say hello. Since she was the newcomer, this was inexcusably rude.

'You can't sit next to the hibachi,' I said finally.

'And why not?' she responded indifferently.

'What's your name anyway?' I asked.

'My name's Toshimi Suganuma.' She didn't say, 'How do you do?'

I was annoyed, but I also felt it was my responsibility as her 'senior' to make her a gift of my superior knowledge and explain how we did things here in the Inoue School.

I tried to make a point. 'When did you start taking lessons?' I wanted her to realise that I had been there longer than she had and that she was supposed to treat me with respect.

But she didn't get it. 'Oh, I don't know. A while ago.'

I was trying to work out what to say to make her understand her deficiencies when she was called away to her lesson.

This was a real problem. I would have to discuss it with Auntie Oima.

I left school as soon as my lesson was over and accomplished my dog, flower, dashimaki routine as quickly as possible. Then I ran the rest of the way home.

When I gave the dashimaki to Auntie Oima, she looked

as if she was about to sing, but I stopped her. 'Don't do *suisui* today. I have a problem and I need to talk to you.' I explained my predicament in great detail.

'Mineko, Toshimi is going to make her debut before you, so she will be one of your Big Sisters one day. This means you have to respect her, and be nice to her. There is no reason for you to tell her what to do. I'm sure that Big Mistress will teach Toshimi everything she needs to know. It's not your responsibility.'

I forgot about this incident until years later. Soon after my debut as a maiko I was called to entertain at a banquet. Yuriko (Meku-chan) and Toshimi, both of whom had become top-class geiko, were in attendance. They joked good-naturedly about how self-important I had been when I was a little girl. I turned bright red from embarrassment. However, they didn't hold it against me. Both became important mentors to me in the coming years, and Yuriko was one of my only friends.

Relationships in Gion Kobu last a long time, and harmony is prized above any other social value. Though characteristic of Japanese society as a whole, the emphasis on peaceful co-existence is even more pronounced in the karyukai. I believe there are two reasons for this. The first is that our lives are so intertwined, people have no choice but to get along.

The other reason is in the nature of the enterprise. Maiko and geiko entertain powerful people from every quarter of society and from all over the world. We are de facto diplomats who have to be able to communicate with anyone.

But this doesn't mean we are doormats. We are expected to be sharp-witted and insightful. Over time, I learned how to express my thoughts and opinions without causing offence to others.

Thirteen

W hen I turned ten in November 1959 I had to appear in the Family Court again. Sour Puss accompanied me. My parents were there when I arrived. I had a lawyer whose name was Mr Kikkawa. He had greasy hair but was the best lawyer in Kyoto.

I was supposed to tell the judge where I wanted to live.

The tension of having to make the choice was still unbearable. Whenever I thought about my parents my heart ached. My father leaned over towards me and said, 'You don't have to do it, Masako. You don't have to stay with them if you don't want to.' I nodded. And then it happened again. I vomited right there in the courtroom.

This time the judge didn't stop the proceedings. Instead, he looked me in the eye and asked point blank: 'Which family do you want to belong to, the Tanakas or the Iwasakis?'

I stood up, took a deep breath, and said in a clear voice, 'I'm going to belong to the Iwasakis.'

'Are you absolutely sure that is what you want?'

'Yes, I am.'

I had already made up my mind what I was going to say but I felt awful when the words came out of my mouth. I felt terrible about hurting my parents. But I said what I said because I loved to dance. That is what tipped the balance in the Iwasakis' favour. The dance had become my life, and I couldn't imagine giving it up for anything or anyone. The reason I decided to become an Iwasaki was so that I could continue learning to dance.

I walked out of the courtroom between my parents, holding tightly onto each one's hand. I felt such guilt at my betrayal that I couldn't bear to look at either of them. I was crying. Out of the corner of my eye I saw that my parents also had tears running down their faces.

Sour Puss hailed a cab and the four of us went back to the okiya.

My father tried to comfort me. 'Maybe this is all for the best, Ma-chan,' he said. 'I am sure you are having more fun living at the Iwasaki okiya than you would at home. There are so many interesting things for you to do here. But if you ever do want to come home, let me know and I will come and get you. Any time, day or night. Just call me.'

I looked at him and said, 'I've died.'

My parents turned to leave and walked away. They were both wearing kimono. As their obis receded into the distance I cried out, 'Dad! Mum!' in my heart. But the words never made it past my lips.

When my father turned back to look at me, I fought the

temptation to run after him and, smiling through my tears, I sadly waved goodbye. I had made my choice.

That night, Auntie Oima was ecstatic. It was official. I was now the Iwasaki successor. When the paperwork was finished I would become the appointed heir. We had a huge dinner, complete with festive dishes like sea bream and red bean rice and expensive fare like steak. Many people came to offer their congratulations and brought me gifts.

The party went on for hours. I couldn't stand it any longer and went into the cupboard. Auntie Oima couldn't stop singing, '*Su-isu-isu-dararattasurasurasuisuisui!*' Even Sour Puss was laughing out loud. Everyone was overjoyed: Aba, Mother Sakaguchi, the okasan (mother) of the branch houses. Even Kuniko.

I had just said goodbye to my mother and father. For good. I couldn't believe everyone saw this as a cause for celebration. I was exhausted and my mind was a complete blank. Without thinking, I took one of the black velvet ribbons from my hair, wrapped it around my neck, pulled as hard as I could, and tried to kill myself. It didn't work. Finally, frustrated, I gave up and dissolved into a puddle of tears.

The next morning I hid the bruise on my neck and dragged myself to school. I felt completely empty. Somehow I made it through that morning and forced myself to go to dance class. When I got there, Big Mistress asked me which dance we were working on.

'*Yozakura (Cherry Blossoms at Night)*,' I replied.

'All right then, show me what you remember.'

I moved into the dance.

She began, sternly, to scold me. 'No, that's wrong, Mineko. And that. And that! Stop it, Mineko, whatever is wrong with you today? Stop it! Stop right now, do you hear me? And don't you dare cry. I can't stand little girls who cry. You are dismissed!'

I couldn't believe it. I had no idea what I had done wrong. I wasn't crying, but I was thoroughly confused. I kept apologising but she wouldn't answer me so finally I left.

I had just received my first, dreaded *otome*, and I had no idea why.

Otome, which means 'Stop!' is a punishment unique to the Inoue School. When the teacher gives you an otome you have to immediately stop and leave the studio. And she doesn't tell you when you will be allowed to return, making it an indefinite suspension. The idea that I might be forbidden to continue dancing was unbearably stressful.

I didn't wait for Kuniko but walked home by myself and went straight into the cupboard, without saying anything to anybody. I was miserable. First the courtroom and now this. Why was Big Mistress so angry?

Auntie Oima came to the cupboard door. 'What happened, Mine-chan?' she called softly.' Why did you come home by yourself?'

Then, when there was no reply: 'Mine-chan, will you be having dinner?'

'Mine-chan, would you like to take a bath?'

I refused to answer.

I heard one of the Sakaguchi maids come into the room

and say that Mother Sakaguchi needed to see Auntie Oima right away. Auntie Oima hurried off.

Mother Sakaguchi, I learned later, came right to the point. 'We have a bit of a crisis,' she told Auntie Oima. 'Ms Aiko just called. Apparently her assistant mixed up the titles of two pieces, one that Mineko had just finished and one that she is learning. Miss Kawabata told Mineko that *Sakuramiyotote* (*Cherry Blossom Viewing*) was *Yozakura* (*Cherry Blossoms at Night*) and vice versa. So Mineko danced the wrong dance today and Aiko gave her an otome. Is Mineko all right?'

'So that's what happened. No, she's not all right. She's in the cupboard and won't talk to me. I think she's really upset.'

'What are we going to do if she threatens to leave?'

'We'll have to convince her not to.'

'Go home and do your best to get her out of the cupboard.'

In the meantime, after thinking about it, I concluded that I must have been given the otome because I wasn't trying hard enough. So, right there inside the cupboard, I started to rehearse the dance I was learning and the dance I had just finished. I practised them for hours, telling myself to concentrate. If I dance these perfectly tomorrow, I thought, Big Mistress will be so surprised that maybe she will forget about the otome.

But, as with many things in Gion Kobu, it was not so simple. I couldn't just go back to class as if nothing had happened. It didn't matter whose fault it was. I had received the otome so my elders had to petition for my continued enrolment. Off we trooped to Shinmonzen – Mother Sakaguchi, Auntie Oima, Mistress Kasama, Sour Puss, Yaeko, Kun-chan and me.

Mother Sakaguchi bowed and addressed Big Mistress. 'I am so sorry for the unfortunate situation that occurred yesterday. We entreat you to let our Mineko remain a student in your esteemed school.'

No one said a word about what had actually happened. The reason wasn't important. What was important was that everyone should save face and that I should be allowed to continue my training without interruption.

'Very well, Mother Sakaguchi, I will do as you ask. Mineko, please show us what you are working on.'

I danced *Cherry Blossom Viewing*. And then, without being asked, I danced *Cherry Blossoms at Night*. I did well. When I finished, the room was quiet. I looked around at the mixture of emotions on the women's faces.

It struck me that the adult world was a very complicated place.

I now understand that Big Mistress employed the otome as a powerful teaching tool. She gave me an otome whenever she wanted to force me to push through to the next level of artistry; she consciously used the terror of the otome to galvanise my spirit. It was a test. Would I come back stronger? Or would I give up? I don't think this is a particularly enlightened educational philosophy, but in my case at least, it always had the desired effect.

Big Mistress never gave otome to mediocre dancers, only to those of us whom she was grooming for major roles.

The only person who suffered actual consequences from my first otome was the teacher who had given me the wrong information. She was never allowed to instruct me again.

My adoption officially came through on 15 April, 1960. As I had been living in the Iwasaki okiya for the last five years, the change in status didn't have a great effect on my daily routine, except for the fact that now I had to sleep upstairs with old Sour Puss in her room.

I had come all the way across the bridge. My childhood home was behind me. The world of the dance lay ahead.

Fourteen

The only pleasant thing about Yaeko being in the Iwasaki okiya was that her son Masayuki sometimes came to visit. Sour Puss asked Masayuki what he wanted for his thirteenth birthday. He was a very good student and confessed that what he wanted more than anything was a world encyclopedia.

He came to the Iwasaki okiya on his birthday, 9 January, so she could give him the present. Masayuki was delighted. We sat in the guesthouse for hours, looking through the fact-filled pages together.

Formal Japanese reception rooms feature an alcove called a *tokonoma*, which is used to display treasured objects. Usually these include a hanging scroll depicting a seasonal motif and flowers artfully arranged in a suitable vase. I still remember the scroll that was hanging in the tokonoma that day. It was a New Year's image, a painting of the sun rising over the mountains. A crane flew across the sun. The cushions we were sitting on were covered in warm brown silk. Had it been summer they would have been covered in cool blue linen.

Six days later, around eleven in the morning, the telephone rang. As soon as I heard it ring I had a horrible premonition. I knew something bad had happened. The phone call was from my father. He told us that Masayuki was missing. That morning he had gone to the store to buy tofu for breakfast and never came home. They couldn't find him anywhere.

Yaeko was attending a luncheon for some foreign ambassadors at Hyotei, an exclusive restaurant that has a 400-year-old history, near Nanzenji. After telling my father where she was, Kuniko, Tomiko and I raced home.

When we got to our neighbourhood we were greeted by a large crowd of policemen and firemen, hovering around the edge of the canal. The officers had found fingernail scratches on the steep embankment, and the pebbles on the bank were disturbed. The officials concluded that Masayuki had tripped and fallen, and, even though they couldn't find a body, they assumed that he had drowned. There was no way anyone could last more than a few minutes in that freezing cold water.

My brain and heart stopped dead. I couldn't believe it. The canal. The one that gave us tiny clams for miso soup. The one with the beautiful cherry blossoms. The one that protected our house from the rest of the world. That canal had swallowed my friend. More than my friend. My nephew. I went numb with shock.

My parents were clearly devastated. My father adored his

grandson and I couldn't bear to look at the pain in his face. I wanted to comfort him but I was no longer his daughter. I hadn't seen my parents in the two years since that day in court when I declared that I was an Iwasaki, not a Tanaka, and I felt awkward. I didn't know how I was supposed to act. I wished that I had died instead of Masayuki.

Yaeko waited until the luncheon was over before coming out to the house. To this day I still can't understand why she continued to sit in that restaurant, eating food and making clever conversation, when she knew that her son was missing. I know the room where she was sitting. It overlooks a garden. The garden has a pond, which is fed by a small stream. The stream's water comes from the same canal that took her son's life.

When Yaeko finally arrived at around three o'clock, she pointed at me and began screaming like a she-devil. 'It should have been you! *You* are the one who should have died, you worthless piece of nothing, not my Masayuki!'

At that moment, I couldn't have agreed with her more. I would have given anything to exchange my life for his. She blamed my parents. They blamed themselves. It was a horrid mess.

I tried to be stoical. I thought that was what my father expected. He wouldn't want me to disgrace myself with tears. And Auntie Oima – she would want me to maintain my composure as well. So I decided that hiding my feelings was a way to honour both families simultaneously.

I would have to be strong.

When I returned to the okiya I refused to allow myself

the sanctuary of the cupboard. Masayuki's body was recovered a week later. It had washed down the canal into the river network of the Kyoto Basin and floated south all the way to Fushimi. We held the traditional all-night vigil over the corpse. And then we had his funeral. The town put up a green wire fence on the embankment of the canal. It was my first experience of death. And one of the last times I ever visited my parents' house.

Yaeko's hatred of me intensified. Now whenever she walked past me she hissed, 'I wish you were dead,' under her breath. I kept the encyclopedia. Masayuki's fingerprints were on every page. I became obsessed with death. What happens when you die? Where was Masayuki? Was there some way I could go there, too? I thought about it all the time. I was so preoccupied that, for once, I neglected my studies and my lessons. Finally, I decided to question all the old men in the neighbourhood. They were closer to death than I was. Maybe one of them would know something.

I asked Mr Vegetable Man, and Uncle Hori my calligraphy teacher, and Mr Nohmura the gilder, and Mr Sugane the laundry man, and the coppersmith. I asked everyone I could think of, but nobody had a definitive answer to my questions about death. I didn't know where else to turn.

Meanwhile, spring was approaching and, with it, the entrance exams for secondary school. Sour Puss wanted me to apply to the prestigious school connected to the Kyoto Women's College, but I wasn't able to focus. In the end I enrolled in the local school close to home.

Yaeko was so furious with my parents that she didn't

want her older son Mamoru to live with them any longer. Yet she was too selfish and irresponsible to find a proper home, like an apartment, where they could live together. She insisted on bringing him to live in the okiya.

This was not the first time that Yaeko had flaunted the rules. She was always bending them. Her very presence was an aberration. The only geiko allowed to reside in the okiya are the atotori and the young geiko who are still under contract. Yaeko was neither. She may have liked to think she was still an Iwasaki, but her divorce wasn't final and her last name was Uehara. She had broken her contract with the okiya when she left to be married, and had no right to live there on either account. As if this was not enough, it is not permitted to re-enter an okiya once you leave it.

Yae overrode all of Auntie Oima and Sour Puss's objections. She moved Mamoru in and kept breaking the rules. She even sneaked her boyfriends up into her room at night. One morning I staggered into the bathroom half-asleep and bumped into some man she had brought home the night before. I screamed. The whole household was thrown into turmoil.

Typical Yaeko.

It was bad form for a man, any man, to spend the night in an okiya because it cast suspicion on the chastity of its inhabitants. Nothing is left unnoticed, or unremarked, in Gion Kobu. Auntie Oima was never happy when there was a man in the house. When one had to stay over-night for some reason, even if he were a close male relative, she made him wait until after lunch before leaving, lest anyone see him depart in the morning and get the wrong idea.

I was twelve at this time; Mamoru was fifteen. My nephew may not have been a full-grown man but his energy changed the atmosphere of the okiya, and it no longer felt like a safe place. He teased me in a way that made me distinctly uncomfortable.

One time he and two of his friends were up in his room. I went in to bring them tea and they grabbed me and pushed me around. I got scared and ran downstairs. They were laughing. Another time I was in the bath by myself and I heard someone in the changing room. I called out, 'Who's there?' Suzu-chan was doing a chore in the garden and her voice came through the window. 'Miss Mineko, are you all right?'

'I'm fine,' I answered.

I heard the door slam and someone run up the outside stairs to the first floor. It had to be Mamoru.

I knew next to nothing about sex. It was never discussed and I wasn't particularly curious. The only man I had ever seen naked was my father and that was so many years ago I barely remembered what he looked like. So it came as a complete shock when, one evening when I was undressing in the changing room, Mamoru sneaked up silently from behind, grabbed me, threw me brutally to the floor, and tried to rape me.

It was a hot summer evening but I froze. My mind went blank and my total being went cold with fear. I was too terrified to scream and barely able to put up a struggle.

Just then, earning my eternal gratitude, Kun-chan walked in to bring me a fresh towel and a change of clothes.

She ripped Mamoru off me and violently threw him aside. I thought she was going to murder him. 'You filthy bastard!' she yelled, transformed from her normally placid self into some kind of fierce guardian deity. 'You dirty, rotten pig! How *dare* you put your hands on Mineko? Get the hell out of here – this instant! I'll kill you if you ever think about touching her again. DO YOU HEAR ME?'

He tore out of there, like a thief in the night. Kuniko tried to lift me up. I was shaking so hard I couldn't even stand. My body was covered with bruises.

She put me to bed. Auntie Oima and Sour Puss were very kind, but I was completely traumatised, caught in a wrenching vice of panic and fear. Auntie Oima summoned Yaeko and Mamoru and, without preamble, commanded them to leave: 'I want you out of here this instant. Now. No excuses. Don't say a word.' Auntie Oima later told me she had never been angrier in her life.

Yaeko refused to leave. She insisted that she had nowhere to go, which, looking back on it, was probably true. No one could stand her. Sour Puss intervened and said she would help find somewhere for Yaeko to go.

Auntie Oima didn't want Mamoru in the same house with me for one minute longer than necessary. She telephoned Mother Sakaguchi for advice. Mother Sakaguchi didn't want us under the same roof either. So the two women came up with a plan.

The next day Auntie Oima called me to her. 'Mine-chan,

I have a great favour to ask. Mother Sakaguchi needs some assistance at home right now and she'd like you to stay with her for a while to help out. Would you mind? We'd really appreciate it.'

It took me no time to answer. 'I'd be happy to do what I can.'

'Thank you, dear. I'll pack up your clothes but you had better get your school things together yourself.'

To tell the truth, I was secretly relieved.

I moved into Mother Sakaguchi's house that afternoon.

It took two weeks for Sour Puss to find Yaeko a house. It was south of Shijo on Nishihanamikohi Street. She loaned her £25,000 to buy it. Yaeko moved there with Mamoru. I tried to avoid my nephew as much as possible, but he always had something nasty to say when we passed each other on the street. Auntie Oima agreed to continue managing Yaeko's career. The benefit of this strategy was that the Iwasaki okiya would not lose face in the community as a result of the incident. Yaeko was being punished, but no one would have to know.

I myself was having a terrible time. The attempted rape still preyed on my mind. I suffered from horrible nightmares and felt constantly on the verge of hysteria. Nausea plagued me. I knew that everyone was really worried about me but I was incapable of pretending that I was all right. Mother Sakaguchi had one of her maids watch over me twenty-four hours a day. This situation went on for months.

Fifteen

I've often wondered why Auntie Oima put up with Yaeko's behaviour for as long as she did when she was so strict about everything else. Was it simply a matter of harmony and face over dissonance and disgrace? Partly, I'm sure. But I think she also felt honour bound to deal decently with Yaeko out of respect for the fact that Yaeko was my sister and I was the atotori. And, whatever her faults, Yaeko was still a member of the Iwasaki okiya family.

Mother Sakaguchi, however, didn't believe that Auntie Oima's punishment of Yaeko went far enough. She called Yaeko to her and meted out a harsher sentence: 'I forbid you to dance in public for the next three years. I have already informed Mistress Aiko of my decision so it is final. Until further notice, you are also banished from our inner circle. You may not step over the threshold of this or any other house in our lineage. We wish no concourse with you. Send me no gifts. Do not trouble yourself with the customary greetings or ritual visits, even at the New Year.'

She paused and looked sternly at my sister. 'And there is one more thing. I forbid you to come anywhere near Mineko. Do you understand? You are to have nothing to do with her. I absolve you of your duties as her Onesan, in fact but not in name. You will attend to her debut in a secondary position. The gentleman from the Suehiroya will tell you where you are to sit on that occasion. Now go. And don't come back!'

No one would have faulted Mother Sakaguchi for expelling Yaeko from Gion Kobu for her activities, but she chose a less drastic punishment, one that effectively curtailed Yaeko's activity for the next few years without bringing dishonour on any of our names, particularly mine.

Living with Mother Sakaguchi was a terrific education in how the geiko functioned. She was a great businesswoman and a real power broker. I like to think of her as the 'godmother' of the neighbourhood. People called upon her constantly, seeking her influence, intervention and advice.

Kanoko Sakaguchi was a true daughter of Gion Kobu. She was not adopted, but was born to the proprietress of the prominent Sakaguchi okiya. The Sakaguchi okiya was known for its musicians and Kanoko became a master of the *ohayashi*, Japanese percussion. She debuted in her teens and grew into a very popular geiko.

Kanoko's mother appointed Kanoko as her atotori. The Sakaguchi okiya was large and prosperous, and Kanoko had many Younger Sisters. But she wanted to concentrate on her music rather than running the okiya. She encouraged the younger geiko in her charge to become independent.

Free to focus on her music, Kanoko quickly rose within the hierarchy of the Gion Kobu. She received certification that gave her the sole authority to teach certain of its dances. In the Gion Kobu system, this means that anyone who wished to perform the ohayashi had to get specific permission from Mother Sakaguchi to do so.

There is a position in the organisation of the Inoue School called a *koken*. The koken are like special guardians. There are five families who hold this honorary title, the Sakaguchi being one of them.

One of the reasons the koken are important is because they are in charge of the selection of the Iemoto. This succession happens only once in two or three generations and has a profound effect on the direction of the School. As a koken, Mother Sakaguchi was instrumental in electing Inoue Yachio IV to her present position. The Iemoto was beholden to Mother Sakaguchi for her support.

But Mother Sakaguchi's influence went beyond Big Mistress. By birth or circumstance she was an authority figure to many of the major players in Gion Kobu, including Mistress Kazama, the dance teacher, Kotei Yoshizumi, the shamisen player, various ochaya owners, officers of the Kabukai and, of course, the okasan of all the Sakaguchi branch okiya.

Mother Sakaguchi was ten years younger than Auntie Oima so would have been around eighty when I went to live with her. Yet she was still vigorous and actively involved in Gion Kobu affairs. Just look at all the care and attention she lavished on my career and wellbeing. I ended up staying with Mother Sakaguchi for nearly eighteen months in all.

The move changed where I slept but not what I did. I still went to school in the morning and to my dancing lessons in the afternoon. I studied hard and practised even harder. By this time I was so entwined with the larger community of Gion Kobu that I hardly noticed the difference, except that I finally had to give up my lifelong habit of suckling on Kuniko or Auntie Oima's breast until I fell asleep.

I continued to do well in school, and became very attached to my schoolteacher of the time. One day he became ill and had to be hospitalised. I was still traumatised by Masayuki's death and was terrified that he was going to meet the same fate. The principal wouldn't tell me where he was, but I nagged him until he wrote down his address and slipped it to me on a piece of paper.

Springing into action, I organised the class. Ignoring the protests of the substitute teacher, we folded 999 origami cranes in a mere three days and strung them all together into a mobile meant to speed our teacher's recovery. Then we folded the last crane, the thousandth one. This one was for our teacher to add to the mobile when he got well. I wasn't allowed to cross Shijo Street so my classmates had to deliver the mobile without me.

When our teacher returned to school two months later, he gave us all pretty pencils as thank you presents. I was enormously relieved that he didn't die.

I moved back into the Iwasaki okiya when I was almost fourteen. In my absence, Tomiko's term of service had expired. When my sister joined the okiya she signed a contract for a six-year term of service. This meant she was basically an employee of the okiya. When her contract was finished she was free to continue working as a geiko, living outside the okiya but under its management, or do something else. She chose to get married.

As a contract geiko, Tomiko remained a Tanaka throughout her sojourn at the okiya. She was therefore encouraged, unlike me, to maintain an active relationship with my parents and siblings, which she did, visiting them regularly. My sister Yoshio got engaged and her fiancé introduced Tomiko to the man whom she ended up marrying.

I missed her, but it was good to be home. I was also looking forward to my school trip, a highlight of every Japanese adolescent's life. We were going to Tokyo. A week before we were set to leave, my tummy began to ache and I went to the lavatory. Something was very wrong. I was bleeding from down there. I must have developed haemorrhoids, a condition that runs in my family. I didn't know what to do. Finally Fusae-chan, one of our apprentices, called in to see if I was all right. I asked her to fetch Auntie Oima, who spoke to me through the door.

'Mine-chan, what's going on in there?'

'Something terrible has happened. I'm bleeding.'

'That's not terrible, Mineko. You are fine. This is good.'

'Haemorrhoids are good?'

'It's not haemorrhoids. You have your period.'

'My what?'

'Your period. You are menstruating. It's perfectly normal. Didn't you learn about this at school?'

'They told us something, but that was a long time ago.'

One might think that living in an all-female society would have prepared me for this sort of thing. But the opposite was true. No one ever discussed intimate matters. I didn't have a clue.

'Let me get Kun-chan to help you. I no longer have any of the things you'll need.'

The household made a big deal of my 'attainment'. This event is generally marked in Japan with a special dinner at home but, because I was the Iwasaki atotori, Auntie Oima turned it into quite an occasion. That night we had a large, festive dinner in the okiya and people came from all over Gion Kobu to pay respects and say congratulations. We gave out boxes of a special sweet called ochobo, a small rounded confection with a red tip on top made to resemble a budding breast.

I found the whole thing terribly embarrassing and, like many girls my age, hated the idea of everyone knowing what had happened to me. How come we kept celebrating things that made me feel bad?

That year, Yaeko finally settled her loans. She repaid Auntie Oima the money she had borrowed in 1952 to cover her debts, and repaid Sour Puss the sum she had borrowed in 1962 to buy a house. Auntie Oima returned the cash to Mother Sakaguchi, to whom it belonged. But then Yaeko completely spoiled the gesture.

In lieu of interest, Yaeko presented Sour Puss with an amethyst obi clasp, and by doing so, completely offended her. Yaeko had purchased the clasp at a jewellery store that we dealt with all the time, well aware that we would know exactly how much it cost. Instead of helping to patch things up, the ostentatious gift was further evidence of Yaeko's vulgarity and lack of comprehension about the way the karyukai was supposed to work.

I myself was beginning to resist the restriction of the rules that dictated every aspect of life in the karyukai. This was only natural. I was fourteen. Without telling my family I did something really wicked. I joined the basketball team. This was no easy feat. I was strictly forbidden to engage in any activity that might cause me physical harm. I lied and told Sour Puss that I had joined the flower arranging club. The poor thing was pleased that I was interested in such a refined pursuit.

I loved the game. The years of dancing had honed my concentration and sense of balance to a fine point. I was a gifted player. My team came in second in the regional tournament that year.

Thank heavens old Sour Puss never found out.

Sixteen

In November 1964, when she was ninety-two years old, Auntie Oima suddenly fell ill and was confined to her futon. My fifteenth birthday came and went. I stayed by her side as much as possible, talking to her, massaging her old and tired muscles. She wouldn't let anyone besides Kuniko or me bathe her or change her bedpan.

In Gion Kobu we begin our New Year preparations in mid-December, before the rest of the country gets started. They start on 13 December, a day we call *Kotohajime*.

The first order of business on Kotohajime is to pay a visit to the Iemoto for a ritual exchange of greetings and gifts. The Iemoto gives each of us our new fan for the coming year. The colour of the fan corresponds to our present rank. In return, in the name of our family, we present her with two items: *okagamisan*, a pair of pounded glutinous rice cakes placed one on top of the other, and a red and white envelope containing cash. The envelope is tied with an intricate decoration made of gold and silver twine. The amount of money is linked to the 'price' of the fan that we received i.e. our status within the school hierarchy – less for children, more for senior geiko. When Kotohajime is over, the Iemoto donates the sweets and money to a school for physically handicapped or mentally retarded children.

On that 13 December I got dressed and dutifully went to pay my Kotohajime visit. I remember feeling a bit nostalgic. This was my last year as an amateur. I was scheduled to take the maiko examination the following autumn when I turned sixteen and, if I passed, would then begin my professional career.

So I was disconcerted when Big Mistress nodded to me and said, 'Mine-chan, there is an exam the day after tomorrow at the Nyokoba and I want you to take it. It starts at ten o'clock, so please be there promptly by nine-thirty.'

I had no choice but to agree, although I didn't really feel like dealing with one more thing on top of Auntie Oima's illness. When I went home and told her the news, however, I couldn't believe the change that came over her. She was like her old self again. Her face broke out in a grin and she actually started singing the *sui-sui* song. For the first time I understood how important it was to Auntie Oima that I become a maiko. It was a powerful realisation. I really hadn't been paying attention.

When Auntie Oima told Sour Puss about the examination, she became even more excited than Auntie Oima.

'Oh my goodness,' she twittered. 'That doesn't leave us much time. Kuniko, cancel my engagements for the rest of the day. Come to think of it, cancel tomorrow and the next day too. All right, Mineko, let's get to work. First, telephone two of the girls and ask them to come over. It's better if you practise in a group. Go on, hurry up, we have to get cracking.'

I tried not to laugh at her officiousness.

'But I'm not taking the exam for real until next year,' I protested. 'This one's no big deal. I basically know the dances.'

'Don't talk nonsense. We have to get to work and we don't have much time. Now kindly telephone your friends – and be quick about it.'

I still didn't see the point but did as I was told.

The girls were glad for the extra attention.

We had been instructed to prepare seven pieces. Sour Puss pulled out her shamisen and began to play. We rehearsed each piece hundreds of times, working day and night, barely stopping to eat or sleep. By the end of the two days I knew every infinitesimal movement of all seven dances by heart. Sour Puss didn't let up for a minute. She was amazing.

On 15 December Sour Puss woke me extra early to make sure that we arrived at the Nyokoba on time. Thirteen girls were sitting and waiting in Studio 2. Everyone was very nervous – except for me. I still hadn't grasped the importance of the moment. Today was the last chance for some of them. If they didn't pass this time, they would have to give up their dreams of becoming a maiko.

We were called in one by one to be tested. The door

was closed so we couldn't see what was going on behind it. This only added to the air of apprehension in the hallway.

We wouldn't know which piece we had to perform until we got inside and, alone, mounted the stage. Then Big Mistress would tell us what to do.

Two of my friends went before me.

'What did you get?' I asked when they came out.

'*Torioi* (*The Story of a Strolling Shamisen Player*),' they both answered.

Piece of cake, I thought. I've got that one. I began to dance *Torioi* in my head, meticulously going over each and every movement. I really didn't understand what everyone was so worried about.

Then it was my turn.

The first part of the exam consisted of opening the door. I did it precisely as I had been taught. By now the mechanical movements had become second nature. They felt liquid and graceful.

I slid open the door, bowed, and asked permission to enter. Then I understood why the other girls were so nervous. Big Mistress wasn't in there by herself. All the Little Mistresses were there, and the master of the Ichirikitei, along with members of the Kabukai. There were also delegates from the Ochaya and the Geiko Associations, and some faces I didn't recognise. Rows of people were sitting in front of the stage, ready to pass judgement.

Trying to maintain my composure, I mounted the stage as calmly as I could.

Big Mistress turned to me and said one word: '*Nanoha* (*The Story of a Butterfly and a Cole Blossom*).'

Oops, I thought. Not *Torioi*. Very well then, this is it. Give it your best shot, Mineko.

I paused for a moment, said, 'Thank you,' acknowledged the panel of judges, and began to dance. I performed the first section of the piece flawlessly, but then, right before the end, I made a minuscule mistake. Mid-pose, I stopped in my tracks, turned to the accompanist and announced, 'I've made a mistake. Please begin again.'

Big Mistress interrupted. 'We would never have noticed if you hadn't said something. Excuse me, everyone, but since Mineko had almost completed the piece, do you mind if she only does the last section again?'

'Of course,' they all responded.

'Mine-chan, just the last part please.'

'Very well,' I said and proceeded to finish the piece, after which I thanked the panel again and left the stage.

Sour Puss was pacing the hallway like a cat. She pounced the second she saw me. 'How did it go?'

'I made a mistake.'

'A mistake?' she hissed. 'What kind of mistake? Was it bad? Do you think you have failed?'

'For sure.'

'Oh dear, I hope not.'

'Why?' I still wasn't taking the thing very seriously.

'Because Auntie Oima will be devastated. She is lying there with bated breath waiting for the results. I was hoping to bring her good news.'

Now I felt really terrible. I had completely forgotten about Auntie Oima. Not only was I a lousy dancer, but I was selfish and disloyal as well. The longer we waited the worse I felt. At last a member of the Kabukai summoned us all into the entranceway of the Nyokoba.

'Here are the results of today's examination. I am pleased to announce that Miss Mineko Iwasaki has taken first place, with a score of ninety-seven points. Congratulations, Mineko.' He proceeded to post a list on the wall. 'Here are the other results. My regrets to those of you who didn't make it.'

I couldn't believe it. I thought there had to be some kind of error. But there it was, in black and white.

'This couldn't be better!' Sour Puss was overjoyed. 'Auntie Oima is going to be beside herself! Really, Mineko, I am so proud of you. What an accomplishment! Let's celebrate before going home, shall we? We'll invite your friends to join us. Where shall we go? Anything you want is fine. The treat's on me.' She was almost babbling.

We invited the gang to *Takarabune* for steak. It took us forever to get there. Sour Puss must have bowed to every person we met along the way and declared: 'Mineko came in first! Thank you so much!'

She was thanking everybody because she believed, as do many Japanese, that it takes a village to raise a child. I was the product of a group effort rather than any given individual. And the group was Gion Kobu.

The owners of the restaurant were old friends and they showered us with food and congratulations. Everyone was having a good time, but I wasn't very happy. One of the girls asked me what was wrong.

'Just shut up and eat your steak,' I muttered.

It's not that I was in a bad mood; there were just so many thoughts and emotions running around inside my head. I was glad I had passed the exam but felt badly for those who failed. I was worried sick about Auntie Oima. And I was thinking about my relationship to Sour Puss.

I had been living in the Iwasaki okiya for ten years now. Masako had adopted me into the family nearly five years ago. I was thinking about the fact that I had never allowed myself to call her 'Mother'.

One time after the adoption papers came through I was fooling around with a water pistol and, in a childish bid for attention, sprayed her. She came after me and said, 'If you were my real child I'd give you a good spanking.' It was like a slap in the face. I had thought I *was* her child. Kind of, anyway. I didn't really belong to my own mother any more. Who *did* I belong to?

When Masako was younger, Auntie Oima had suggested to her that she try to have a child. The karyukai functions to promote the independence of women and there is no stigma attached to being a single mother. As I mentioned earlier, it is easier to raise girls than boys in the karyukai but many women have raised sons there as well. Auntie Oima was, of course, hoping that Masako would produce a daughter, someone to carry on the family name, an atotori.

But Masako refused to consider it. She had never completely come to terms with the fact that she herself was illegitimate, and didn't want to put someone else in the same position. Also, she was physically debilitated from the TB and wasn't sure she was strong enough to bear a child.

When I was adopted, I decided that I would never call her 'Mother', but now I wasn't so sure. What about the last two days? – how hard she had worked for me? How much she had wanted me to succeed? A real mother could not have done more.

Maybe the time has come to change my mind, I thought.

When we finished the meal I took the plunge. I looked directly at her and said, 'Mum, let's go home.'

The look of surprise that flashed across her face lasted only an instant but I'll never forget it. 'Yes, shall we?' she smiled. 'Thank you all for coming. I'm so pleased you could join us.'

As we walked back to the Iwasaki okiya, she told me, 'This has been one of the best days of my life.'

Once home, we rushed into Auntie Oima's room to tell her the good news, and I had the presence of mind to thank her for all her efforts on my behalf.

Auntie Oima was thrilled, but tried to hide it. 'I never had any doubt that you would pass – none at all,' she said. 'Now we have to plan your wardrobe. We'll start tomorrow. Masako, we've got to call Eriman and Saito and a host of others. Let's make a list. We have so much to do!'

Auntie Oima was dying but didn't miss a beat. This is what she had been living for, and she vowed that my debut would be spectacular. I was happy that she was happy, but had mixed emotions about becoming a maiko. I still didn't think it was what I wanted to do. It's true that I wanted to keep dancing, but I also wanted to carry on at school and complete my education.

After the test, events started moving so quickly that I had little time to indulge in reflection. It was already 15 December. Mother Sakaguchi, Auntie Oima, and Mama Masako decided that I would become a *minarai*, or apprentice maiko, on 15 February and make my formal debut, or *misedashi*, on 26 March.

The fact that I was becoming a maiko a year early meant that I would start classes at the Nyokoba before leaving secondary school on 15 March. And if I was to appear in next spring's *Miyako Odori* I would have to be available for press engagements starting the following month.

The Iwasaki okiya was abuzz with preparations for my coming out as well as the approach of the New Year. Our resources were stretched. Auntie Oima was bedridden and had to be cared for. The okiya had to be thoroughly cleaned from top to bottom. There was a constant stream of purveyors coming in to consult on various aspects of my wardrobe. Kun-chan, Aba, and Mama Masako had their hands full and I spent every free second with Auntie Oima. Tomiko came by frequently to assist in the madness. She was pregnant with the first of her two sons, but kindly helped in the arrangements for my coming out.

I was aware that the time I was spending with Auntie Oima was precious. She made a point of telling me how pleased she was that I had decided to call Masako 'Mother'. 'Mineko, I know that Masako is a difficult person but she is a very good one. She has such a pure heart that she sometimes comes across as too serious and straightforward. But you can always trust her. So please be good to her. She doesn't have an evil bone in her body. Not like Yaeko.'

I did my best to reassure her. 'I understand, Auntie Oima. Please don't worry about us. We'll be fine. Here, let me give you a massage.'

One is a minarai for only a short period of a month or two. Minarai means learning by observing. This is a chance for the soon-to-be maiko to gain first-hand experience of the ochaya. She wears a professional costume and attends nightly banquets. She observes the intricate nuances of behaviour, etiquette, deportment and conversational skill that she will soon have to demonstrate herself.

The minarai is sponsored by an ochaya (her *minaraijaya*), though she is free to attend banquets at other venues. She dresses and reports to her ochaya every evening for work. The owner organises her engagements. This is convenient because the owner, in his or her role of mentor, is on the spot to answer any questions that may arise. It is not uncommon for owner and minarai to form a bond that lasts for years.

One of the first decisions my elders had to make when I passed the unexpected exam was which ochaya would be entrusted with my care. They had a number of options. Sakaguchi women customarily apprenticed at the Tomiyo, the Iwasakis at the Mankiku, and Yaeko had done her minarai at the Minomatsu. For some reason, my elders chose the

Fusanoya for me. I'm sure the reason had something to do with Gion Kobu politics at the time.

On 9 January the Kabukai issued a sealed document listing the names of the geiko who would appear in that year's *Miyako Odori*. My name was among them. It was now official.

I was informed that the photo-shoot for the publicity brochure would take place on 26 January. This meant the Iwasaki okiya had to prepare an authentic ensemble for me to wear by that date. The hurricane pace of the preparations became a whirlwind.

On 21 January I returned from my dance lesson and went to share my day with Auntie Oima. As though she had been waiting for me to come home, she passed away as soon as I sat down next to her. Kun-chan was there too. We were so numb from shock that neither of us cried. I refused to believe that she was really gone.

I remember Auntie Oima's funeral in shades of black and white, like an old movie. It was a freezing cold morning. Snow was falling. The ground was carpeted with white. Hundreds of mourners gathered in the Iwasaki okiya. They were all wearing sombre black mourning kimono.

A cloth runner led from the genkan to the altar room. The whole surface was covered with a 3-inch high carpet of salt. It was a pathway of salt, pure white salt.

Mama Masako sat at the head of the room. I sat next to her; Kuniko at my side. The casket lay in front of the altar, Buddhist priests chanting sutras before it.

After the funeral we accompanied the casket to the

crematorium. We waited two hours while they cremated her. Then we picked up some of her charred bones with special chopsticks and placed them in an urn. The ashes were white. We carried the urn back to the Iwasaki okiya and placed it on the altar. The priests came again and we, the family, had a private service.

The stark contrasts of the day seemed to reflect the intense clarity and dignity of Auntie Oima's life.

Mama Masako was now the proprietress of the Iwasaki okiya.

We continued our preparations for my coming out. I had to get ready to participate in the planned photo-shoot on 26 January, which happened to be the seventh day after Auntie Oima's death, the day of her first memorial service.

That morning I went to a master hairdresser and had my hair done. Then Mother Sakaguchi came to the okiya to make up my neck and face. I sat before her, feeling regal and grown-up in my first formal hairstyle. She looked at me with an achingly tender expression of pride. In that instant I truly realised that Auntie Oima was dead, and I burst out crying. Finally. The healing had begun. I cried for two hours before Mother Sakaguchi could begin to apply my make-up, and kept everybody waiting.

Forty-nine days after her death we buried Auntie Oima's urn in the Iwasaki gravesite at Otani cemetery.

Seventeen

The aesthetics of the ochaya derive from the traditional Japanese tea ceremony, a demanding artistic discipline that is more correctly translated as 'the way of tea'.

The ceremonies are intricately scripted rituals that celebrate the simple act of enjoying a cup of tea with a small group of friends, a pleasant respite from the cares of the everyday world. It takes an extraordinary amount of artifice to create the ideal simplicity of the tea ceremony. The teahouse itself and every hand-crafted object used in it is an artwork that has been created with utmost care. The host prepares bowls of tea for his guests in a series of minutely choreographed and endlessly practised movements. Nothing is left to chance.

So too at the ochaya. Everything possible is done to ensure that the guests have an exquisite experience. No detail is overlooked. An event at an ochaya is called an *ozashiki*. This loosely translates as 'banquet', or 'dinner party', and is also the name of the private room in which the event is held.

An ozashiki is an occasion for a host and his or her guests to enjoy the very best in cuisine, relaxation, stimulating conversation and refined entertainment that the ochaya can provide. An ozashiki lasts for a few hours, takes place in a totally private and pristine space and, like the tea ceremony, ideally supplies a break from daily affairs. The ochaya provides the setting, the maiko and geiko act as catalysts, but it is the sophistication of the guests that determines the tone of the evening.

A person can only become a customer of an ochaya through personal referral. One can't walk in off the street. New customers are introduced to the system by clients who already have a good standing in the karyukai. This leads to an inherent process of self-selection whereby any guest who has the wherewithal to host a banquet in an ochaya in Gion Kobu is, almost by definition, someone who is trustworthy, learned, and well-cultured. It is not uncommon for parents to bring their young adult children to banquets as part of their education. So a family may have a relationship with a certain ochaya that stretches back generations.

A regular habitué of the Gion Kobu enters into a steady relationship with one ochaya. In certain cases a customer may patronise two establishments, one for business entertaining and the other for informal socialising, but most often utilises one ochaya for both purposes.

A strong bond of loyalty develops between an ochaya and its regular customers, many of whom host ozashiki at least once a week, if not more often. Similarly, customers develop real relationships with the geiko of whom they are most fond. We get to know our regular customers very well. Some of the dearest relationships of my life began in the ozashiki. My favourite customers were professionals who were expert in some field of knowledge. The most enjoyable ozashiki for me personally were those in which I learned something.

There were some customers I liked so much that I always found time to attend their ozashiki, no matter how tightly my schedule was booked. And others I tried my best to avoid. The bottom line, though, is that the geiko has been hired to amuse the host of the ozashiki and his or her guests. She is there to make people feel good. When a geiko enters an ozashiki she is required to go over to whoever is seated in the place of honour and engage that person in conversation. No matter what she is feeling, her expression must declare: 'I couldn't wait to come right over and speak to you.' If her face says, 'I can't stand you,' she doesn't deserve to be a geiko. It is her job to find something likeable about everyone.

Sometimes I had to be nice to people whom I found physically repulsive. This was hard because repulsion is a difficult reaction to conceal. But the customers had paid for my company. The least I could do was treat every one of them graciously. Sublimating one's personal likes and dislikes under a veneer of gentility is one of the fundamental challenges of the profession.

In the old days, customers tended to be aficionados of the arts and students of the shamisen or traditional art or Japanese dance. They had thus been trained to understand what they were seeing and were eager to engage in the sort of lively artistic dialogue at which maiko and geiko excel. These days, unfortunately, people of means may no longer have the time and interest to pursue such hobbies. However, the beauty and mastery of the maiko and geiko stands on its own and can be appreciated by anyone.

Conversation at a banquet is wide ranging, and geiko are presumed to be knowledgeable about current events and contemporary literature as well as thoroughly grounded in traditional art forms such as the tea ceremony, flower arranging, poetry, calligraphy and painting. The first forty or fifty minutes of a banquet are normally devoted to a pleasant discussion of these topics.

Serving women (*naikai*) present the banquet, assisted by maids, though the geiko will pour *sake*. Needless to say, the cuisine must be excellent. Ochaya do not prepare their own food but rely on the many gourmet restaurants and catering services (*shidashi*) in the area to provide feasts commensurate with the host's tastes and income.

The fee for a banquet at an ochaya is not inexpensive. An ozashiki costs about £325 an hour. This pays for the use of the room and the services of the ochaya staff, but it does *not* include the food and drink that is ordered, nor the fees for the services of the geiko. A two-hour party with a full dinner for a few guests and three or four geiko in attendance can easily cost well in excess of £1,000.

The ochaya must meet the discriminating standards of customers from the top ranks of Japanese and international society. Historically based on the refined aesthetic of the tea ceremony, the ochaya embodies the best of traditional Japanese architecture and interior design. Each room must have a tatami floor and a tokonoma replete with a monthly appropriate hanging scroll and a suitable arrangement of flowers in the right vase. These amenities are completely changed for each guest.

At some point the geiko perform. A maiko or *tachikata* geiko will dance. A *jikata* geiko will play the shamisen and sing. After the performance, conversation often turns to artistic matters. The geiko may tell an amusing story or lead the group in a drinking game.

A geiko's fee is calculated in units of time known as *hanadai*, or 'flower charges', usually quarters of an hour, which are then billed to the client. In addition to the hanadai, customers also give the geiko cash tips (*goshugi*), which they place in small white envelopes and may tuck into her obi or sleeve. She is free to keep these for herself.

At the end of the night, the ochaya calculates the hanadai for all the maiko and geiko who have attended banquets there that evening. They write the tallies down on slips of paper that they place in a box in the entryway of the ochaya. The next morning a representative of the *kenban*, or financial affairs office, makes the rounds of the ochaya to collect all the slips from the night before. These are tallied and reported to the Kabukai. The kenban is an independent organisation that performs this service on behalf of the Geiko Association.

The kenban checks with the okiya to make sure that the accounts agree, and, if no mistake has been made, calculates the distribution of income. It tells the ochaya how much is due it to pay taxes and monthly fees. It then specifies the amount that the ochaya is to pay the okiya.

The ochaya, in turn, keeps its own accounts and bills its customers on a regular basis. This used to be done on a yearly basis but is now done once a month. After being paid, the ochaya then settles with the okiya.

The okasan of the okiya notes the amount received in the geiko's ledger, deducts fees and expenditures, and transfers the remainder to the geiko's account.

This transparent system of accounting means that we know which geiko did the most business on any given day. It is always clear who is Number One.

15 February, 1965 was a big day for me. I began rehearsals for the *Miyako Odori*, started full-time classes at the Nyokoba and began my apprenticeship as a minarai at the Fusanoya ochaya, which lasted for about a month.

Mother Sakaguchi came to the okiya to oversee the process of getting me dressed and to do my make-up herself. It was quite a production.

A maiko in full costume closely approximates the Japanese ideal of feminine beauty.

She has the classic looks of a Heian princess, as though she might have stepped out of an eleventh-century scroll painting. Her face is a perfect oval. Her skin is white and flawless, her hair black as a raven's wing. Her brows are half moons, her mouth a delicate rosebud. Her neck is long and sensuous, her figure gently rounded.

I went to the hairdresser and had my hair done up in

the *wareshinobu* style, the first hairstyle a maiko wears. The hair is swept up and sculpted into a mass on the top of the head that is secured by red silk bands (*kanoko*) front and back and decorated with *kanzashi*, the stick-pin ornaments so distinctive of the karyukai look. It is said that this simple, elegant style showcases the curve of the young girl's neck and the freshness of her features to their best advantage.

After finishing at the hairdresser's, I went to the barber's to have my face shaved, a common practice among Japanese women. I first had my face shaved when I turned one year old, the same time I had my first haircut, and have had it done once a month since then.

After becoming a maiko I had my hair done once every five days. To preserve its shape, I slept on a rectangular lacquered wooden pillow topped with a narrow cushion. At first the pillow kept me awake but I soon got used to it. Other girls found it more difficult. The okiya had a trick to keep us from removing the pillow during the night. The maids would sprinkle rice bran around the pillow. If a girl removed the pillow, bits of bran stuck like glue to the pomade in her hair and the next morning she had to make an unhappy trip back to the hairdresser's.

I wore two hairpins tipped with silk plum blossoms (because it was February) on the sides of the back of the bun, a pair of silver flutters (*bira*) on the sides in front, an orange blossom pin (*tachibana*) on top, and a long pin tipped with balls of red coral (*akadama*) and jade, inserted horizontally through the base.

Mother Sakaguchi applied the maiko's distinctive white

make-up to my face and neck. This make-up has an interest-ing history. Originally it was worn by male aristocrats when they had an audience with the Emperor. In pre-modern times the Emperor, considered a sacred presence, received his subjects while hidden from their sight by a thin scrim. The audience chamber was lit by candlelight. The white make-up reflected whatever light there was, making it easier for the Emperor to distinguish who was who.

Dancers and actors later took up the practice. Not only does the white make-up look good on stage, but it also echoes the value placed on light skin. In olden days the make-up contained zinc, which was very bad for one's health. But this is no longer the case.

Mother Sakaguchi next brushed pink powder on my cheeks and eyebrows. She put a spot of red lipstick on my lower lip. (A year later I began to wear lipstick on my upper lip as well.) Then it was time to get dressed.

The kimono that a maiko wears is called a *hikizuri*. It differs from an ordinary kimono in that it has long sleeves and a wide train, and is worn slung low on the back of the neck. The hem of the train is weighted and fans out behind in a lovely arc. The hikizuri is secured with a particularly long obi (over twenty feet in length) that is tied at the back with both ends dangling down. A minarai's kimono is similar to that of a maiko, but neither the train nor the obi is as long; the dangling portion of the obi is half the length of the maiko's.

My kimono was made out of figured satin in variegated turquoise. The heavy hem of the train was dyed in shades of burnt orange, against which floated a drift of pine needles, maple leaves, cherry blossoms and chrysanthemum petals. My obi was made of black damask decorated with swallowtail butterflies. I wore a matching obi clasp of a swallowtail butterfly fashioned out of silver.

I carried the traditional handbag called a *kago*, which has a basket weave base topped by a drawstring pouch of colourful tie-dyed silk, *shibori*. Shibori is made by tying silk into a myriad of minute knots with thread before it is dyed. The result is a stunning dappled effect. Kyoto is famous for this technique. It is the one that was practised by my mother.

The shibori of my handbag was pale peach and sported a design of cabbage butterflies. It held my dancing fan, decorated with the three red diamonds of the Konoe family (close advisers to the Emperor) painted on a gold background, a red and white hand towel decorated in a matching pattern, a boxwood comb, and various other accessories. All of these were encased in covers made from the same silk as the bag, and all of them were monogrammed.

At last I was dressed and ready to go. I stepped down into my okobo and the maid slid open the front door. I was about to step over the lintel when I stopped in surprise. The street was mobbed with people, packed shoulder to shoulder. There was no way I was going out into that.

I turned around in confusion.

'Kun-chan, I don't know what's going on but there are a million people in the street. Can I wait until they've gone?'

'Don't be silly, Mineko. They are here to see you.'

I knew that people were looking forward to my debut as a maiko but had no idea of the degree of their interest. Many of the locals had been anticipating this moment for years.

Voices called from the outside: 'Come out, Mineko! Let us see how beautiful you are!'

'I can't face them,' I panicked. 'I'll just wait until the crowd thins.'

'Mineko, these people are not going anywhere. Ignore them if you must, but it is high time to get going. You can't be late on your first day.'

I still refused. I didn't want all those people looking at me. Kuniko was getting frustrated. The walker from the Fusanoya was waiting outside to escort me, and she was becoming annoyed. Kuniko was trying to placate her and get me moving at the same time.

Finally, she read me the riot act. 'You have to do it for Auntie Oima. This is what she always wanted. Don't you dare disappoint her!'

I knew she was right. I had no choice.

I turned again towards the door, took a deep breath and thought, All right, Dad, Mum. All right, Auntie Oima. Here I go! I let out a soft determined grunt and lifted my foot over the threshold.

Another bridge. Another passage.

The crowd burst into a deafening round of applause. People called out words of congratulations and praise but I was too mortified to hear them. I kept my face down, eyes hidden, all the way to the Fusanoya. The whole route was clogged with well-wishers and it was quite late by the time we wended our way through them. I didn't see them, but I am sure my parents were there.

The master (*otosan*, or father) of the ochaya immediately scolded me for being late. 'There is no excuse for such tardiness, young lady, especially on your first day. It shows a lack of dedication and focus. You are a minarai now. Act like one.'

It was clear that he was taking his responsibilities towards me seriously.

'Yes, sir,' I answered crisply.

'And stop using standard Japanese. Speak our language. Say *hei* instead of *hae*.'

'*Hae*, please forgive me.'

'You mean *hei, eraisunmahen*. Don't stop working on this until you sound like a proper geiko.'

'*Hae*.'

If you remember, this is the same criticism I received from Big Mistress when I was five. It took years until I was truly fluent in the mellifluous, poetically vague and, for me, difficult idiom of the district. Now it is hard for me to speak anything else.

The okasan of the Fusanoya was more encouraging. 'Don't worry, dear. It may take a while, but I am sure you will master it in no time. Just do your best.'

I responded well to her kindness. She became a guiding light, a pilot who helped me navigate the treacherous waters that lay ahead.

Eighteen

That night I attended my first ozashiki. The guest of honour was a gentleman from the West. The translator explained to him that I was an apprentice maiko and that this was my first appearance in public at a banquet. The guest turned to ask me a question and I did my best to answer him in my schoolgirl English.

'Do you ever go to see American movies?'

'Yes, I do.'

'Do you know the names of any American actors?'

'I know James Dean.'

'What about directors?'

'I know the name of one director. His name is Elia Kazan.'

'Why, thank you. That's me. I'm Elia Kazan.'

'No! Really? I had no idea,' I exclaimed in Japanese. The theme song from *East of Eden* was popular at the time. Everybody was humming it. This seemed like an auspicious beginning to my career.

But a cloud soon loomed on the horizon. The translator told Mr Kazan that I was planning on being a dancer and he asked if he could see me dance. This wasn't normally done, since I hadn't yet made my formal debut, but I agreed and sent for an accompanist (*jikata*).

She and I met in the next room to prepare.

'What number do you want me to play?' she whispered.

I drew an absolute blank.

'Oh, umm,' I fumbled.

'How about *Gionkouta* (*The Ballad of the Gion*)?'

'I don't know that one.'

'Well, what about *The Seasons in Kyoto*?'

'I haven't learned that one yet.'

'*Akebono* (*Dawn*)?'

'Don't know that one either.'

'You're Fumichiyo's daughter, aren't you? You must be able to dance *something*.'

We were supposed to keep our voices down but hers kept getting louder and louder. I was afraid the guests would overhear.

'This is my first banquet so I don't know what to do,' I confessed. 'Please decide for me.'

'You mean you haven't even started to learn the maiko dances yet?'

I shook my head.

'Well, in that case we'll have to work with what we have. What are you learning right now?'

I recited a list. '*Shakkyou* (*A Story about a Lion and her Cubs*), *Matsuzukushi* (*A Story about a Pine Tree*), *Shisha* (*The*

Story of a Contest among Four Companions of the Emperor Riding in Four Oxcarts), Nanoha (The Story of the Butterfly and the Cole Blossom).' None of these dances are in the standard maiko repertoire.

'I don't have my book with me today, and I'm not sure if I remember how to play any of those by heart. Do you know *Imperial Horse Cart?*'

'Yes, I do. Let's try that one.'

I didn't have a lot of confidence in her ability to remember the song and, in fact, she did make a few mistakes. I was a wreck, but the guests didn't appear to know the difference. They seemed delighted with the performance. I was exhausted.

My second day's journey into the world as a geiko wasn't as difficult as the first. I was able to hold my head a little higher and arrived at the Fusanoya on time.

The ochaya had accepted a reservation for me to attend a dinner at the *Tsuruya* Restaurant in Okazaki. Geiko do not entertain only at ochaya, but also perform at private dinners in exclusive restaurants, hotel ballrooms and the like. The okasan of the Fusanoya accompanied me to the event.

It is customary for the most junior geiko to enter a banquet room first. The okasan of the Fusanoya told me what to do. 'Open the door, carry in the earthenware sake bottle, and bow to the guests.'

As soon as I opened the door, my attention flew to the magnificent display of dolls that was set on a platform next to the far wall. These miniatures of the Imperial Court are part of the Girls Day celebration that takes place in the early spring. Without thinking I made a beeline for the dolls, walking right in front of the ten guests. 'These are so beautiful,' I gushed.

The Fusanoya okasan became rattled and reprimanded me in a hoarse whisper, 'Mineko! Serve the guests!'

'Oops. Of course.' The flask wasn't in my hand. I looked around and there it was, sitting forlornly by the door, where I had left it. Luckily the guests were charmed rather than offended by my ineptitude. Some of the people who were there on that day still chuckle about it, apparently.

I got dressed and went to the Fusanoya every afternoon. When I wasn't otherwise engaged I ate dinner with okasan and otosan and their daughter Chi-chan in the living room of the ochaya. We played cards until it was time for me to return to the okiya at ten.

One night we received a call from the okasan of the ochaya Tomiyo asking me to come over. When I got there the okasan ushered me into a banquet room. It had a stage and on the stage there were at least fifteen maiko lined up next to each other. I was asked to join them. I felt shy and tried to conceal myself in the shadow of a pillar.

There were ten people sitting in the middle of the room. One of them said, 'Excuse me, you there by the pillar. Come forward. Sit down. Now stand. Turn to the side.' I had no idea what this was all about but I did as I was told.

'Great,' he said. 'She's perfect. I'm going to use her as the model for this year's poster.'

The man was the president of the Kimono Dealers Association. He had the power to decide who was going to be chosen as the model for their annual poster. These large images, three feet by nine feet, are hung in every kimono and accessory store throughout Japan. Being chosen for this honour is every young maiko's dream.

The model for that year's poster had already been chosen so I didn't know what he was talking about.

I went back to the Fusanoya.

'Mother, I have to model for some photograph.'

'Which one?'

'I'm not sure. Something or other.'

'Mine-chan, I think we need to have a little talk. Father tells me that you've been chosen to be the centrefold in the *Miyako Odori* programme. That's a great honour, you know. And now you've been picked for something else. I don't want to put a damper on all this good news, but I'm worried that people are going to be jealous of you. I want you to be careful. Girls can be very spiteful.'

'Then let one of them do it, if it's so important. I don't care.'

'I'm afraid it doesn't work that way.'

'But I don't want them to be horrid to me!'

'I know, Mineko. There isn't much you can do to avoid it, but I want you to be aware of the envy you are arousing. I don't want you to be surprised.'

'I still don't really understand.'

'I wish I could explain.'

'I hate complicated stuff like this. I like everything to be clear and simple.'

If only I had known. The okasan's words were a gentle

portent of the excruciating torment that I was destined to suffer for the next five years.

It started the very next morning when I got to class. Everyone ignored me. I mean *everyone*.

It turned out that the president of the Kimono Dealers Association had spurned the maiko he had picked earlier in favour of me. People were infuriated by what they saw as my premature vault into a top position. I wasn't even a maiko yet. I was still a minarai. Even girls who I thought were my friends wouldn't talk to me. I was hurt and angry. I hadn't done anything wrong!

But as I soon learned, it didn't matter. Like many all-female societies, the Gion Kobu is fraught with intrigue, backstabbing and vicious competitive relationships. The rigidity of the system may have caused me years of frustration, but the years of rivalry caused me true sadness.

I still didn't understand why someone would want to hurt somebody else – especially if that person hadn't done anything to make them feel bad. I tried to be pragmatic and come up with a plan. I worked on it for days, picturing every angle.

What might these envious girls do? And how would I respond? If someone tried to grab my foot, should I lift it so high that they couldn't reach it? I thought it all through, and came up with a few ideas. Instead of giving into their jealousy and minimising my skills, I decided, I would attempt to become the best dancer that I could possibly be. With luck, I would transform jealousy into admiration. Then they would want to become like me and be my friend. I vowed to study even harder, to practise longer hours. I wouldn't give up until I was Number One!

I simply had to make everybody like me.

Right – if I wanted everyone to like me, the first thing I had to do was identify my weaknesses and correct them. I was serious about this in the way that only an adolescent can be.

My days and nights were full of activity, but I stole whatever time I could for my intellectual housekeeping. I sat by myself in the dark of the cupboard or the silence of the altar room and pondered. I talked to Auntie Oima.

Here are some of the faults I came up with:

I have a short temper.

When I'm faced with a difficult decision I often do the opposite of what I want to do.

I'm too quick. I want to finish everything right away.

I have no patience.

And a partial list of my solutions:

I have to remain calm.

I have to remain steadfast.

I have to maintain a kind and gentle expression on my face like Auntie Oima.

I have to smile more.

I have to be professional. That means I have to attend more ozashiki than anyone else. I must never refuse a reservation. I have to take my job seriously and do it well.

I have to be Number One.

Basically, this became my creed.

I was fifteen.

Nineteen

Mama Masako really came into her own when she started managing the okiya. Handling the everyday details of the business gave her great satisfaction: keeping the ledgers, arranging the schedules, counting the money. She was amazingly well-organised and ran the okiya like an efficient machine.

Mama Masako was also a frugal banker who oversaw how every yen of income was spent. Her one indulgence was home appliances. We always had the newest vacuum cleaner, the roomiest refrigerator, the biggest colour TV. We were the first people in Gion Kobu to install an air conditioner.

Unfortunately, her clear-headed common sense evaporated around men. Not only did she pick ugly ones, she was always falling in love with inappropriate men who didn't love her back.

Mama Masako wore her heart on her sleeve. When she was in love she glowed. When the relationship went wrong she didn't bother to fix her hair and cried a lot. I'd pat her shoulder: 'I'm sure you are going to meet Mr Right any day now.' She never stopped hoping. She never found him.

One of Mama Masako's first tasks as proprietress of the okiya was to prepare for my coming out.

Misedashi, the term used for a maiko's debut, means 'open for business' and indicates that the maiko is prepared to begin working as a professional. I had my misedashi on 26 March, 1965. There were sixty-three other maiko working at the time. I was number sixty-four.

I woke up at six o'clock in the morning, took a bath, and went to the hairdresser's to have my hair done in the wareshinobu style. When I returned we had a special breakfast of red bean rice and sea bream. I drank as little tea and water as possible, because it is very difficult to go to the toilet once one is dressed.

Mother Sakaguchi arrived at nine o'clock to put on my make-up. Custom dictates that one's Onesan performs this task but, true to her word, Mother Sakaguchi refused to allow Yaeko near me. She did it herself. First, she prepared my throat, neck, upper back and face by painting them with *binsuke* oil paste, a kind of pomade that acts as a foundation. Then she covered the area with white make-up, leaving three vertical strips on the back of my neck unpainted to accentuate its length and fragility. Maiko and geiko are given two lines on the neck when wearing 'ordinary' costumes and three lines when wearing formal kimono.

Mother Sakaguchi continued by painting my chin, the bridge of my nose and my upper chest. She took peachy pink polishing powder and applied it to my cheeks and around my eyes, then reapplied the white powder over everything. She redid my eyebrows in red, then pencilled them in with black. A spot of pink lipstick on my lower lip came next.

Then she put in my hair ornaments. I had a red silk band called an *arimachikanoko* in my chignon, and at the crown, a *kanokodome* band and pins made from coral, jade and silver, two silver flutters in front that had the family crest of the okiya worked into the design, and the tortoiseshell ornaments called *chirikan*. The latter are very special. They are only worn once in a maiko's lifetime, during the first three days of her debut.

Next I was dressed in the standard undergarments. The first two are rectangles of bleached white cotton, one worn tight around the hips and the other around the chest. This latter flattens and smoothes the line of the kimono. Next comes a long cotton hip wrap, like a half-slip, then a pair of long bloomers to preserve modesty should the front fold of the kimono open.

Next comes the *hadajuban*, a loose, blouse-like garment that follows the lines of the kimono. A maiko's hadajuban has a red collar. Over this I wore the full-length under robe, the *nagajuban*. Mine was made from tie-dyed silk figured with a fan-shaped pattern and embroidered with an assortment of flowers.

A maiko's ensemble features a distinctive collar (*eri*) that is hand sewn onto the nagajuban for each wearing. These red collars tell a story in and of themselves. They are made from silk that has been finely embroidered with white, silver and gold thread. The younger one is, the less dense the embroidery and the more visible the red of the silk. As one matures, the appliqué becomes heavier until little red (a symbol of childhood) can be seen. The progression continues until the day one 'turns one's collar' from maiko to geiko and begins to wear a white collar instead of a red one.

I had five collars made every year, two for summer out of silk gauze and three for winter out of crepe. Each one cost well over £1,000. I kept them all and even now maintain the collection in my home. That first collar, the one I wore on my misedashi, was decorated with a 'Prince Genji's Carriage' motif done in silver and gold thread.

After the nagajuban the dresser placed the formal crested *hikizuri* kimono over my shoulders. The robe itself was made of black figured silk covered in a floral Imperial Palace pattern. It was decorated with five crests: one on the back, two on the lapel panels, and two on the outer portion of the sleeves. Each family in Japan has a *mon*, or crest, which it uses on formal occasions. The Iwasaki crest is a stylised five-petalled bellflower.

My obi was a work of art that had taken three years to create. It was made from handwoven damask embroidered with muted and bright golden maple leaves and was over twenty feet long. It had cost thousands of pounds. The obi was tied so that both ends dangled down almost to the ground. It was held secure with an *obiage*, a band of silk crepe that is worn on the outside. As customary, mine was made of red silk and embroidered with the crest of the okiya. (An obi clasp is not worn with a formal crested kimono.)

I carried a handbag similar to the one I carried as a minarai. It held my fan, a hand towel, lipstick, comb, and small cushion. Every item had its own carrying case made from Eriman red silk and monogrammed in white with the characters for *Mineko*.

A few of the items I wore that day had been in the Iwasaki okiya for generations, but many of them, twenty at least, had been especially commissioned for the occasion. I don't have the exact figures, but I'm sure one could have built a house for what it cost to put it all together. I imagine the sum was well over £50,000.

When I was ready, a delegation from the okiya accompanied me on my round of formal visits. The dresser, as so often on ritual occasions, came with us to act as a kind of master of ceremonies. My first obligation was to pay my respects to the Iemoto.

When we arrived at Shinmonzen the dresser announced in a deep voice: 'May I present Miss Mineko, younger sister to Miss Yaechiyo, on the occasion of her misedashi. We ask you for your recognition and best wishes.'

'I offer her my heartiest congratulations,' Big Mistress announced from the foyer, followed by the felicitations of the rest of the staff. 'We entreat you to work hard and do your best,' they chorused.

'Yes, thank you, I will,' I said in my family's Japanese.

'There you go again.' Big Mistress caught it instantly. 'A

geiko says *hei* and *ookini*.' Ookini actually means 'thank you'. We use it like 'excuse me'.

Thus chastised, I continued on my rounds. We went to pay our respects to the owners of ochaya, to senior geiko, and to important customers. I bowed and asked for everyone's support. On that first day alone we called in at thirty-seven separate places.

At one point we stopped at a hall to perform the *osakazuki* ritual by which Yaeko and I would formalise our bond. The Suehiroya had arranged the ceremony. When we entered the room, the dresser Suehiroya asked Mother Sakaguchi to take the place of honour in front of the tokonoma. He sat me next to her, Mother Masako next to me, and then the heads of other branch houses. Yaeko, who normally would have been seated next to me, was assigned an inferior position. We carried on with the trading of cups. I'm sure the attendants were baffled by the seating arrangements. They didn't understand that it was a privilege for Yaeko to be there at all.

I wore the formal misedashi ensemble for three days, and then exchanged it for a new outfit marking the second phase of my debut. This outfit was not black and was not emblazoned with crests. The body of the outer kimono was made from periwinkle-blue silk and was named *Pine Wind*. The hem of the train was the beige of a sandy beach, with tie-dyed pine trees and embroidered seashells scattered across it. The obi was deep orange satin damask patterned with golden cranes.

My memory is usually acute, but the first six days of my

misedashi are one long dizzying blur. I must have made hundreds of visits and appearances. The Miyako Odori opened seven days after I came out, and I had to appear on stage in my first truly professional role. I felt overwhelmed, and remember complaining to Kuniko. 'Kun-chan, when am I going to have some time off?'

'I have no idea,' she answered.

'But when am I going to learn all I have to learn? I'm still not good enough. I don't even know *Gionkouta* (*The Ballad of the Gion*). Will I have to follow everybody else for ever? How am I going to work up into a solo? It's all going too fast.'

But there was no way to halt the moving tide. It just kept pushing me forward. Now that I was an official maiko I no longer went to the Fusanoya to receive my assignments. Requests for engagements came in directly to the okiya and Mama Masako handled them all.

The first request I received as a maiko to attend an ozashiki came from Ichirikitei, the most famous ochaya in Gion Kobu. A number of important historical meetings and incidents have taken place in the private rooms of the Ichirikitei, so much so that it has assumed a legendary quality. In fact, the Ichirikitei often appears as the setting for the action in novels and plays.

This has not always benefited Gion Kobu. Some of the fiction has served to propagate the notion that courtesans ply their trade in the area and that geiko spend the night with their customers. Once an idea like this is planted in the general culture it takes on a life of its own. I understand that there are some scholars of Japan in foreign countries who also believe these misconceptions to be true.

But I was innocent of all this as I made my entrance into the banquet room that night. The host of the ozashiki was the business magnate Sazo Idemistsu. He was entertaining the film director Zenzo Matsuyama and his wife, the actress Hideko Takamine. Yaeko was already there when I arrived.

'This is your younger sister?' Ms Takamine asked. 'Isn't she just adorable?'

Yaeko drew her lips into that thin smile of hers. 'Really? You think she's adorable? Which part of her do you think is cute?'

'What do you mean? Everything about her is precious.'

'Oh, I don't know. I think it's just because she's so young. And, to tell you the truth, she's not a very nice person. Don't let her fool you.'

I couldn't believe what I was hearing. I'd never heard of an Older Sister disparaging her Younger Sister in front of clients. I experienced a sharp stab of regret that Satoharu wasn't my Onesan. She would never do something like this.

My old flight mechanism took over and I excused myself. I was too old to hide in a cupboard so I went to the ladies room. I couldn't stand being embarrassed this way in front of strangers. As soon I was alone I started to cry, but immediately forced myself to stop. This would never do. I pulled myself together, went back to the banquet room, and acted like nothing had happened.

In a few minutes Yaeko attacked again.

'Mineko is only here,' she said, 'because she has some very powerful people behind her. She hasn't done anything to deserve her good fortune, so I don't expect she'll last very long. I wouldn't be surprised if she dies on the vine.'

'Then you need to protect her,' Ms Takamine said kindly.

'Fat chance,' said Yaeko.

At that point the head *naikai* of the ochaya, a good-natured woman named Bu-chan, called into the room. 'Excuse me, Mineko-san, it's time for your next appointment.'

As soon as I got outside she looked at me quizzically and asked, 'What in the world is wrong with Yaeko? She is your Onesan, right? Why is she being so mean to you?'

'I wish I knew,' I answered. I had no way to begin to explain.

'Anyway, the next guest is a regular patron here so you should be able to take it a little easier . . .'

'Thank you. I mean, *ookini*,' I corrected myself.

Bu-chan ushered me into another room. 'May I introduce Mineko-chan,' she announced. 'She has recently become a maiko.'

'Well then, Mineko-chan, welcome. Let us have a good look at you. Aren't you pretty? Would you like to have some sake?'

'No, thank you. It's against the law here to drink before you're twenty.'

'Not even a tiny bit?'

'No, I can't. But I'm happy to pretend. May I have a cup, please?' I was like a little kid at a tea party.

'Here you go.'

'Thank you . . . oops, *ookini*.'

I felt myself relax. And with the release came a renewed threat of tears.

'Now, now, dear, what's wrong? Did I do something to upset you?'

'No, I'm terribly sorry. It's nothing, really.' I couldn't tell him it was my own sister who had made me feel this way.

He tried to cheer me up by changing the subject. 'What it is your favourite thing to do, Mine-chan?'

'I love to dance.'

'How nice. And where did you come from?'

'From over there.'

'Over where?'

'From the other room.'

He found this very amusing. 'No, I mean where were you born?'

'Kyoto.'

'But you speak such standard Japanese.'

'I haven't been able to lose my accent.'

He smiled at my topsy-turviness. 'I know, the Kyoto dialect is difficult to master. Feel free to speak to me anyway you wish.'

I got confused between the two and answered him in a mixed-up combination of both. He kept smiling. 'Mine-chan, I think you've made a new conquest today. I hope you'll consider me a friend, and a fan!'

What a sweet man. I later learned that he was Jiro Ushio, the CEO of Ushio Electric. Ushio-san restored my mood and confidence for that evening, but I couldn't escape the pall cast by Yaeko's negative shadow. Our bond as maiko and Onesan was looser than most, but I still had to comply with the basic proprieties.

For example, one of a maiko's duties is to regularly tidy up her Onesan's dressing table. Accordingly, soon after my misedashi, I stopped by her house on Nishihanamikoji Street one day on the way home from school. I had never been there before.

I went into the house and saw a maid bent over cleaning something. She seemed vaguely familiar. I looked again. It was my mother! She cried out, 'Ma-chan!' just as Yaeko walked into the room and screamed, 'This is the bitch who sold us and killed Masayuki!' I felt a sharp pain in my chest. I was about to hurl back, 'I'm going to kill you!' when my mother caught my eye and I knew I must stop before I made it all worse. I started to cry and then simply ran out of the house.

I never went back. Some proprieties were just not worth it. From then on, I tried to avoid contact with Yaeko whenever humanly possible.

Twenty

For years I considered myself to be a busy person, but now things were spinning out of control. Between attending classes at the Nyokoba, rehearsing for public dance performances, and entertaining every evening at ozashiki, I barely had time to breathe. My days began at dawn and didn't end until 2 or 3 a.m. the following morning.

I set my stereo for 6 a.m. to play some classical music or spoken text, and I listened for a while before I got up. The first thing I did was rehearse whatever dance I was working on, to focus my mind on the tasks ahead. It was an unusual life for a fifteen year old. I wasn't interested in boys. Mamoru had ruined that for me. Nor did I have any friends, besides Big John. I didn't trust any of the other girls enough to get close to them. The truth is, all I ever thought about was my career.

I never ate breakfast because I found it impaired my ability to concentrate. I left for the Nyokoba at 8.10 a.m. every morning. Let me tell you the story of how the Nyokoba came into existence.

In 1872 a Peruvian ship named the *Maria Luz* docked in the port of Yokohama. It was carrying a number of Chinese slaves who managed to escape their captors and apply to the Meiji government for asylum. The government, saying it did not have a policy of recognising slavery, set the men free and sent them back to China. This brought a storm of protest from the Peruvian government, who claimed that Japan had its own de facto system of slavery in its licensing of women who worked in the pleasure quarters.

The Meiji government, which was striving to enter the world stage as a modern country, was extremely sensitive to international opinion. In order to pacify the Peruvians, it issued an Emancipation Act that abolished the obligatory terms of service (*nenki-boko*) under which many of the women worked. In the process, the perception of the role of the *oiran* (courtesan) and the *geisha* (entertainer) became intertwined and confused. It still is.

Three years later, in 1875, the matter came up formally before an international tribunal that was presided over by the Tsar of Russia. It was the first time Japan had ever been involved in human rights litigation and it won the case, but it was too late to correct the misconception that geiko were slaves.

In response to the Emancipation Act, Jiroemon Sugiura, ninth generation of the ochaya Ichirikitei, Inoue Yachiyo III, Iemoto of the Inoue School, Nobuatsu Hase, Governor of Kyoto, and Masanao Uemura, Councillor, founded an association known as the Gion Kobu Female Professional Training Company. The name was shortened to the Kabukai, or Performers Association. The organisation's charter was to advance the self-sufficiency, independence and social position of women working as artists and entertainers. Its motto was *We sell art, not bodies*.

The Gion Kobu is run by a consortium of three groups: the Kabukai, the Ochaya Association, and the Geiko Association. The consortium founded a vocational school to train the geiko. Before the war, girls who began professional training at six (five by modern reckoning) might become a maiko or geiko as young as eleven or twelve. After the war, in 1952, the Foundation became an educational foundation and the name of the school was changed to the Yasaka Nyokoba Academy. Due to educational reform, girls now have to complete their secondary education before entering the Nyokoba, and cannot become maiko until they turn fifteen.

The Nyokoba teaches the disciplines a geiko is required to master: dance, music, comportment, calligraphy, tea ceremony and flower arrangement, and is annexed to the Kaburenjo Theatre. Its teachers rank among the greatest artists in Japan. Many of the Faculty were designated 'Living National Treasures' (like the Iemoto) or 'Important Cultural Assets'. Unfortunately, it teaches no academic subjects.

To return to my morning's routine: each day I left the house at ten past eight in time to reach the Nyokoba by twenty past so I would be there before Big Mistress arrived at around eight-thirty. That gave me ten minutes to set out her teaching things and prepare a cup of tea for her arrival. I wasn't just being polite by doing this, or trying to curry favour in any way. I simply wanted to have everything ready for her so that I could get the first lesson.

Two dance lessons a day awaited me – the first from Big Mistress and the second from one of the Little Mistresses. If I didn't get an early lesson with Big Mistress it was difficult to find time for everything else, since besides the other dance lesson, I had to fit in music, tea ceremony and Noh dance. And I also had to leave enough time to pay the obligatory calls before returning to the okiya for lunch.

These calls were an essential part of my job. At that time there were about 150 ochaya in Gion Kobu, and though I primarily appeared at ten or so, I regularly did business with forty or fifty of them. Every day I tried to visit as many places as possible. I thanked the owners of the ochaya I had been to the night before and double-checked the arrangements for the coming evening. I couldn't bear to have any free periods when I was working, and on the rare occasions when I had a few minutes open I would try to book the time myself.

Lunch was at 12.30. While we were eating, Mama Masako and Aunt Taji detailed the evening's appointments and told us what they knew about the customers we would be entertaining.

Each day was different. Sometimes I'd have to be ready to go out at three, other days not until five or six. Some days I had to dress for a photo-shoot in the morning (I'd wear my costume to school) or travel to an event in a distant city. But even when I had to go out of town, I tried to return to Kyoto in time to work that evening.

I felt compelled to work as much as humanly possible. It was the only way I was going to become Number One. I was in and out of the house so often that the family nicknamed me 'the homing pigeon'. Each night I entertained at as many ozashiki as time would allow and didn't get home until one or two in the morning. My schedule was in total violation of the Child Labour Laws, but I wanted to work and didn't care.

When I finally got home I changed into casual kimono, took off my make-up, and rehearsed the previous morning's dance lesson again so I didn't forget it. Then I enjoyed a nice hot bath and read for a while to unwind. I rarely went to sleep before 3 a.m.

It was difficult to maintain this pace on three hours' sleep a night but I managed somehow. I thought it was unseemly for a maiko to be seen napping in public so I never slept when I was dressed in costume, even when travelling on a plane or the bullet train. That was one of the hard parts.

One day I was attending a kimono fashion show at a department store. I wasn't dressed as a maiko, so was able to let down my guard that extra little bit. I was so exhausted that I fell sound asleep on my feet. But I didn't close my eyes. They were wide open.

Twenty-one

I have always regretted the fact that I had to stop my education when I was fifteen. I didn't understand why the Nyokoba taught no academic subjects. We were being prepared to entertain world leaders but not being given the language skills to communicate with them. It seemed completely irrational.

Soon after becoming a maiko I went to the Kabukai and lodged a complaint about the lack of foreign language education. I was told to find myself a tutor, which I did, but they clearly weren't getting the point. However, being a novice member of the karyukai did provide me with an unusual education, one that I can't imagine having had anywhere else. I met all kinds of brilliant and accomplished people, some of whom became my trusted friends.

Meanwhile, my geographical boundaries did not expand as quickly as my intellectual horizons. I rarely ventured out of the neighbourhood. Mama Masako was as protective of me as Auntie Oima had been. Gion Kobu lies east of the

Kamo River, Kyoto's central artery. Downtown Kyoto, the commercial hub of the city, lies on the other side. I was not allowed to cross the river by myself until I was eighteen, or to venture outside the district without a chaperone.

My customers were my tickets to the outside world. They were my real teachers. One night, I was summoned to an ozashiki at the ochaya Tomiyo that was being hosted by one of its regular patrons, the Noh drama costume designer Kayoh Wakamatsu. Mr Wakamatsu was known as an aficionado of geiko and our world.

I readied myself for my entrance. I placed the flask of sake on its tray, slid open the door, and said, 'Ookini', which actually means thank you, and can also be used as a polite greeting. There was quite a party going on. Seven or eight of my Onesan were already in the room with him.

One of them said, 'You slid open the door incorrectly.'

'I'm so sorry,' I replied. I slid the door closed and tried again.

No one complained.

I said, 'Ookini,' again and entered the room.

'You entered the room incorrectly.'

And then, 'The way you're holding the tray is all wrong.'

And then, 'That's not the right way to hold the sake flask.'

I was getting frustrated but tried to keep my cool. I went back out into the hall to try again.

The okasan of the Tomiyo pulled me aside. 'Mine-chan, what's going on?'

'My Onesan are kindly offering me instructions on how to do everything correctly,' I answered. I knew they were really being cruel. I just wanted to see how far things would go before the guest or okasan intervened.

'Oh please,' she said. 'They're just teasing you. Go on in there and don't pay them any mind.'

This time no one said a word.

Mr Wakamatsu asked me, nicely, to bring him a large writing brush, an ink stick and an ink stone. I did as he requested. He then asked me to prepare the ink. I ground the stick against the stone and carefully added the right amount of water. When the ink was the right consistency, I dipped the brush in it and handed it to him. He asked the ringleader of the bunch, Miss S, to stand up in front of him.

Miss S was wearing a white kimono decorated with a pine motif. Mr Wakamatsu lifted the brush and looked her in the face. 'You have all treated Mineko disgracefully but I'm holding you personally responsible,' he said, and with that, he proceeded to slash the brush across the front of her kimono, leaving thick black strokes in its wake.

'Go away, all of you,' he said disgustedly. 'I never want to see any of you again. Please leave!'

The geiko shuffled out of the room en masse.

The okasan heard the commotion and came running. 'Wa-san,' (his nickname), he panted, 'what in the world has happened?'

'I will not put up with this kind of nastiness. Please don't book any of that bunch for me again.'

'Of course, Wa-san. Whatever you wish.'

This experience left a strong impression on me. It made me both sad and happy. I was sad that my Onesan would treat me like that. I was worried that I had more of this kind of thing ahead of me. But I was encouraged by Wa-san's kindness. It made me feel that I was not alone. And he had not only noticed my discomfort, but had gone out of his way to act on my behalf. Wa-san was an incredibly nice man. The next day he sent Miss S three kimono and brocade obi, care of the ochaya. These actions endeared him to me for ever. He became one of my favourite customers (*gohiiki*) and I became one of his favourite maiko.

A while later I was talking to two of the other girls who were also frequent companions of his.

'Wa-san is so good to the three of us, why don't we do something for him? Maybe we should get him a present.'

'That's a nice idea. But what should we get him?'

'Hmmm.' We all thought hard. And then I smiled. 'I've got it!'

'What?'

'Let's do the Beatles.'

They stared at me blankly.

'What's a beatle?'

'You'll see. Just trust me on this one, OK?'

The next day, after class, the three of us got in a taxi and I directed the driver to a store on the corner of Higashioji Nijo. My friends started giggling as soon as we pulled up to the shop. It was a wig store. Wa-san was completely bald, so I thought a wig would make a great present. We chose a blond one, laughing the whole time we picked it out. We couldn't decide where he'd stick the pin.

The next time he called us to an ozashiki, we bore the present excitedly into the room and placed it in front of him. We bowed formally, and I had one of my friends make a little speech.

'Wa-san, thank you so much for all your kindness. We have brought you something to express our gratitude. Please accept it as a token of our affection and esteem.'

'Oh my! You shouldn't have!'

He unwrapped the big hairy mass. At first he had no idea what it was but it fell into shape when he held it up in the air. He put the wig on his head and, grinning, asked, 'Well, what do you think?'

'It looks great!' we all chorused back. 'Really terrific!'

We handed him a mirror.

One of Wa-san's guests arrived in the midst of the hubbub. 'What's going on?' he asked. 'It's awfully lively in here this evening.'

'Welcome, Mr O,' said Wa-san. 'Come in and join the party. How do I look?'

We looked over at Mr O, only to see that, by some strange coincidence, his own toupée was missing! None of us could resist staring at his head. Mr O put his hand to his scalp, instinctively covered his head with the newspaper he was carrying, and ran hurriedly back down the stairs. He returned twenty minutes later. 'That was a surprise,' he said. 'I dropped it in the entrance of the Miyako Hotel.' His toupée was back, but it was on crooked.

The following evening, Wa-san booked me again. His wife and children were with him. His wife was effusive. 'Thank you so much for the splendid present you gave my husband. He hasn't been in such a good mood in years,' Mrs Wakamatsu told me cheerfully. 'I'd love to have you over to the house sometime in return. Why don't you come by one evening to catch fireflies?'

I was almost embarrassed that our jokey little gift had caused such a big reaction.

One of the misconceptions about the karyukai is that it caters solely to men. This simply isn't true. Women host ozashiki too, and often attend them as guests.

It is true that the majority of our customers are men, but we often get to know their families. My clients regularly brought their wives and children to visit me in the ochaya and to watch me perform on stage. Wives seemed to like to go to the *Miyako Odori* in particular, and often invited me to their homes on special occasions like New Year's Day. A husband might be presiding over a stuffy ozashiki of business executives in one room while his wife and her girlfriends were laughing it up in another. I would finish with the gentlemen as soon as decorum allowed and happily glide down the hall to join the ladies.

It wasn't uncommon for me to know someone's entire family. Sometimes customers booked ozashiki for family reunions, especially around the New Year. Or a grandfather might host an ozashiki for his newborn grandchild and, while the proud parents were enjoying themselves, we geiko would vie to hold the baby. At times we joked that the ochaya were like high class 'family restaurants'.

As I have noted before, the culture of the karyukai fosters long-term relationships that are based on confidence and trust. The bond that is forged over time between an ochaya, a regular customer, and his or her favourite geiko can be very strong.

What is said and done in the privacy of an ozashiki may be divorced from the reality of the outside world, but the relationships that develop within it are very real. I was so young when I started that, over the years, I became very close to many of my regular customers and their families.

I have a good memory for dates, and became famous for remembering my clients' birthdays, their wives' birthdays, and their wedding anniversaries. At one point I retained this information for over 100 of my best customers. I always had a stash of little presents handy so I could give my male customers something to take home to their wives if perchance they had forgotten an important date.

Twenty-two

Before I tell you about some of the difficult experiences I had as a maiko, I'd like to describe some of the wonderful ones. I met many great people along the way, but two men stand out above the rest.

First and foremost is the distinguished philosopher and aesthetician Dr Tetsuzo Tanigawa. Soon after my debut, I had the good fortune to attend an ozashiki at which Dr Tanigawa was a guest.

'It's been over fifty years since I visited Gion Kobu,' he greeted me by way of introduction.

I thought he was joking. He didn't look old enough for that to be true. But as I chatted with him and his host, the president of a big publishing company, I realised that Dr Tanigawa had to be well into his seventies.

I had no idea what an important man Dr Tanigawa was when I first met him. It was clear that he was very erudite, but he wasn't a snob. He had an open manner that invited conversation. When I asked him a question about something, he listened to my question with genuine interest and thought for a few moments before speaking. His answer was clear, pointed and precise. I eagerly asked him something else. Again, he gave me a serious, considered answer. I loved this.

It was almost time for my next appointment but I didn't want to go. I slipped out of the room for a moment and told the okasan to please say that I wasn't feeling well and cancel my other appointments, something I had never done before.

I went back into the ozashiki and we continued our conversation. When Dr Tanigawa rose to leave I told him how much I had enjoyed meeting him and that I hoped I would have the opportunity to see him again some day.

'I, too, have enjoyed our conversation very much,' he answered, 'and think you are a delightful young woman. Please consider me a fan. I have to attend a series of monthly symposia here in the city, and will try to visit you again. Think up some more questions for me!'

'That'll be easy. Please come again, as soon as you can.'

'I'll make sure of it. But for now, let me bid you farewell.'

Dr Tanigawa used the English word 'fan', a word very much in vogue at the time.

Although he used the term generically, I actually had a large number of fan clubs, even among maiko and geiko in other karyukai in Kyoto and geisha throughout the country. (Maiko only exist in Kyoto.)

Dr Tanigawa was true to his promise and returned to

the ochaya some days later. During our next conversation I asked him questions about himself. He was forthcoming in his answers and I learned quite a bit about his long and impressive career.

Dr Tanigawa, it turned out, was one year older than my father. Over the years he had taught Aesthetics and Philosophy at universities throughout Japan, including the Kyoto Art University where my father himself had studied. In addition, Dr Tanigawa had served as the Director of the National Museum of Nara, the National Museum of Kyoto, and the National Museum of Tokyo. No wonder he knew so much about everything! He was also a member of the elite Japan Art Academy and the father of the poet Shuntaro Tanigawa, who was so famous that even I knew who he was.

When I asked Dr Tanigawa about his academic background, he told me that he had decided to go to Kyoto instead of Tokyo University in order to study with the great philosopher Kitaro Nishida. He loved Kyoto and Gion Kobu, and knew them well because of his days as a student here.

Whenever I knew Dr Tanigawa was coming I refused all other engagements so that I could devote myself fully to being in his company. We formed a friendship that was to continue until his death in the early 1990s. I didn't think of my appointments with him as business transactions. They felt more like tutorials with my favourite professor.

I peppered him mercilessly with questions, and he continued to answer me seriously, always clearly and to the point. Dr Tanigawa taught me how to think. He never foisted his own opinions on me but rather, encouraged me to reason things out for myself. We talked endlessly about art and aesthetics. Being an artist, I wanted to train myself to recognise beauty in all its forms.

'How do I look at a piece of art?' I asked.

'You have only to see what you see and feel what you feel,' was his honest and succinct answer.

'Is beauty only in the eye of the beholder?'

'No, Mineko, beauty is universal. There is an absolute principle in this world that underlies the appearance and disappearance of all phenomena. That is what we call karma. It is constant and immutable, and gives rise to universal values like beauty and morality.'

This teaching became the core concept of my personal philosophy.

One evening Dr Tanigawa was dining with the president of another publishing company, and this gentleman started a conversation about aesthetics, using a lot of difficult words. He asked Dr Tanigawa, 'How can I evaluate a piece of art so that other people will think I am a professional?'

What a sleazy question, I thought.

Dr Tanigawa amazed me by giving him the exact answer he had given me. 'You have only to see what you see and feel what you feel.'

I couldn't believe it. Here I was, this barely educated fifteen-year-old girl, and Dr Tanigawa was giving the president of a big company the same advice he had given me. I was very moved.

Dr Tanigawa taught me how to find the truth by looking

inside myself. I think this is the greatest gift that anyone has ever given me. I loved him dearly.

In March 1987, Dr Tanigawa's new book *Doubts at 90* was published. I went to the Okura Hotel in Tokyo to attend a publication party with a hundred of his closest friends, and felt proud to be included among them.

'Do you really still have doubts,' I asked him, 'even at over ninety?'

'Some things we can never be sure of,' he replied, 'even if we live to be a hundred years. This proves that we are human.'

In his final years I used to visit Dr Tanigawa at his home in Tokyo whenever I had the chance. One day I was teasing him light-heartedly and pretended to steal an ancient Egyptian fly, made of gold, from his collection. He said, 'Each piece in my collection has already been promised to a museum. These artefacts belong in the public eye, where they can teach us what they have to say about art and culture. So please return it to me immediately.'

To make up for my embarrassing gaffe, I commissioned a box for the amulet that I designed myself. The outside of the box was made of Chinese quince, the inside of paulownia, and the whole was lined with amethyst silk. Dr Tanigawa was very pleased with the gift, and kept the amulet in its special box from then on.

Another brilliant man who left a strong impression on my young mind was Dr Hideki Yukawa. Dr Yukawa was a Professor of Physics at Kyoto University who had won the

1949 Nobel Prize in Physics for predicting the existence of the elementary particle meson. He was someone else who took my questions seriously.

Dr Yukawa tended to get drowsy when he drank sake. One time he fell asleep and I had to rouse him.

'Wake up, Dr Yukawa. It's not your bedtime yet.'

His eyes were all bleary and his face was crinkled. 'What do you want? I'm so sleepy.'

'I want you to explain to me about Physics. What is it? And tell me what you had to do to win that big prize. You know, the Nobel one.'

I was way out of my depth, but he didn't laugh at me. He sat up and patiently answered my questions in great detail, though I'm not sure how much I actually understood.

Twenty-three

U nfortunately, not all my early encounters in the ochaya were pleasant or instructive. One night I was summoned to a certain ozashiki. The host was very anxious I attend, I was told, but for some reason I had a bad feeling about the engagement and sure enough, when I got there, trouble was waiting. A geiko named Miss K was present, and she was already drunk as usual.

In Gion Kobu, upon entering an ozashiki, a geiko first bows to her Elder Sisters before she bows to the customers. Accordingly, I bowed to Miss K and greeted her politely. 'Good evening, Onesan.' Then I turned and bowed to the host.

He greeted me in return. 'It's so nice to see you again.'

I looked up and recognised him as one of the men who had been at the infamous banquet when I ran over to look at the dolls before greeting the guests. It had only been a matter of weeks, but so much had happened in that short time that it felt like ages. 'My, it seems like a long time since we last met,' I said politely. 'Thank you so much for inviting me to be with you this evening.'

At that point Miss K cut in, her words slurred. 'What are you talking about, a long time? A long time since what?'

'Excuse me?' I had no idea what she was talking about.

'Speaking of which, what is it with that Onesan of yours?' she went on aggressively. 'What's her problem? She's not even a good dancer. Why is she always acting like she's better than everybody else?'

'I'm terribly sorry if she's done something to offend you.'

Miss K was puffing away on a cigarette, surrounded by a cloud of smoke. 'You're sorry – what does that mean?' she drawled. 'Your being sorry doesn't change a thing.'

'Why don't I call in to discuss this with you tomorrow?' I was uncomfortable and noticed that the customer was looking increasingly displeased. This was not what he was paying for.

He tried to take control of the situation. 'Now, now, Miss K, I came here to enjoy myself. Let's change the subject, shall we?'

But she refused to let it go. 'No, let's not. I'm only trying to help Mineko. I don't want her to turn out like her terrible Onesan.'

He tried again. 'I'm sure that will never happen.'

'And what do you know about it?' she demanded. 'Why don't you just shut up!'

Justifiably upset, the customer raised his voice. 'Miss K, how dare you talk to me in that way?'

Oh dear! The only way I could think to extricate us all was to keep apologising for Yaeko.

'*Nesan*', I said hastily. 'I promise I'll speak to Yaeko about this immediately and tell her how angry you are. We are so sorry that we have upset you.'

She answered with a non-sequitur. 'What's the matter with you? Can't you see that I'm smoking?'

'Oh, of course. Excuse me. I'll bring you an ashtray right away.' When I went to stand up, Miss K put her hand on my arm.

'No, it's all right. There's one right here. Give me your hand for a moment.'

I thought she was going to pass me an ashtray that needed emptying. Instead she took hold of my left wrist and flicked her ashes into my open palm. She kept my hand in a tight grasp so that I couldn't pull away. The customer was horrified and called out for the okasan. Miss K refused to let go of my hand.

I remembered Auntie Oima telling me over and over that a proper geiko always remains calm, no matter what happens. I thought to myself, This is like a spiritual exercise. If I think the ashes are hot they will be hot; if I think they are nothing, they will be nothing. *Focus*. As the okasan came bustling through the door, Miss K proceeded to grind out the stub of her cigarette in my palm and let go of my hand. I know this sounds like an exaggeration but it really happened.

'Thank you,' I said, not knowing how else to respond. 'I'll come and see you tomorrow.'

'Good. I think I'll be going now.'

She was too drunk to stand up. The okasan half carried/half dragged her out of the room. I excused myself and went to the kitchen for a chunk of ice. Gripping it tightly in my burnt hand, I re-entered the room and greeted the customer again as though nothing was amiss.

I bowed. 'I am so sorry about the time with the dolls. Please forgive me.'

He was very gracious but the atmosphere was a little sombre. Luckily, the okasan soon escorted some veteran geiko into the room and they skilfully livened up the party.

And I had followed two important rules:

Always show respect to one's Older Sisters.

Never display conflict or rude behaviour in front of customers.

But I needed to show Miss K that I was not intimidated by her appalling actions. So the next day I took the initiative and paid her a visit. My hand was bandaged and I was in a lot of pain, but I pretended it wasn't her fault.

'Onesan, I'm so sorry for the trouble last night.'

'Yeah, fine. What did you do to your hand?'

'Oh, I'm so clumsy. I wasn't looking where I was going and I tripped. It's nothing. But I wanted to thank you for all the advice you gave me last night. I will take your words to heart and try to follow them in the future.'

'Fine, whatever.' She was clearly mortified and amazed that I had the gumption to act as if nothing had happened. 'Would you care for a cup of tea?'

GEISHA OF GION

'That's very kind of you, but I really must be going. I haven't finished my lessons for today. Goodbye for now.'

I had taken the upper hand. She never bothered me again.

When I began my career, besides dealing with difficult characters, I had to adjust to the rigours of an extremely demanding schedule that included daily classes, nightly ozashiki and regular public performances.

Look at my first six months. On 15 February I went into rehearsals for my first *Miyako Odori*. I became a maiko on 26 March. The *Miyako Odori* opened on 1 April, seven days later, and ran for a solid month. Then I danced in a series of special performances at the New Kabukiza Theatre in Osaka for the month of May. As soon as that was finished, I went straight into rehearsal for the *Rokkagai* performances in June.

I couldn't wait to participate in the Rokkagai. The word refers to the five karyukai and is the one time a year when all the karyukai of Kyoto get together and put on a group performance that showcases our different styles of dance. There used to be six karyukai in Kyoto. Now there are only five because the Shimabara area is no longer active.

Naively, I was looking forward to getting to know the other girls and feeling a sense of community spirit. But I was soon disappointed. The whole operation simmered with competitiveness and barely disguised rivalry. The order in which the karyukai appear on the programme is considered its de facto ranking for that year. Gion Kobu retains the annual privilege of appearing first so is spared the infighting, but it was disturbing to see the level of conflict. It forever dashed my fantasy of 'one happy family'.

I was quickly becoming the most popular maiko in Kyoto, which meant I received numerous requests to appear at ozashiki at ochaya in other karyukai besides Gion Kobu. People who had the means to do so wanted to get a look at me, and if the invitation was important enough, Mama Masako would accept. This traipsing about didn't seem odd to me. I cheerfully believed that anything that was good for the business of the karyukai was good for everyone involved.

But not everyone in Gion Kobu shared this belief. Some maiko and geiko felt I was intruding into other karyukai and would snidely ask: 'Which karyukai did you say you were from again?'

Again, I have always liked things clear and simple, and found all the jockeying for rank and position silly. In hindsight it is easy to say that I was able to take this viewpoint because I was in such a powerful position, but at the time I honestly didn't understand the reason for all the drama. And I didn't like it at all. I kept trying to use my influence to get the officials of the Kabukai to listen to me.

Snapping photos of maiko is a favourite tourist and paparazzi pastime in Kyoto, and I was often surrounded by photographers as I made my way from one event to the other. One day I went to Kyoto Station to take a train to Tokyo, and found that my face was everywhere. The kiosks were selling shopping bags advertising Kyoto with my picture on them. I had never seen the photo before and had certainly not given my permission for it to be used commercially. I was furious. The next day, I stormed into the Kabukai.

'How dare someone use my picture without my authorisation?' I demanded.

I was fifteen but the man behind the desk spoke to me as if I was a child of four.

'Now, now, Mine-chan, don't worry your pretty little head about such grown-up matters. Think of it as the price of fame.'

Needless to say, I wasn't satisfied by his response. I went back after class the next day and badgered the official until he let me speak with the director. But the latter wasn't much help. He told me repeatedly that he would look into it but nothing ever happened.

This kind of thing went on for years.

I never let my growing dissatisfaction interfere with my dedication. By the time the Rokkagai performances were over in mid-June I was completely exhausted. I was supposed to go right into rehearsals for the *Yukatakai*, a summer series of dance put on by the Inoue School, but my body couldn't take it. I came down with an acute case of appendicitis and had to have an appendectomy. I was supposed to stay in the hospital for ten days. Kuniko never left my side, though I slept for the first four days and don't remember them at all.

Kuniko later told me that I kept going over my schedule in my sleep. 'I have to be at the Ichirikitei at six sharp and then go to the Tomiyo by seven.'

I finally woke up.

The consultant came to examine me and asked if I had passed gas.

'Gas?' I asked.

'Yes, gas. Has any come out yet?'

'Come out? From where?'

'What I mean is, have you broken wind? Have you farted?'

'Excuse me,' I replied indignantly. 'I don't do things like that.'

But I did ask Kuniko if she had noticed anything gassy about me and she said she hadn't heard or smelled a thing. The doctor decided to mark it down anyway.

Mama Masako came to visit. 'How are you feeling, my child?' she asked kindly. Then, with a wicked grin, she said, 'You know, you shouldn't laugh when you have stitches because it really hurts.' She put her hands up to her head and twisted her face into a completely loopy expression. 'What do you think of this one?' she said. 'And this?'

The whole performance was so uncharacteristic that I found it hysterically funny and couldn't stop laughing. It hurt so much that I had tears rolling down my face.

'Please stop,' I begged.

'Usually when I come to visit, you are sleeping and I am bored. But this is fun. I must come back again.'

'You don't have to,' I said. 'And please tell everybody to stop sending me all these flowers.'

There were so many bouquets in the room that the scent was no longer pleasant: it was downright cloying.

Fortunately, Mama Masako convinced my friends to bring me *manga* instead, the thick comic books that Japanese teenagers devour like sweets. This was absolutely the best thing about being in the hospital. I got to spend hours reading, something I never had the free time to do at home. I just lay there relaxing, reading, laughing, hurting.

During the ten days I was in the hospital I was hoping that I could get out one day early. I had wanted to experience *ochaohiku* for many years and decided to try it. The okiya had already distributed fliers all over Gion Kobu announcing that I was unavailable for those ten days so no requests would come in for appearances. This gave me the chance to finally do ochaohiku.

As part of her job a geiko dresses every evening even if she has no scheduled appointments, so that she can respond immediately to any request that might come into the okiya. The term ochaohiku is used for those times when a geiko has to dress up with nowhere to go. In other words, the store is open but there are no customers.

I had been booked solid ever since I started to work so had never had the opportunity to do ochaohiku. I thought I should experience it at least once.

First I took a luxurious bath. It felt good to be in our spacious bathhouse after the confines of the hospital. I taped over my scar so it wouldn't get wet and gratefully doused myself with hot water from the large cedar tub. I lowered myself gingerly into the steaming water and soaked until my skin was supple. Then I got out of the tub and, with a bucket and hot water from a tap in the wall, washed thoroughly with soap and water. Next I rubbed myself all over with a net pouch filled with rice bran. Rice bran contains a significant amount of Vitamin B and is great for the skin. Then I got back in the tub for a final soak.

The family members and Kuniko were the only okiya residents allowed to use the bathhouse. Everyone else went to the local public bath, which was the norm at the time. Few Japanese could afford to maintain a bathhouse at home. Relaxed from my bath, I went to have my hair done.

'I thought you weren't supposed to go back to work until tomorrow,' my hairdresser said when she saw me.

'I know,' I said. 'But I thought I would try my hand at ochaohiku.'

She looked at me strangely but did what I asked. I then contacted the Suehiroya and asked my otokoshi to come and dress me. He too thought it was odd but went along with my request. When I was all ready to go I sat down and waited. Nothing happened, of course, because I was off duty. But I learned something very important. I didn't like being idle. I found sitting around in the heavy costume exhausting. It was much easier to be busy, I realised.

Twenty-four

T he next day I went into rehearsal for the *Yukatakai*, the summer dances, and life returned to normal.

That night, still feeling weak and vulnerable, I attended a scheduled ozashiki. As I bowed in greeting, one of the guests, who was pretending to be drunk, pushed me over on the floor. I landed on my back and was just about to get up when he grabbed hold of the padded hem of my kimono and lifted the skirt all the way up to my thighs, exposing my legs and undergarments. He then took hold of my legs and dragged me around the floor like a rag doll. Everybody started laughing, including the other maiko and geiko who were in the room.

Livid with rage and embarrassment, I jumped up, pulled my skirt together and headed straight for the kitchen. There I borrowed a sashimi knife from one of the maids, placed it on a tray and went back to the banquet room.

'All right, everybody, stop it right there. Nobody move!'

'Please, Mine-chan, I was only playing around. I didn't mean anything.'

The okasan came running in after me. 'Stop, Mine-chan. Don't!'

I paid no attention to her. I was furious. Speaking slowly and calmly, I said: 'Stay where you are. I want you all to listen very carefully to what I have to say. I'm going to wound this gentleman. I may even kill him. I want you all to realise how deeply humiliated I feel.'

Then I went up to my assailant and shoved the knife against the base of his throat.

'Stab the body and it heals,' I said, 'but injure the heart and the wound lasts a lifetime. You have wounded my pride and I do not suffer disgrace lightly. I will not forget what happened here tonight for as long as I live. But you are not worth going to jail over, so I'll let you go. This time. But don't you *ever* do anything like this again!'

With that I thrust the knife point-down into the tatami next to where the guest was sitting and, with my head held high, I marched out of the room.

The next day I was having lunch in the cafeteria at school when one of the maiko who had been in the room the previous night sat down next to me. She told me how the geiko had planned the whole thing and put the customer up to it. Apparently, they had all been laughing about how much fun it would be to humiliate me. The poor girl felt terrible. She hadn't wanted to go along with it but didn't know what to do.

My cool fury did not put an end to the harassment. In fact, it got worse. The hostility took many forms; some were crueller than others. For example, my props and accessories (fans, parasols, tea whisks, etc) were constantly disappearing. Other geiko were rude or ignored me at banquets. People called the okiya and left messages purposely misdirecting me to appointments.

The hem of a maiko's kimono is padded with batting to give the train its proper heft and shape. One night someone stuck needles into the padding. After being pricked innumerable times, I went home and sadly pulled twenty-two needles out of the hem of my beautiful kimono.

The longer these incidents continued, the more difficult it was for me to trust anyone or to take anything for granted. And when I did make a mistake, the punishment never seemed to fit the crime. One evening I arrived at an ochaya. It was dark and I couldn't see who was passing me in the hallway. It turned out to be the okasan, and she was furious at me for not greeting her properly. To chastise me, she forbade me from entering her ochaya for an entire year. I dealt with the harassment as best as I could. In the end, I believe it made me a stronger person.

Although I didn't have one friend among my own age group, some of the older geiko, all of whom were very secure in their own success, went out of their way to be kind. They were among the few who relished the fact that I was such a phenomenon.

The accounting system of the Gion Kobu immediately translates one's popularity into concrete numeric terms. The amount of *hanadai* one earns is equal to the demand for one's services, and the total is a matter of public record. It didn't take long for my sales to reach the top. I occupied this position almost every week of the five years I was a maiko.

The word we use to refer to our total earnings is *mizuage* (not to be confused with the coming of age ceremony). The geiko who has the highest mizuage for the previous year is publicly recognised during the annual commencement ceremony that takes place at the Nyokoba School on 7 January. I was recognised that first year.

Right from the beginning I was hired to attend an inordinate number of ozashiki. I visited an average of ten ochaya in an evening, and attended as many ozashiki as I could in each one, rarely spending more than thirty minutes total in any given house. It was not unusual for me to join a party for five minutes or less before I had to get to my next commitment.

Because I was so popular, customers were billed for a full hour of my time even if I was only with them for a few minutes. In this way, I accumulated many more hanadai than time units worked. Every night. I don't have the exact figures, but I believe I was earning over a quarter of a million pounds per year. This was a good deal of money in 1960's Japan. Especially for a fifteen year old.

Yet I didn't take my work in the ozashiki that seriously. I still saw the ozashiki as simply a venue for my dancing, and didn't bother very much about taking care of the customers. If I was enjoying myself, I decided, then they were probably having a good time too, and I didn't go out of my way to try to please them.

But the geiko were another matter. I wanted their respect

and friendship and I did try to please them. At the very least, I wanted them to like me. But nothing I did seemed to work. The more popular I became with the customers, the more alienated I grew from the other geiko. Most of them treated me shabbily, from the youngest maiko to the older, veteran geiko. I was increasingly frustrated and depressed. Then I had a brainstorm.

Because I only had time to stay at any given banquet for a short while, there was quite a bit of time left over that needed to be filled by other geiko. So I decided to try to orchestrate the company myself by asking the okasan of the ochaya to invite certain geiko to attend the ozashiki for which I was booked. I coordinated all of this on my way home from the Nyokoba in the afternoon.

'Okasan, tonight for my engagement with so-and-so, I was wondering if you could ask this one and that one to help me out . . .' The okasan would then call around to the okiya and say that Mineko had specifically asked for so-and-so to work with her that evening. I booked three to five additional geiko per banquet. Multiply this by the number of banquets I attended and the numbers quickly add up. This was work these geiko might not otherwise have received and their appreciation eventually wore down their envy.

When their purses began to fill as a result of my asking for them, they couldn't help but start to treat me better. The harassment gradually began to abate. This only furthered my resolve to stay on top. My clever strategy would only work as long as I was Number One.

That helped with the women but not the men. I had to learn how to defend myself from them as well. With the women I tried to be friendly and obliging. With the men I was tough.

One day I was returning from Shimogamo Shrine where I had performed a New Year's dance. It was 5 January, and I was carrying a 'demon-dispelling arrow', a talisman that Shinto Shrines sell at the New Year to ward off evil spirits. A middle-aged gentleman was walking towards me. As he brushed past, he turned and, without warning, started to fondle me all over.

Grabbing the man's right wrist I stabbed the bamboo arrow into the back of his hand. The tip was pointed in notches, so I knew it was very painful. I ground it down as hard as I could, drawing blood. The man tried to pull his hand away but I hung on with all my might. Staring at him coldly, I announced: 'We have two choices here. We can go to the police, or you can vow right here and now that you will never do anything like this again, *ever*, to anyone. It's up to you. What's it going to be?'

He answered immediately, his voice a strangled cry. 'I promise I will never do it again. Please let me go.'

'Whenever you are tempted to hurt anyone else,' I told him, 'I want you to look at the scar from this and stop.'

Another time Yuriko and I were walking along Hanamikoji Street when, out of the corner of my eye, I noticed three men closing in on us. They looked drunk. Before I could act, one of the men grabbed me from behind and pinned my arms behind my back. The other two started to go after Yuriko and I shouted at her to run. She took off and ducked into an alleyway.

Meanwhile, the man who had his arms around me bent down and started to lick the nape of my neck. I was totally disgusted. 'It's not a good idea to mess with a woman of today,' I hissed. 'You'd better be careful from now on.' Then I forced myself to go limp. When he relaxed his hold, I grabbed his left hand and sank my teeth into his wrist. He immediately let out a scream and released me. Blood was dripping from his hand. The other two men were staring at me in wide-eyed amazement. All three fled.

My lips were covered in blood. I was steps away from the okiya when a bunch of men came swaggering down the street, clearly trying to impress the women they were with. The men surrounded me, leering and snickering; then they started to touch me. One of the bamboo strips of the basket I was carrying had broken and was sticking out of the bottom. I snapped it off with my free hand and started waving it in front of my attackers.

I shouted at them: 'So you think you're clever, do you, you idiots!' Then I took the pointed end of the bamboo and started to claw at the face of the most aggressive of the men. The others moved away and I ran off into the house.

Another time a man tried to molest me at the corner of Shinbashi and Hanamikoji Street. I squirmed out of his clutches, took off one of my *okobo* and threw it at him, hitting him square on the head. Once when I was walking from one ochaya to another, a drunken man came up behind me, grabbed hold of me, and dropped a live cigarette butt down the nape of my kimono. I couldn't reach behind to get it out so I chased after him and made him take it out himself. It really hurt. I hurried home and took off my kimono. In the mirror I could see a big fat blister on the back of my neck. Taking a needle, I punctured the skin to let out the fluid, then redid my make-up so it didn't show. By some miracle I was able to make it to my next engagement on time. But enough was enough. I started to travel everywhere by taxi, even if my engagements were only a few hundred feet apart.

Occasionally I ran into problems on the inside of ochaya as well as outside them. The vast majority of our customers were perfect gentleman, but every now and then there was a bad apple.

One man came to Gion Kobu almost every night and spent a fortune on ozashiki. He had a bad reputation among the maiko and geiko and I tried to avoid him whenever possible. One night I was waiting next to the kitchen for a flask of hot sake when this man came up to me and started to feel the front of my kimono. 'Where are your tits, Mine-chan? Right about here?'

I had no idea if he got away with this kind of behaviour with the other girls, but he certainly wasn't going to get away with it with me.

The altar room was right next to the kitchen, and in it I saw a set of wooden blocks lying on a cushion. These blocks are used to beat time when chanting sutras and are quite heavy. I went in, picked up one of the blocks, and turned towards the obnoxious man. I must have looked quite menacing because he took off down the corridor. I ran after him. He sprinted into the garden and I followed, shoeless, long train trailing behind me.

I chased him up and down the stairs to the first floor of the ochaya, not bothering to imagine how this scene must have looked to the other guests. When I finally caught up with him, back near the kitchen, I whacked him on the head with the block. It made a hollow sound. 'Serves you right!' I cried.

The man just happened to go bald soon after that.

Twenty-five

I didn't need the numbers to tell me that I had become the most popular maiko in Gion Kobu; I only had to look at my schedule. It was booked for a year and a half in advance.

My schedule was so tight that a prospective client had to confirm any tentative booking a month before the engagement and, although I always left a couple of slots open for emergencies, these were invariably taken a week in advance. If I did happen to have a few minutes open in my evening's schedule I would book them on my way home from the Nyokoba, promising five minutes here or ten minutes there. I had Kuniko write down these extra jobs in my appointment ledger while I was eating lunch.

Basically, I was booked solid for the entire five years that I was a maiko. I worked seven days a week, three hundred and sixty-five days a year, from the time I was fifteen until I was twenty-one. I never took a day off. I worked every Saturday and Sunday. I worked New Year's Eve and New Year's Day.

I was the only person in the Iwasaki okiya who didn't take any days off during this time and, for all I know, I may have been the only one in Gion Kobu as well. At least it was better than not working.

I really didn't know how to have fun. Sometimes I went out with friends when I had a bit of free time, but I found being in public exhausting. The moment I stepped outside the door I became 'Mineko of Gion Kobu'. Admirers surrounded me wherever I went and I felt compelled to act the part. I was always 'on'. If someone wanted to take a picture with me I let him. If someone wanted an autograph I gave it to her. It never stopped.

I was afraid that if I didn't maintain the professional demeanour of a maiko at all times I would simply fall apart. In truth, I was much happier at home by myself, thinking my own thoughts, reading a book, or listening to music. That was the only way I could truly relax.

It's hard to imagine living in a world where everyone — your friends, your sisters, even your mother — is your rival. I found it very disorienting. I wasn't able to distinguish friend from foe; I never knew who or what to believe. Inevitably, all of this took a psychological toll and I began to experience emotional problems. I suffered periodic anxiety, insomnia, and difficulty speaking.

I was afraid that if I didn't lighten up, I was going to get really ill, so I decided to become funnier. I bought a bunch of records of comic stories and listened to them every day. Then I made up my own little routines and tried them out at ozashiki. I pretended that the banquet room was a playground, and that I was there to have a good time.

This tactic really helped. I began to feel better and was able to pay more attention to what was going on in the room. Dance and the other art forms can be taught, but the way to make an ozashiki sparkle cannot. This is something that takes a certain aptitude and years of experience.

Each ozashiki is different, even within the same ochaya. One can tell much about the status of the guests from how the room has been arranged. How valuable is the scroll hanging in the tokonoma? What dishes are on the table? Where is the food from? A trained geiko grasps these nuances the moment she walks into an ozashiki and modulates her behaviour accordingly. The aesthetic training I received from my parents gave me a head start in this direction.

A geiko must also know how to steer the entertainment. Does the host enjoy watching dance, engaging in witty conversation, or playing amusing games? When we get to know a customer we commit his or her personal likes and dislikes to memory so that we can better serve them in the future.

Ochaya are not only used for entertaining. They are also used as venues for sensitive business and political discussions. An ozashiki provides a secluded environment where the participants know they will be comfortable and their privacy will be protected.

Auntie Oima once told me that the reason our hair ornaments have pointed ends is so that we can use them to defend our customers from attack. And that the coral ones worn in the colder months can be used to test the safety of the sake: coral breaks apart in the presence of poison.

Sometimes the most valuable service a geiko can perform is to become part of the wall, to become invisible. If appropriate, she will position herself near the entrance to the room and let the host know when someone is approaching by making a small signal. Or, if asked to do so, she will inform anyone who is approaching that the guests do not wish to be disturbed.

One of the specialised jobs in the teahouse is that of the sake heater, or *okanban*. The latter fills a flask with sake and places it into a pan of simmering water to warm it. It sounds simple, but each guest likes his or her sake served at a certain temperature. The okanban's skill is to calculate how many degrees of heat will be lost as the sake travels from kitchen to banquet room so it is the correct temperature when it arrives. This is no small feat. I liked the job of fetching sake because I enjoyed talking to the okanban. They were always full of interesting, behind-the-scenes information.

As I mentioned before, teahouses tend to have multi-generational relationships with their best clients. One of the ways the ochaya engenders this loyalty is by hiring their client's progeny as temporary employees. Assistant okanban is a popular position.

For example, a young man starting college in Kyoto might apply for this job, on his father's recommendation, in order to help him meet expenses. Everyone benefits from this arrangement. The young man learns how the culture of the ochaya functions from the inside out. He sees how much effort is involved in even the simplest ozashiki and gets to know the local maiko and geiko. The father is helping to educate his son in the sophisticated ways of the adult world. And the ochaya is investing in a future client.

I continued to devote as much energy as possible to my dance classes. Now that I was a professional dancer I felt that I was finally making real progress, so it came as a shock when I received my second otome. It was during rehearsal for the Yukatakai, the summer dances in which all the Gion Kobu geiko participate. I was seventeen at the time. We were rehearsing a group number, when suddenly Big Mistress stopped the action, called my name and told me to leave the stage. I couldn't believe it. I hadn't made a mistake. The girl next to me had.

I found Mama Masako and stormed, 'That's it – I'm leaving! I got another otome and this one wasn't my fault either!'

Without missing a beat, Mama Masako said evenly, 'Fine. Go ahead. I mean, you didn't even make a mistake. How dare she embarrass you in front of everybody? You poor thing!'

She was spurring me on. Mama Masako could certainly see right through me. She knew that I always did the opposite of what she told me to do.

'No, I mean it, Mama, I'm really going to leave.'

'That makes sense. It's exactly what I'd do if I were in your position.'

'But if I do leave, then I shall lose face. Maybe I should fool everybody and keep on going. I don't know . . .'

'Well, that is another option . . .'

Just then Yaeko walked into the room. She had been eavesdropping on our conversation.

'You've really done it this time, Mineko. You have shamed us all.' She meant that my disgrace would cause a loss of face for every geiko associated with our lineage.

But Mama Masako brushed her off. 'This is none of your business, Yaeko. Would you mind going into the other room for a minute?'

Yaeko's lips curled into a thin smile. 'Of course it's my business. Her bad behaviour is an embarrassment to me as well.'

Mama said flatly, 'Yae, don't be ridiculous. Would you please get out of here?'

'Since when do you boss me around?'

'This is between Mineko and me. I want you to stay out of it.'

'Well, if that's how you feel, I'm terribly sorry to have bothered you. Far be it from me to intrude on you and your precious Mineko. Not that she's worth it.'

Yaeko huffed out of the room but her words lingered in my mind. Maybe I was so bad that I really should leave.

'Forgive me, Mama,' I said contritely. 'I'm really sorry. Perhaps it is better if I give up.'

'Whatever you decide to do is all right with me.'

'But what if it's like Yaeko says? What if I've brought disgrace upon the house?'

'That's not a good enough reason. You said it yourself a few minutes ago: you might lose more face if you leave. If I were you, I would talk to Big Mistress – see what she has to say. I bet she wants you to continue.'

'You think so? Thank you, Mama. That's what I'll do.'

Mama Masako telephoned Mother Sakaguchi, who came rushing over in a car.

As usual, our contingent sat facing their contingent. Everyone bowed. I was waiting for Mother Sakaguchi to defend my innocence.

'Mistress Aiko, I must tell you how grateful I am that you scolded Mineko like that. This is the kind of censure she needs to become a true dancer. On her behalf, may I ask most humbly for your continued consideration and guidance?'

As if on cue, the Iwasaki contingent bowed down again. I was a heartbeat behind, just time enough to think, What's going on here? Then I got it. In a flash. Big Mistress was testing me again. Using the otome to push me forwards. She wanted me to understand that the most important thing was to keep on dancing. An occasional reprimand was nothing in light of what I might be able to achieve, or what I stood to lose. My arrogance and schoolgirl superiority had no place in all this. And in that instant something changed. I started to see the bigger picture. I felt a new level of commitment to what I was doing. That was when I really became a dancer.

I have no idea what Mama Masako told Mother Sakaguchi when she called her, or how Mother Sakaguchi reacted, or what she said to Mistress Aiko before we all met together. But, through her eloquent display of humility, Mother Sakaguchi was also sending me a crucial message. She was showing me how professionals dealt with their differences in a way that was non-reactive and beneficial for all concerned. I had seen countless examples of this before, but until that moment, had never really understood it. I was so proud of the skilful way Mother Sakaguchi handled the situation. Big Mistress may have given me the initial scolding, but the real lesson came from Mother Sakaguchi.

I still had a long way to go before I was an adult, but I knew then that I wanted to be as good a person as the women who were in that room. Big Mistress thanked Madam Sakaguchi for coming and, with her staff in tow, accompanied Mother Sakaguchi to the entryway to bid her goodbye.

Right before she got into the car, Mother Sakaguchi bent down and whispered quietly into my ear: 'Mine-chan, work hard.'

'Yes, I promise.'

When we got home, I went around the okiya and brought all the mirrors I could find into my room. I arranged them along the walls so that I could view myself from every angle and started to dance. From that moment on I practised like a madwoman. I changed into dance clothes as soon as I walked into the house at night and rehearsed until I couldn't keep my eyes open any longer. Some nights I only got one hour of sleep.

I looked at myself as critically as I could. I tried to analyse every aspect of my movements, tried to perfect every gesture. But something was missing, some element of expressiveness. I thought about it long and hard. What could it be? Finally, it dawned on me that the problem was emotional, not physical.

The problem was that I had never been in love. My dancing lacked a depth of feeling that would only come after I had experienced romantic passion. How could I portray authentic love or loss when I didn't know them?

This realisation was very scary, because whenever I thought about physical love I thought about the time my nephew tried to rape me and my mind stopped cold. I was still stuck in the terror of that moment. I was afraid that something was seriously wrong with me. Had I been so damaged that I would never be able to have a normal relationship? And this wasn't the only obstacle standing between me and intimacy. There was something deeper, potentially more insidious.

The fact was, I didn't like people. I hadn't when I was a little girl and I still didn't. My distaste for other people hindered me professionally as well as personally. It was my biggest shortcoming as a maiko. But I had no choice. I had to force myself to pretend that I liked everyone.

I feel such poignancy when I look back and see my younger self, this unworldly girl trying so hard to please, yet not wanting anyone to come near.

The relationship between the sexes, always a mystery, is confusing to most adolescents, but I was truly at sea. I had so little experience with men or boys that I had no intuitive feel for how to project warmth without inviting intimacy. It was imperative that I be friendly to everyone. But if I was too nice, the customer got the wrong idea, and that was the last thing I wanted to happen. It was years before I learned how to tread a middle path between making men happy and keeping them away. In the beginning, before I knew how to send the right signals, I made a lot of mistakes.

One time a customer, a very wealthy young man, said to me, 'I'm going abroad to study. I'd like you to come with me. Any objections?'

I was flabbergasted. He announced his plans for me as though they had already been decided. I didn't know what to say.

Men who are familiar with the ways of Gion Kobu understand the unspoken rules and rarely break them. But sometimes, especially if the man was as naive as this fellow was, one would misinterpret my kindness and take it too personally. I was left with no choice but to deal with him head on. I explained to him that I was just doing my job, and that, although I thought he was a nice man, I hadn't meant to give him the impression that I was interested in him.

Another time a young customer brought me an expensive doll from his hometown. He was so excited about giving me the present that he couldn't wait until his next ozashiki. He brought it to the okiya and knocked on the door.

This was a total breach of etiquette but I felt sorry for

him, even though it was rather creepy. I couldn't believe he was naive enough to think he had the right to come to my home. Still, I tried to be polite.

'Thank you anyway, but I don't care much for dolls. Please give it to someone else who will appreciate it.'

A rumour soon spread among my regular customers that I hated dolls.

Once I was on assignment in Tokyo when my client took me to a shop that specialised in name-brand luxury items.

'Pick out anything you want,' he said.

I rarely accepted gifts from clients so I declined and said I was happy just to look around. I saw a watch that I liked and mumbled unconsciously to myself, 'Nice watch.' The next day the customer had the watch delivered to my hotel. I returned it immediately. It was a good reminder that I could never let down my guard.

These incidents all happened when I was sixteen or seventeen and are testaments to my immaturity and inexperience. They show how much I still had to learn.

Sometimes my innocence led to real embarrassment.

The first New Year after becoming a maiko I was invited to attend the *Hatsugama* (first tea ceremony of the year) at the Urasenke Tea School, the premier bastion of aesthetic correctness in Japan. It was an honour to be invited, and I was on my best behaviour in front of the distinguished group of attendees.

Geiko study the tea ceremony in order to absorb the

graciousness that it imparts, but we also must be prepared to perform the ceremony publicly at the annual *Miyako Odori*.

There is an enormous tearoom in the Kaburenjo that holds 300 guests. On her appointed day, a geiko enacts the ceremony five times before each performance, at fifteen-minute intervals, to accommodate the 1450 audience members. She herself only prepares tea for the two people who have been invited to participate as guests of honour. The other 298 people are served by women who have prepared the tea in an anteroom. Every geiko must study tea, and there is thus a close relationship between the Urasenke Tea School and the Gion Kobu.

At the Hatsugama, we were seated in a long row around a large room, and an attendant began passing an interesting-looking cup from guest to guest. The cup had a pointed stem and no base, like a golf tee or a mushroom. There was no way to put the cup down. You had to drink whatever was in it. What fun, I thought, and when it came to me I drank the contents in one gulp.

It was disgusting. I had never tasted anything so awful. I thought I was going to vomit. My face must have shown what I was feeling because Mrs Kayoko Sen, the wife of the previous director of the Urasenke Tea School, who was always very nice to me, laughed and said, 'What's the matter, Mine-chan? Don't you like the sake?'

Sake? At first I grimaced. And then I panicked. *I had just broken the law! Oh my God, what if I was arrested?* My father had put such fear of the law in me that I was terrified of committing crimes. *What was I going to do now?* But then the cup came round my way again and nobody seemed to think anything was wrong. I didn't want to make a scene in front of all these important people so I held my breath and gulped it down again. By the time the party was over I had had a lot of sake.

I started to feel strange, but managed to perform my dance without incident. I attended my usual number of banquets in the evening and got through those as well. But the moment I returned home and walked into the vestibule of the okiya I fell flat on my face. Everyone there made a big fuss of me as they helped me take off my costume and put me into my futon.

The next day I woke up at 6 a.m. as usual but was immediately overcome by an intense feeling of shame and self-loathing. What had I done last night? I couldn't remember anything that happened after I left the tea school. I couldn't remember anything about any of the ozashiki I had attended.

I wanted to crawl into a hole and die. Not only had I broken the law but maybe I had behaved disgracefully as well. It was almost too much to bear. I didn't want to face anyone.

Eventually I forced myself to get up and go to class. I took my lesson with Big Mistress, but was convinced that everybody was looking at me in a strange way. I was unbearably uncomfortable. I asked to be excused from the rest of my classes and fled back to the okiya. As soon as I walked through the door I went straight into the cupboard. I rocked myself and chanted, 'I'm sorry. Forgive me. I'll never do it again,' over and over again in my head, like a mantra.

I hadn't taken sanctuary in the cupboard for quite a while and stayed there for the entire afternoon. I finally came out when it was time to get dressed for work.

This was the last time I allowed myself the comfort of my childhood refuge. I never went back inside the cupboard again.

I wonder why I was so hard on myself. It was something about my father, something about feeling so alone. I completely believed that the answer to everything was self-discipline.

I believed that self-discipline was the key to beauty.

Twenty-six

After I had been a maiko for more than two years, the time was approaching for my *mizuage*, the ceremony that celebrates a maiko's moving up. A maiko changes her hairstyle five times to symbolise the steps she takes in becoming a geiko. At her mizuage ceremony, the topknot is symbolically cut to denote her transition from girlhood to young womanhood and she assumes a more adult hairstyle.

When I asked Mama Masako if I was supposed to ask my customers to pay for the expenses of the mizuage ceremony she just laughed and said, 'What are you talking about? I have raised you to be an independent, professional woman. We don't need men to help with this. The okiya can take care of it, no problem at all.'

Mama Masako was very careful about money. Although I was not knowledgeable in that area, I always wanted to feel that I was carrying my weight.

'Then what do I have to do?'

'Not much. You have to get a new hairstyle. Then we'll

hold a *sakazuki* ceremony to mark the occasion and give out gifts to the main and branch families, including those little sweets that embarrassed you so much when you were fourteen.'

Thus my mizuage ceremony took place in October, 1967, when I was seventeen. We did a formal round of visits to make the announcement and present gifts to all our 'relations' in Gion Kobu. I said goodbye to the wareshinobu hairstyle I had worn for the last two and a half years and began to wear the *ofuku* style, the everyday style of the senior maiko. There were two other styles I was required to wear on special occasions: the *yakko*, for when I was in formal kimono, and the *katsuyama*, for one month before and after the Gion Festival in July.

The change in hairstyle meant that I had entered the latter stages of my career as a maiko. My regular customers took this as a signal that I was nearing marriageable age and started to approach me with proposals. Not for themselves, of course, but for their sons and grandsons.

The geiko of Gion Kobu make famously prized wives for rich and powerful men. One couldn't ask for a more beautiful or sophisticated hostess, especially if one travels in diplomatic or international business circles. And a geiko brings with her the cornucopia of connections she has cultivated over her career, which can be very important for a young man starting out.

From the geiko's point of view, she needs a partner who is as interesting as the men she meets every night of the week. Most have no desire to leave their eyrie of glamour and openness for the constriction of a middle-class existence. And geiko are used to having a lot of money. I have seen instances where working geiko married for love and basically kept their husbands. These relationships were rarely successful.

What about the women who are the mistresses of married patrons? Those stories could fill another volume. The classic tale is that of a wife lying on her deathbed. She calls the geiko to her side and thanks her tearfully for taking such good care of her husband. Then she dies, the geiko becomes the man's second wife, and they live happily ever after.

It is rarely that straightforward.

I remember one particularly disturbing incident. Two geiko were having an affair with the same man, a big sake merchant. They each took it upon themselves to pay uninvited visits to his wife to implore her to separate from him. Caught in the impossible dilemma of the ensuing uproar, the man committed suicide.

I received more than ten serious proposals from men who asked that I consider their son or grandson as a potential husband but I refused them all. I had just turned eighteen (a very young eighteen) and I couldn't begin to take the idea of marriage seriously. First of all, I couldn't imagine a life in which I wasn't dancing.

Over the next few years I did go out on a number of dates with hopeful young men. I was used to such sophisticated company, however, that age-appropriate men seemed pretty dull and boring. After the movies and a cup of tea I could never wait to get home.

After the mizuage ceremony, the next major rite of passage in the life of a maiko is her *erikae* ceremony, or 'turning of the collar'. This is when the maiko exchanges the red embroidered collar of the 'child' dancer for the white collar of the adult geiko. This transition normally occurs around the age of twenty. After that, a geiko must be able to stand on the strength of her artistic accomplishments.

I was planning to have my erikae on my twentieth birthday, in 1969. But Osaka was planning a World Exposition for the following year and the powers that be wanted as many maiko as possible available to entertain the great number of dignitaries they were expecting to attend. Accordingly, they asked for the cooperation of the Kabukai and, in turn, the Kabukai asked everyone in my class to put off becoming a geiko for one more year.

I entertained many important people that year. In April 1970 I was invited to an informal banquet for Prince Charles. The party took place at the Kitcho restaurant in Sagano, generally considered the best restaurant in Japan.

It was a lovely, sunny afternoon and Prince Charles seemed to be having a very nice time. He ate everything he was offered and declared it all delicious. We were sitting in the garden. The master of the establishment was grilling up some tiny sweetfish, a local speciality, on the outdoor brazier. I was fanning myself with one of my favourite fans. Prince Charles smiled at me and said, 'May I have a look at that for a moment?' I handed it to him.

Before I knew what was happening, Prince Charles whipped out a pen and wrote his autograph '*70 Charles*

across the face of my fan. Oh no! I thought, aghast. I loved
that fan. I couldn't believe he had signed it without asking
me. I don't care who he is, I thought. That is really rude.
He began to hand it back to me, obviously thinking that I
would be pleased by his gesture.

In my best English I said, 'I would be honoured if you
would accept this fan as a gift from me. It is one of my
favourites.'

He looked perplexed. 'Don't you want my autograph?'

'No, thank you.'

'I've never heard anyone say that before.'

'In that case, please take the fan and give it to someone
who wants your autograph. When I leave here I have to
attend another banquet, and it would be rude to the host if
I am carrying something with someone else's signature on
it. If you don't wish to take it with you, I will be happy to
take care of it.'

'Well, yes, thank you.' He still looked confused, so I
kept hold of the ruined fan.

I didn't have time to run home and get another one so I
telephoned the house and had a maid bring one to my next
engagement. I handed her Charles's fan and told her to get
rid of it. Later on, I ran into another maiko who had been
at the garden party.

'Mine-chan – what happened to that fan?' she asked.

'I'm not sure. Why?'

'Because if you don't want it, I'd really like to have it.'

'You should have said something before. I think it's
already been thrown away.'

She immediately telephoned to enquire but, unfortunately, it was too late. The maid had done as I asked and disposed of it. My friend lamented the loss of the souvenir, but I didn't feel that way at all. It just felt to me as though Prince Charles had defaced something precious.

Twenty-seven

I had never been as busy as I was the year of the Osaka Expo. I had so many engagements with foreign visitors that I felt like an employee of the Ministry of Foreign Affairs or the Imperial Household Agency. Then one of my friends fell ill and I agreed to stand in for her at the *Miyako Odori*. This strained my schedule to bursting point. On top of that, one of the Iwasaki okiya's maiko, whose name was Chiyoe, eloped, and we had to take over the duties caused by her sudden disappearance.

Finally, there was another geiko who was causing us problems. Her name was Yaemaru and she was impossible. She was one of Yaeko's other Younger Sisters – though she was older than me. The two of them deserved each other. Yaemaru was a heavy drinker who got falling down drunk almost every night. The maids were forever having to drag her home from wherever she happened to pass out, her hair dishevelled and her kimono in disarray. She was quite a character.

Whenever Auntie Oima or Mama Masako threatened her with reprisal she would beg their forgiveness and promise to be better. Things would be calm for a week or so and then she'd be reeling around again. This went on for years.

You are probably wondering why they put up with such undisciplined behaviour. The reason is simple. Yaemaru was the best *taiko* drummer in Gion Kobu, one of the best ever. She played an integral role in the *Miyako Odori* and everyone depended on her to perform, but we were never sure if she was going to make it. She'd stagger into the theatre late, nursing a hangover, but then the moment she picked up her drumsticks she underwent some kind of transformation. She was magnificent. No one else could touch her.

So even though Yaemaru was a constant headache, Auntie Oima and Mama Masako had overlooked her faults and taken good care of her. But that spring she was causing a lot of trouble. And then Chiyoe took off with her lover, leaving behind nothing but unpaid debts, as Yaeko had done, several years before.

As the atotori, I was keenly aware of my financial responsibility to the okiya. When Yaemaru was too drunk to work or Chiyoe left us in the lurch, I felt under pressure to work even harder. Even though I knew little about money, I was aware that I was the main support of the household.

That spring, I appeared in the *Miyako Odori* thirty-eight days out of forty. At the end, I was so exhausted I could barely stand up. One day I lay down in the maids' room off the tearoom, then Big Mistress came in to check on me.

'Mine-chan, how are you?' she asked anxiously. 'You

don't look very well. I think you should see the doctor.'

'Thank you for your concern, but I'm fine, really,' I told her, 'I'm just a little tired. I'm sure I'll feel better in a bit.'

The truth was that I felt awful. I was moaning as I made my way to the stage and lay down on a pillow in the wings while I was waiting to go on. Mysteriously, I was fine while I was on stage.

I'm all right, I thought. I'm probably just tired. Today's performance will be over soon, and then I'll go home and take a nap. I'll be fine.

I got through the rest of the day and went home. I lay down for a while and then got up, let myself be dressed, and went out to keep my evening appointments.

I was about to make my entrance into an ozashiki when I suddenly felt extremely light and buoyant. I heard a loud crashing sound come from somewhere.

The next thing I knew, I was lying in a bed and Dr Yanai was staring down at me. I knew he was scheduled to attend the ozashiki.

'What are you doing here?' I asked him. 'Why aren't you at the party?'

'Because you passed out and I brought you here to my clinic.'

'I did? Surely not.' The only thing I could remember was that feeling of buoyancy. I had no sense of the passage of time.

'Yes, Mineko, you did. I'm afraid you have a problem. Your blood pressure is up to a hundred and sixty.'

'Really?' I didn't have a clue what that meant.

'I want you to go to Kyoto University Hospital tomorrow and get a thorough examination.'

'No, I'm fine. I've just been working very hard and let myself get overly tired. I think I'll go back to the ozashiki now. Would you like to come back with me?'

'Mine-chan, listen to this old quack. You have to take care of yourself. I want you to go home now and get to bed. Promise me you'll go to the hospital tomorrow.'

'But I'm fine.'

'Mine-chan, you are not listening.'

'Because I'm fine.'

'You're not fine. You could die if you keep this up.'

'Ah, the beautiful always die young.'

Now he looked annoyed. 'This isn't a joking matter.'

'I'm sorry, Doctor. I do appreciate your kindness. Would you please call a taxi for me?'

'And where do you plan to go?'

'I just need to go back to the ozashiki for a minute so that I can apologise to everyone.'

'Never mind that, young lady. You go home. I'll return to the ozashiki and make your apologies for you.'

I went home for a little while, but then it was time for another ozashiki and I felt all right so I decided to go. As soon as I got there, though, I started to feel weak and shaky again. Now even I was getting concerned. Maybe there really *was* something wrong and I needed to have myself checked out. But I didn't know when I would have the time to fit it in.

The next day I spoke to Mama Masako. 'Mama, I'm not

sure but I think something is wrong with me. I don't want to cause any problems for the okiya, but do you think it would be all right if I took a few days off?'

'Of course it is, Mine-chan. Don't worry about work. Nothing is more important than your health. We'll go to the hospital first thing tomorrow to find out what's going on, and then we'll see where we go from there.'

'But I don't want to take a lot of time off!' I protested 'I mean, I don't want to get behind in my lessons, and if I stop going to ozashiki I'll lose my spot. Somebody else will be number one.'

'It might be nice to give one of the other girls a chance for a change,' she said wisely.

'You wouldn't mind?'

'Not at all.'

That's as far as we got in the conversation before I nodded off again.

The next morning Kuniko took me to Kyoto University Hospital. The name of the Chief Medical Officer was Dr Nakano. He made me drink a whole pitcher of water in order to test my urine. But it took forever until I could pee, over three hours. The doctor tested my urine on a strip of lab paper. The paper turned deep green. I remember because it was one of my favourite colours.

They put me in an examination room and Dr Nakano came in with about ten students. 'Take off your top,' he said.

The only man who had ever seen me naked was my father, and that was many years ago. I wasn't about to get undressed in front of all these strangers. Dr Nakano saw my hesitation and barked at me, 'Do as I say, young lady. These people are all going to be doctors and are here to observe procedure. Now pretend I'm the only one in the room and strip from the waist up.'

'I wouldn't take off my top even if you were the only one in the room,' I replied.

He was exasperated. 'Stop wasting my time and do as I say.'

I screwed up my face and followed his command. Nothing happened. I am not sure what I was expecting, but the doctor and the students kept on with their business.

Once I realised they weren't interested in my body I forgot about them and looked around the room. There was a strange-looking machine with many wires protruding from it in one corner. A nurse came in and started to plaster my torso with round adhesive things to hook me up to the machine.

The doctor turned on the device. It spewed forth a length of graph paper that had two lines running along it. One of them was straight and the other one went up and down.

'That's a pretty line,' I said. 'The straight one.'

'I'm afraid it's not very pretty for you. It means that your left kidney isn't working.'

'Why not?'

'We'll have to see. But it may mean that you need an operation. I shall have do some more tests.'

All I could hear was the word 'operation'.

'Excuse me, but I think I'd better go home and discuss this with my mother.'

'Can you come back tomorrow?'

'I'm not exactly sure what my plans are.'

'Miss Iwasaki, you have to take care of this immediately. Or you could develop a real problem.'

'What kind of problem?'

'We might have to remove one of your kidneys.'

I still didn't grasp the gravity of the situation. 'I never even knew that I had two kidneys,' I told him. 'Isn't one enough? Do I really need both of them?'

'Yes, you do. Living with one kidney isn't easy. It means dialysis and the likelihood of damage to other internal organs. It is very serious. I need to do more tests as soon as possible.'

'Could you do them now?'

'Yes, if you are prepared to check-in to the hospital.'

'Check-in? You mean I have to stay overnight?'

'Of course. You'll probably be here for about a week.'

I felt as if he had punched me in the stomach.

'Doctor, I'm afraid I don't have that kind of time. I could maybe give you three days, but it would be better for me if you could finish in two.'

'It will take as long as it takes. Now go and make arrangements to check-in here as soon as you can.'

I felt powerless, like a carp on a cutting board ready to be sliced into sashimi.

When the doctors did a battery of tests, they discovered that my tonsils were severely infected and that the overload of bacteria in my system was causing the kidney failure. Before doing anything else, they decided to perform a tonsillectomy to see if that would alleviate the problem. I was immediately scheduled for surgery.

The first thing I saw when I was wheeled into the operating room was a man in a white coat aiming a camera at my face. Without thinking, I flashed him my biggest smile.

The doctor spoke to me sharply. 'Please don't pay attention to the camera and kindly stop smiling. I need pictures of this operation for a surgical conference. Now, open wide . . .'

The nurse standing next to me suppressed a giggle. But, due to the nature of my work, I couldn't take my eye off the camera. It was all quite amusing. For a minute, anyway. They had given me a local anaesthetic and right after the doctor started operating I suddenly had a full-blown allergic reaction. My entire body broke out in a rash. I itched all over and was exceedingly uncomfortable. All I could think about was getting out of there and going home.

I refused to stay in the hospital after the operation. 'There's nothing wrong with my legs,' I insisted, and arranged to receive further treatment on an outpatient basis.

I went home but I was still very unwell. My throat was killing me. I couldn't swallow; I couldn't talk. The pain and the fever left me so limp that I stayed in bed, motionless, for three days. When I was finally strong enough to stand up Kuniko took me back to the hospital for a check-up. On the way home we passed a coffee shop and I was assaulted by the delicious smell of hotcakes. I had been on a liquid diet for over a week and felt my first stab of hunger. I thought this meant I was almost better. But I still couldn't speak so I wrote down on my pad *I'm hungry* and showed it to Kuniko.

'That's great,' she replied. 'Let's go home and tell everyone the good news.'

My nose wanted to follow the aroma of the hotcakes but I let her lead me home. Kuniko reported on my hunger pains to Mama Masako, who replied, 'Then I suppose it's a good thing we're not having sukiyaki tonight.' She had that wicked grin on her face. Around dinnertime the fragrance of sauté-ing beef came wafting up to my room from the kitchen. I went stomping down there and wrote on my pad, *Something stinks*.

'What, this?' Mama pretended surprise. 'It smells pretty good to me!'

You are still an old Sour Puss, I scribbled back. *Making something so delicious when you know I can't eat anything!*

She got so caught up in our little battle that she went to write down her next retort.

I pulled the pad out of her hand. *There's no reason for you to write anything down*, I wrote. *My ears are working just fine.*

'Oh, you're right.' She burst out laughing at her own silliness.

I asked for a glass of milk, took one swallow and the pain was so great that it radiated out to the tips of my hair. I went to bed hungry. My friends were nice enough to visit but I was frustrated because I couldn't talk to them. I wasn't having a very good time. One friend stopped by with a huge bouquet of cosmos, which were out of season at the time.

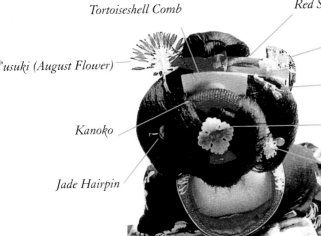

Tortoiseshell Comb

Red Silk Frontal Band

Silver Flutters

usuki (August Flower)

Opal Hairpin

Kanoko

Kanoko Pin

Jade Hairpin

Tortoiseshell Hairpin

The wareshinobu hairstyle.

Entertaining Prince Charles.

Mama Masako, aged forty-four.

In front of the Iwasaki okiya.

With my dresser Suehiroya.

With Dr Tanigawa.

The sakko hairstyle. This was also my last day as a maiko.

The day I became a geiko, fans sent many hand-painted messages of congratulations, which we hung in the entrance to the okiya.

On stage during the Miyako Odori.

A summer portrait.

Between performances at the Kaburento Theater, aged twenty-three.

As Murasaki Shikibu during the Festival of the Ages, aged eighteen.

In the garden of an ochaya.

Performing a tea ceremony at the Miyako Odori.

With Toshio in Atlantic City.

With Yuriko in Hakata.

Rehearsing the Suntory commercial.

My final performance, aged twenty-nine.

A summer ensemble (August).

'Thanks,' I said, 'but what I'd really like is something light (a euphemism for money).'

'That's not very grateful of you. After I went to all the trouble to bring you these flowers.'

'No, I meant light as in food. I'm starving.'

'Then why don't you eat something?'

'If I could eat anything then I wouldn't be starving.'

'You poor thing. But I bet these cosmos have the power to make you feel better,' she said mysteriously. 'I didn't buy them myself. *Somebody* asked me to bring them to you. So concentrate on the cosmos and see what happens.'

'I'll do that,' I said. 'I used to talk to them when I was a little girl.'

I had a serious conversation with the flowers and they told me where they came from. I was right. They were from the man who was secreted away in my heart.

I missed him so much, I couldn't wait to see him again. But, at the same time, I was scared of him. Whenever I thought of him, a little door in my heart banged shut and I felt like crying. I had no idea what was going on.

Had my nephew ruined me for life? Was I too scared to ever have a physical relationship with a man? Whenever I started to think about getting close to someone I remembered the feeling of Mamoru's horrible embrace and my body went rigid with fear. My real problem isn't in my throat or kidneys, I thought to myself. The doctor should have operated on my heart instead.

There wasn't anyone I could talk to about how I was feeling.

Twenty-eight

H is stage name was Shintaro Katsu, and I met him when I was fifteen at one of the first ozashiki I attended after becoming a maiko. He had asked one of the older maiko to introduce me to him. When she did so, she used his real name, Toshio. Toshio at that time was the biggest movie star in Japan. I knew his name, but as I hardly ever went to the movies, I didn't recognise his face. Anyway, I wasn't impressed. When I first met him, he was dressed any old how, in a creased *yukata* (cotton kimono), which was too informal for an ozashiki, and he still had pancake make-up on his neck.

I was only in the ozashiki for about five minutes and didn't speak to him directly. I remember thinking, What an unsavoury person. I hoped he wouldn't ask for me again.

A few days later I stopped by the ochaya on my way home from school and bumped into Toshio, who was there with his wife; he introduced me to her. She is a famous actress and I was pleased to meet her.

Toshio was in the habit of coming to Gion Kobu almost every night. In fact, he asked for me frequently. I refused as often as I could, but karyukai decorum demanded that I appear once in a while. I specifically asked the okasan of the ochaya to keep me away from him, but there was only so much she could do. It was business, after all, and the okasan had to cater to the reasonable requests of her customers.

On one occasion, Toshio asked the accompanist if he could borrow her shamisen for a minute. She handed it to him and he started to play a ballad called 'Nagare' ('Flowing'). I couldn't believe it! He was incredibly talented. I got goose bumps all over.

'Wherever did you learn to play like that?' I asked him. It was the first natural thing I ever said to him.

'Actually, my father is the Iemoto of the Kineya School of Shamisen Balladry and I have been playing since I was a little boy.'

'I'm very impressed. What other secrets are you hiding?' The scales fell from my eyes and I saw him in a whole new light. There was more here than met the eye.

For fun, I announced that I would only attend his ozashiki if he would play the shamisen for me when I was there. It was an impertinent request on my part, but, from then on, whenever I entered an ozashiki he was hosting there was a shamisen sitting there ready to be played. Things continued like this for three years. He asked for me continually, I went occasionally, and when I did, it was mostly to hear him play.

One night, when I was eighteen, I was carrying sake

from the kitchen to an ozashiki. I was about to walk up the staircase to the first floor when I noticed Toshio coming down it. I was embarrassed to be caught so obviously in the open, because earlier on I had refused to attend his ozashiki that evening. He bounded down the stairs and took the tray from my hands.

'Mineko, come here a minute,' he said, and pressed me into one of the maids' rooms.

Before I saw it coming he put his arms around me and kissed me full on the lips.

'Yeech, stop!' I struggled free. 'The only person allowed to do that is Big John, my dog.'

It was my first kiss. And I didn't find it appealing at all. I thought I was having an allergic reaction, since my skin prickled, my hair stood on end, and I broke out in a cold sweat. After moving through shock and fear, I quickly arrived at a state of burning anger.

'How dare you!' I hissed. 'Don't you ever touch me again. *Ever!*'

'Oh, Mine-chan, don't you like me even a little bit?'

'Like? What do you mean, *like*? Like has nothing to do with it!' I am ashamed to admit it now, but at eighteen I still believed that kissing could make you pregnant. I was scared to death.

I ran into the office and, in vehement tones, told the okasan everything. 'I never want to see him again, no matter how many times he asks for me. He's disgusting and his manners are despicable.'

She told me I was overreacting. 'Mine-chan, you have to

grow up a little bit here. It was an innocent kiss, nothing to get so riled up over. Toshio is an important customer, and I want you to go easier on him.'

She explained away my fears and over the next few weeks convinced me that it was safe to accept one of his repeated requests for an appearance.

I entered the ozashiki with reservations, but Toshio was clearly repentant. He promised not to lay a finger on me. I resumed my routine of honouring, on average, one out of his five requests.

One evening he playfully asked, 'I know I'm not allowed to touch you, but would you put one, just one, of your fingers on my knee? In return for all my hard work on the shamisen?'

I acted as if I was touching something contaminated and gingerly rested the tip of my index finger on the top of his knee. It was like a game.

After three months with the index finger he said, 'What about three fingers?'

Then, 'What about five fingers?'

And later, 'What about your whole palm?'

Then one night he got serious. 'Mineko, I think I'm falling in love with you.'

I was too inexperienced to know the difference between flirting and the real thing. I thought he was just joking around.

'Oh please, Toshio-san, how can that be? I'm not interested in married men. Besides, if you're married you are already in love!'

'That's not necessarily true, Mineko. Love and marriage don't always go together.'

'Well, I wouldn't know. But you shouldn't fool around like this, even for a joke. Your wife would feel terrible if she heard and I'm sure you would never want to hurt her, or your children. Your first responsibility is to make them happy.'

The only adult male I had ever known was my father. All my ideas about love and responsibility came from him.

'Mineko, I didn't want this to happen. It just did.'

'Well, there is nothing we can do about it so you had better forget the whole thing right now.'

'And how do you propose I do that?'

'I have no idea – it's not my problem. But I'm sure you'll do just fine. Anyway, you aren't what I'm looking for. I'm looking for a grand passion, someone who will sweep me off my feet and teach me all about love. And then I'm going to become a really great dancer.'

'So what is he like, this grand passion of yours?'

'I'm not sure because I haven't found him yet. But I know a few things about him. He is not married. He is very knowledgeable about art so that I can talk to him about what I'm doing. He will never try to stop me dancing. And he is very clever, because I have so many questions. I think he is a professional of some sort.' I blurted out my whole laundry list of requirements. I clearly had in mind someone as sophisticated as my father or Dr Tanigawa.

Toshio-san looked crestfallen. 'But what about me?'

'What about you?'

'Do I have a chance?'

'It doesn't sound like it, does it?'

'So, you're saying you don't like me very much – is that it?'

'Of course I like you. But I'm talking about something else. I'm talking about the love of my life.'

'What if I got divorced?'

'That's no answer. I don't want to hurt anybody.'

'But my wife and I are not in love with each other.'

'Then why did you get married?'

'She was in love with somebody else. I saw it as a challenge and decided to steal her away from him.'

Now I was getting annoyed. 'That's the stupidest thing I've ever heard.'

'I know. You see why I want a divorce.'

'What about your children? I could never love anyone who treated his children like that.' Toshio was twice as old as I was, but the more we talked, the more I felt like I was the adult. 'I don't think we should talk about this any more,' I told him. 'We're just going around in circles. This discussion is over.'

'I'm sorry, Mineko, but I'm not willing to give up. I am going to keep trying.'

I decided to throw down a challenge of my own. Maybe if I played completely hard to get he would tire of the game and forget about me.

'If you really love me then I want you to prove it. Remember the poet Onono Komachi? How she made Officer Fukakusa visit her for one hundred nights before she would give him her hand? Well, I want you to visit Gion Kobu every night for the next three years. Every night, without exception. Most of the time I won't attend your ozashiki but I will always check on whether or not you came. If you complete this task we can talk again.'

I never thought in a million years that he was actually going to do it.

But he did. He came to Gion Kobu every single night for the next three years, even on major holidays like New Year's Day. And he always requested that I make an appearance at his ozashiki. This I did once or twice a week. During these years we developed a very civilised friendship. I danced. He played the shamisen. We talked mostly about art.

Toshio was a very talented man. His upbringing gave him a firm grounding in the aesthetic principles that I was trying to master. It turned out he was a kind and lively teacher and, once he started to take me seriously, a perfect gentleman. He never again went beyond the boundaries of propriety and I no longer felt any sexual threat in his presence. In fact, he became one of my favourite customers.

Meanwhile, I was slowly and surely falling under his spell. Eventually I recognised that I was feeling something for him I had never felt for anyone else. I wasn't sure what it was, but I had the sneaking suspicion that it was sexual attraction. It *was* attraction. I felt attracted to him. This is what people were talking about.

This is where we were when he asked my friend to deliver the bouquet of cosmos to my bedside. It was his sweet way of continuing to honour his promise to visit me every day.

When I realised the flowers were from Toshio I was filled with emotion. I didn't know if this was love, but it was definitely something. I got a tight feeling in my chest whenever I thought about him, and I thought about him all the time. It made me feel shy and awkward. I wanted to talk to him about what was going on but I had no idea what to say. I think that the little door in my heart was beginning to crack open. And I was fighting it every step of the way.

After ten days I felt well enough to dance again. I still couldn't speak, but Mama announced that I was available to entertain and called the dresser.

I made up a bunch of note cards on which I wrote short phrases such as *How nice to see you*, *It's been a long time*, *Thank you*, *I'm fine*, *I'd love to dance*, and *Everything is working except my voice*. I got through ten days of ozashiki using the cards. It was fun, actually. The cards and my pantomime added an extra element of whimsy that the guests seemed to enjoy.

It took all of those ten days for the pain in my throat to go away, until at last I was able to swallow without discomfort. My kidney came back from its vacation and began to function properly again. I was better.

The most disturbing after-effect of the ordeal was how much weight I had lost. I was down to 86 pounds. As noted, the full maiko ensemble weighs 30 to 40 pounds, so you can imagine how difficult it was for me to move around and dance when I was in costume. But I was so happy to be up and about that I persevered, and ate as much as I could. If I couldn't carry the weight of the kimono I couldn't work.

Even though I was weak, I managed to accomplish quite

a bit during this period because there was so much going on. I appeared a number of times on the stage at Exposition Plaza. I was in a movie, one that was directed by Kon Ichikawa and written by Zenzo Matsuyama, one of my very first customers. The movie played in Kyoto at the government Monopoly Theatre but I was so busy that I never got to see it.

Twenty-nine

In the early 1970s Japan was emerging onto the international stage as an economic power. This change was reflected in the nature of my work. As a representative of traditional Japanese culture, I was fortunate to meet and interact with leaders from all over the world. I'll never forget one encounter that jolted my notion of our insularity.

I was invited to an ozashiki at the Kyoyamato Restaurant. The hosts were the Japanese Ambassador to Saudi Arabia and his wife, and the guests of honour were the Arabian Minister of Oil, Mr Yamani, and his number four wife. Mrs Yamani was wearing the largest diamond I had ever seen. It was huge. She told me it was 30 carats. No one in the room could keep their eyes off it. Our hostess was wearing a small diamond on her finger, and I noticed her turn the ring around so that the stone was hidden in her palm, as though she was ashamed by its size. This bothered me. In Japanese, I spoke right up.

'Madam, your hospitality today, lavish as it may be, is still characterised by the humble aesthetic ideals of the tea ceremony. Please don't hide the beauty of your diamond. There is no reason to conceal its brilliance from our guests, whose greatest asset is their oil. And, for all we know, Mrs Yamani's stone might be a hunk of crystal. In either event, it isn't as radiant as yours.'

Without missing a beat Mr Yamani laughed and said, 'How clever of you to recognise crystal when you see it.'

He spoke Japanese! I was impressed. His riposte showed not only that he grasped the deeper meaning of what I was saying, in a language that most Japanese believed was practically impossible for foreigners to understand, but that he was savvy enough to respond with quick wit and good humour. What a sharp mind! I felt as if I had crossed swords with a master.

I never did find out whether or not that diamond was real!

The Osaka Expo was over on 30 September, 1970. I was now free to celebrate the next rite of passage and turn my collar from maiko to geiko. It was time to become an adult.

I asked Mama Masako: 'I hear it takes a lot of money to prepare for an *erikae* – all the new kimono and things. What can I do to help?'

'You? Why, nothing. The business has it covered, so just leave it all up to me.'

'But all my customers have been asking me how much I want them to give me for my erikae and I've been telling them at least two thousand pounds. Was that wrong of me? I'm sorry if it was.'

'No, Mineko, that's all right. Your regular clients will expect to contribute something – that's part of the tradition and it makes them feel good. Plus, they can brag about it to their friends. So don't worry. As Auntie Oima used to say, "You can never have too much money." Though, I must say, you are not letting them off cheap.'

I have no idea how I came up with that figure. These things just popped out of my mouth. 'In that case I'll leave it alone and see what happens.'

According to Mama, my customers contributed a small fortune to my erikae. I never heard the details.

On 1 October I had my hairstyle changed into the *sakko*, which a maiko wears for the final month of her career. Then, at midnight on 1 November, Mama Masako and Kuniko cut off the tie binding my topknot. My days as a maiko were over.

Most girls experience this cutting with much nostalgia and emotion, but I went through it coolly. I ended my career as a maiko with as much ambivalence as I had begun it, but for different reasons. I still loved being a dancer, but I was discontented with the old-fashioned and conservative ways in which the whole geiko system was organised. I had been outspoken in my views since I was a teenager, and had gone repeatedly to the Kabukai to complain. So far no one was taking my concerns seriously. Maybe now that I was becoming an adult they would listen.

I took the day off to prepare for my erikae. It was a cold

day, and Mama Masako and I were sitting around the brazier putting the finishing touches to my new ensemble.

'Mama?' I said.

'Yes?'

'Umm, never mind.'

'Never mind what? What were you going to say?'

'No, forget about it. I was just thinking.'

'About what? Don't leave me hanging. It's annoying.'

I wasn't trying to irritate her. I just couldn't get the words out. 'I'm not sure if you are the right person to talk to.'

'But I'm your mother.'

'I know, and I really respect you when it comes to anything about work, but this is different. I don't know if I should talk about it.'

'Mineko, I am Fumichiyo Iwasaki. You can ask me anything.'

'But all of the men you get involved with look like dried-up old squid, and then they break up with you and you hang onto the lamp-post in front of the grocery store and cry. It's so embarrassing. And everybody in the neighbourhood sees you and says, "Poor Fumichiyo has been dumped again".'

This was all true. Mama Masako was forty-seven and still hadn't settled into a steady relationship. Nothing had changed. She was constantly falling in love, then alienating her lovers with her acerbic tongue. And she did cling onto the lamp-post and cry. I've got lots of witnesses!

'That's not a very nice thing to say', she said, ruffled. 'Looks like I'm not the only one around here who has a nasty streak. But enough about me. What's going on with you?'

'I was just wondering what it feels like when you fall in love.'

Her hands stopped working and her body came to attention. 'Why, Mineko? Have you found somebody?'

'Maybe.'

'Really? Who is he?'

'It hurts too much to talk about it.'

'It will stop hurting if you talk about it.'

'It hurts just to think of his face.'

'This sounds serious.'

'Do you think so?'

'I'd like to meet him. Why don't you introduce us?'

'No way. First of all, you are a terrible judge of men. And, secondly, you might try to steal him from me.'

'Mineko, I'm not Yaeko. I promise you, I would never get involved with one of your boyfriends.'

'But you always make yourself look so beautiful whenever you are going to meet some man. If I do introduce you, would you agree to meet him looking like yourself?'

'Yes, my dear, of course. If it makes you happy, I'll go in everyday clothes.'

'In that case, I'll see what I can do.'

And with that, we finished making the preparations for my transition from maiko to geiko.

My erikae took place on 2 November, 1970, my twenty-first birthday.

The first kimono I wore as a geiko was a formal crested one made of black silk, embellished with a pattern of tie-dyed and embroidered seashells. My obi was white silk damask with a geometric pattern figured in red, blue and gold.

We commissioned two more kimono for me to wear during the initial period. One was made of yellow silk decorated with phoenixes embroidered in gold-leaf thread. The obi was rusty vermilion brocade patterned with peonies. The other was made of muted green silk, with an embroidered pattern of pine and imperial carts worked in gold. The obi was black brocade with a chrysanthemum pattern.

The collars sewn onto my *nagajuban* were now white, signifying that I had left behind the childlike qualities of a maiko. I was grown up. It was time to take responsibility for my life.

Around the time of my erikae, Dr Tanigawa approached me with a very exciting proposition. Kunihito Shimonaka, the president of Heibon Publishing, wanted to devote an entire edition of his magazine *The Sun* to the history and traditions of Gion Kobu. Dr Tanigawa recommended to Mr Shimonaka that I work on the project. I readily agreed to participate, as did a number of my friends.

We worked under the editorial supervision of Takeshi Yasuda and before long I felt like a bona fide journalist. We met as a team once a month and the project took a full year to complete. The special edition was published as the June issue and came out in May 1972; it sold out immediately and was reprinted any number of times.

The project gave me an enormous sense of accomplishment and satisfaction, and I began to see that there might be a life for me outside the silken confines of Gion Kobu. But I was working as hard as a geiko as I had as a maiko, maintaining a full schedule of nightly ozashiki and regular public performances on top of the other work.

One evening I was called to the Tomiyo ochaya. Mr Motoyama, president of the fashion concern Sun Motoyama, was hosting an ozashiki for Aldo Gucci, the Italian fashion designer.

I dressed with particular care that evening. The body of my kimono was black silk crepe. The hem bore an exquisite scene of cranes huddling in their nest. My obi was the dusk red of salt shallows, dyed with a pattern of maple trees.

While I was sitting next to Mr Gucci he accidentally spilled soy sauce on my kimono. I knew he felt terrible, so I tried to think of a quick way to make him feel better. I turned to him and, as though it were not an odd request, asked, 'Mr Gucci, it is such an honour for me to meet you. May I be so bold as to ask for your autograph?'

He agreed and reached for a pen.

'Could you sign my kimono? Here, on the lining of my sleeve?'

Mr Gucci signed the red silk with a flourish of black ink. Since the kimono was effectively ruined it made no difference to me if he defaced it further. The important thing was that he felt good about our interaction.

I still have that kimono. I had always hoped to give it to

him one day but, unfortunately, never had the opportunity to meet him again.

A geiko's kimono is a work of art and I would never wear one that wasn't absolutely perfect. All the kimono worn by maiko and geiko are one of a kind. Many of them are given names, like paintings, and are treasured as such. This is why I have such a vivid memory of everything I ever wore.

When I was in active service I commissioned a new kimono every week and would rarely wear any kimono more than four or five times. I have no idea how many kimono I actually owned during my career, but I imagine it was over three hundred. And each one, not including the enormously expensive robes commissioned for special occasions, cost between £3,000 and £5,000.

Kimono were my passion and I took an active role in their design and conception. My greatest pleasure was to meet with the venerable Mr Iida at Takashimaya, or Mr Saito at Gofukya, or the skilled staff of Eriman and Ichizo, to talk about my ideas for new patterns and colour combinations.

Once I appeared in a new outfit it was invariably copied by other geiko, and I gave my worn kimono away freely to Older and Younger Sisters whenever they asked. We are trained from childhood to remember kimono the way one might remember any work of art. So we always knew when someone was wearing a kimono that had previously been owned by someone else. This was an important indication of one's position within the hierarchy.

All of this may seem extravagant but it is, in fact, the linchpin of a much larger enterprise.

The kimono business is one of the most important industries in Kyoto. I may have been in a position to order more kimono than other geiko, but we all needed a constant supply. Imagine how many kimono the maiko and geiko of Gion Kobu and the other four karyukai collectively order every year? The livelihoods of thousands of artisans, from the dyers of Yuzen silk to the designers of hair ornaments, depend on these orders. The customers who frequent Gion Kobu may not buy kimono themselves, but a large percentage of the money they leave behind goes to the direct support of these craftspeople. In this way, I always felt we were a vital force in keeping these traditional industries alive.

I never thought of kimono in terms of money. They were an essential component of my craft, and the finer the kimono I was wearing, the better I was fulfilling the obligations of my job. Customers come to Gion Kobu to enjoy the appearance of the maiko and geiko as well as their artistic accomplishments. And no matter how accomplished one may be, the hard work is to no avail if one doesn't have the proper clothes in which to appear in public.

In any event, I was still foggy about the whole notion of money. I rarely saw it, seldom touched it, and never paid for anything myself. I did get all those envelopes, the ones with the cash tips in them and realise now that I was probably receiving thousands of dollars every night, but frankly, I wasn't paying attention. I often pulled an envelope out of my sleeve and gave it away as a tip myself, to the *kanban* in the kitchen or to the shoe man in the entranceway of the ochaya.

But there were always more. When I got home at night and took off my kimono, little white envelopes would come tumbling out all over the floor. I never opened these to see how much was inside, just handed over the evening's take to the staff of the okiya as my way of saying thanks, because I couldn't make the nightly transformation into 'Mineko of the Iwasaki' without all of them.

I knew that the term '100,000 yen' (about £650) was used often when people were discussing financial matters. I was becoming curious about these things and one day I asked Mama Masako, 'What does 100,000 yen look like?' She pulled a wallet out of her obi and showed me ten 10,000 yen notes.

'It doesn't look like much,' I said doubtfully. 'I suppose I should be working harder.'

Thirty

I was unworldly in many ways, but now that I was an adult, I felt I should move out of the okiya and try to live on my own. When I told Mama, she was sceptical but didn't try to stop me. 'That's an interesting idea,' she said. 'You are welcome to try, Mine-chan, though I doubt you will be able to handle it.'

In February 1971, when I was twenty-one, I rented a large apartment on Kitashirawa Ave. The rent was around £650 a month, an exorbitant sum at that time. I hired professionals to move me in and decorate the apartment.

As soon as I was settled, one of my girlfriends came to visit. 'Mineko, this is fabulous,' she enthused. 'Congratulations.'

'Thank you, Mari. May I offer you a cup of tea?'

'That would be lovely, thank you.'

I felt so grown up. Beaming proudly, I went into the kitchen to prepare the tea. I put water in the kettle and placed it on top of the stove. But nothing happened. The burner didn't light. I wasn't sure what to do. I had never actually used a stove before!

'What's taking so long?' Mari poked her head into the kitchen.

'Oh, sorry,' I said. 'The gas isn't coming out and the flame isn't lighting.'

'That's because you have to do this,' she said, and flicked on the burner.

I was very impressed. *It was like magic!*

She tells this story to this day. It still gets a big laugh.

One day, I decided to clean the apartment and got the vacuum out of the closet. I pushed it but it didn't start to move. I thought it must be broken and phoned home. Our appliance man came rushing over to see what was wrong. He quickly sized up the situation.

'Mine-chan, the thing about electrical appliances is that you have to take the plug and stick it into an outlet or they won't work.'

'You mean it isn't broken?' Even I was embarrassed at that one.

Next I decided to cook a meal. First the rice. I had already been to the rice shop and placed my order. I went to the shiny new rice canister sitting on top of the counter and opened it. But there was nothing inside! I phoned home.

'My order from Tomiya's never arrived. Did you forget to pay the bill?'

Mama called the shop and the proprietor, with whom we had done business for years, came over right away.

As soon as I saw him I started to complain. 'Really,

Gramps. You shouldn't tease me this way. I really need my order.'

'It's sitting right here in the entranceway, in this bag. The one that says *rice* on it.'

'But why isn't it in the container? I took the lid off and it was empty.'

'Mine-chan, my job is to deliver the rice to your door. You are supposed to put it in the container yourself.'

Oh dear. I had so much to learn.

Before I moved I went to a big department store and charged everything I needed to the okiya's account: furniture, bedding, cooking utensils and dishes. I never looked at the price tag on anything. Mama was horrified when she got the bills but paid them anyway.

However, at that time (before credit cards) we still paid for small purchases in cash. I couldn't charge things like groceries. These I would have to shop for myself. Accordingly, Mama gave me an allowance for incidentals. 'You'll need money for food,' she said and handed me £3,000. I put the money in my purse and went out shopping in the neighbourhood. I found the butcher, and the grocer, and the fish store. I had no idea how much anything cost but assumed I had enough to get what I wanted.

The first shop I went into was a vegetable store. I bought potatoes and carrots and a *daikon* radish. I peeled off a 10,000-yen note (around £65) and gave it to the shopkeeper. My heart was racing. It was the first time I had ever given somebody real money to pay for something.

After handing him the note I picked up my purchases and proudly left the shop. But the shopkeeper came running after me, yelling something. I was sure I had made some terrible blunder and started apologising vociferously. 'I'm so sorry – I'm just not used to this. I didn't mean to make a mistake. Please forgive me.'

The man must have thought I was out of my mind.

'I have no idea what you are talking about, Miss. But you forgot your change.'

'Change? What change?'

'Your change, Miss. I'm sorry but please take it. I'm busy. I don't have time for these games.'

And that's how I learned about change.

Now I was really shopping!

Returning home, full of a sense of accomplishment, I decided to make a meal. The first thing I cooked was a huge pot of *nikujaga*, a kind of meat and potato stew. I made enough for ten people. It took me from noon until four o'clock. When I thought it looked done I wrapped it up, called a cab and carried it carefully to the okiya.

'I've cooked something for you all,' I announced proudly. 'Come on, everybody, eat and enjoy!'

My family dutifully sat around the table and sampled the fare. They each took a mouthful and exchanged looks among themselves. Nobody said a word and nobody was chewing.

Finally Kuniko spoke up. 'It's not bad for your first try.'

Mama and Auntie Taji were looking at their plates. They still hadn't said anything. I was insistent.

'Relish and be thankful for whatever you are served. Isn't that what the Buddha taught. Isn't it?'

Mama said, 'That's true, but everything has its limits.'

'Meaning what, exactly?'

'Mineko, did you bother to taste this before serving it to us?'

'I didn't have to. I could tell it was good from the way it smelled.' Shows you what I knew about cooking.

'Here. You take a bite.'

It was absolutely the strangest thing I have ever tasted. I was actually impressed with myself that I could have concocted something that tasted so weird.

My first reaction was to spit it out, but I held back. If the others had managed to get down one or two mouthfuls, then I would, too. I remembered my father's dictum: 'The samurai betrays no weakness when starving.' But this time I changed it to, 'The samurai betrays no weakness when eating,' and swallowed hard.

Standing up, I said, 'Oh dear. I definitely need more practice,' and started to leave.

'What shall we do with the leftovers?' Kuniko called after me.

'Bin them,' I chuckled, as I hurried out of the door. My prospects for independent living did not look good.

I still came to the okiya every day to get dressed for work. Mama kept asking when she was going to meet my beau. I hadn't spent any time with Toshio outside of the ochaya, but our three-year contract would be up that May. I decided that I'd better get her opinion, so I made arrangements to introduce them.

If I reminded her once, I reminded her a hundred times: 'Promise me you will dress as simply as possible.'

She came out looking as if she was going to a wedding. She was wearing a formal black kimono.

'Mama! What are you doing in that get-up?' I burst out. 'After you promised! Please go back to your room and change into something simpler.'

'But why? Don't you want me to look nice when I meet your friend?'

'Just change. *Please.*'

'Into what?'

'Any old thing will do.'

'I don't understand you, Mineko. Most girls want their mothers to look pretty.'

'Well, I don't. Especially if you look prettier than I do.'

We were sniping at each other before we even left the house.

We met at Toshio's customary ochaya. The meeting didn't go well. I was totally unhinged. Thinking of Toshio as a customer was one thing; thinking of him as my boyfriend was another matter entirely. I became painfully self-conscious, couldn't think of anything to say, was blushing from head to toe and my mind was as white as a blank sheet of paper. It was agony.

My hand shook as I went to serve the sake. My professional composure had completely disappeared. When we got home, Mama taunted me mercilessly. 'Mine-chan, I've never seen you in such a state. It was a riot, everybody. Our cool princess was blushing to the roots of her hair. She was trembling so badly she could hardly pour the sake. And she was tongue-tied. This is great. I think I've finally found your weak spot.'

I had known all along that introducing them would be a mistake.

Thirty-one

On 23 May, 1971, three years to the day that I laid down my challenge, I received a message from Toshio through the okasan of his ochaya asking me to meet him at the Ishibeikoji Inn. The message said there was no need for me to come in costume. This meant it was a private meeting, not an ozashiki. Plus it was noontime.

So I wore a simple kimono of black Oshima pongee patterned with red roses, and a red and white obi patterned with embroidered maple leaves done in black.

When I arrived at the inn Toshio was playing mahjong with a group of his friends. The game soon finished and the other people left. Except for that one stolen kiss, it was the first time I had ever been alone in a room with him.

He came right to the point.

'I have come to see you every night for the last three years, just as you asked. Now I want to talk about us. Do I stand a chance? What are you thinking?'

I wasn't thinking. I was feeling. I knew he had a wife and

children, but right then it didn't seem to make a difference. I couldn't help myself. I answered honestly.

'I'm not sure. I mean, this has never happened to me before. But I think I'm in love with you.'

'In that case,' he said, 'I think we should make the proper arrangements so that we can be together.'

I demurely cast my eyes downward and silently nodded yes. We got up and went directly to see the okasan of the ochaya. She listened while he explained the situation. I can't imagine that she was surprised by what he had to say.

'Toshio-san, you are one of my most valued customers,' she responded, 'and the two of you truly seem to care about each other. For these reasons, I will agree to become party to this discussion. However, things must go through the proper channels. If you want to be with Mineko, you must first receive permission from her family.'

I knew the rules. I was in such a tizzy that I had forgotten them.

The 'flower and willow world' is a society apart, complete with its own rules and regulations, its own rites and rituals. It allows for sexual relationships outside of marriage, but only if those relationships adhere to certain guidelines.

Most long-term relationships in Japan, such as those between man and wife and teacher and disciple, are arranged by a third party who continues to act as a go-between even after the two have been joined. Thus, Mother Sakaguchi arranged my apprenticeship to the Iemoto and remained ready to intervene whenever there was a problem. The okasan of the ochaya was making a serious commitment when she agreed to be a 'party to the discussion'. It effectively meant that she was accepting the role as our go-between. On her advice we immediately went to the okiya to confer with Mama.

'I believe that people who love each other should be together,' she said, ever the romantic.

Toshio promised Mama Masako that he was going to divorce his wife. Mama Masako gave us her blessing.

Begging illness, I cancelled all my appointments for the rest of the day and returned with Toshio to the inn. We went to his room. Neither of us said much at first. We just sat there, resting in each other's presence. Finally we began to speak, bits and pieces of conversation. Out of habit, our talk turned to aesthetics. The afternoon gradually faded into evening.

A maid served us dinner in the room. I could hardly swallow a thing. Then she returned to tell us that the bath was ready. I had already bathed twice that day, once when I got up in the morning and once before I got dressed to come and see Toshio, so I declined.

I wasn't planning on spending the night and was surprised when the maid laid out two sets of futon, side by side. I wasn't sure what to do so I kept talking. Knowing his unending interest in the arts, I brought up one topic after another: music, dance, the theatre. Before I knew it, midnight had come and gone.

Toshio said, 'Mineko, don't you want to get some sleep?'

'Thanks,' I said, with as much energy as I could manage,

'but I don't sleep much. I'm still wide awake, but please, why don't you lie down and rest?'

I was struggling to keep my eyes open and hoping that Toshio would simply fall asleep so I wouldn't have to make any kind of decision. He stretched out on top of one of the futon, without getting under the covers, and kept right on talking. I stayed where I was, sitting at the low table. Neither of us changed position until the sky began to brighten.

When I couldn't hold my head up any longer, I decided to stretch out for a little while but promised myself I wouldn't fall asleep. I lay down gingerly on the second futon. I thought it was rude to turn my back on Toshio so I lay facing him, curled up like a shrimp. He asked me to come closer.

'I'm terribly sorry,' I answered, 'but I don't think I can do that.'

So he made the first move. He edged closer. Then he put his arms around me and pulled me to him in a snug embrace. I lay there stiff as a board, though inside I was trembling and trying not to cry. We barely moved from that position until the sun was up.

'I have to get to class,' I said, and got up to leave, thus ending our first night together.

Now that I was a fully-fledged geiko I began to take some time off, a week in February after the *Setsubun* holiday and another one in the summer. That year I planned on taking a short vacation when the Gion Matsuri was over. Toshio had to go to Brazil on business. We decided to take advantage of this unexpected opportunity and rendezvous in New York City when he was finished.

Toshio flew into Kennedy on his way home to Japan, and I took a Pan Am flight to meet him at the airport. He had to wait for me for six hours. Toshio wasn't used to waiting for anything, though he was definitely in the habit of making other people wait for him. I half-expected him not to be there when I arrived, but he was. I was overjoyed to see him standing there when I walked off the plane.

We went to the Waldorf-Astoria Hotel. We ran into Elizabeth Taylor in the lobby while we were checking in and chatted for a few moments. But we couldn't wait to get up to the room, and rushed off as soon as it was polite to do so. I couldn't wait to be alone with him. When the bellboy shut the door, I turned towards Toshio, who promptly burst out crying. I had never seen a grown man weep like that before.

'Oh, my darling, whatever happened?' I asked, concerned. 'What's wrong?'

'I've tried everything I can think of, but my wife absolutely refuses to give me a divorce. I don't know what else to do. It doesn't seem to matter what I do. Or what I say.'

Toshio sounded on the edge of despair. He talked to me for hours. About his wife. About his children. About his anguish over the whole situation. I was too concerned for him to think about myself. I couldn't stand seeing his pain, and, at last, I reached out to him. For the first time. I put my arms around him and felt him sink fully into my embrace. This intense closeness, I thought, this is love. This is it.

I put two final conditions on our relationship.

'I will stay with you as long as it takes to convince her. But you have to promise me two things. You will never keep secrets from me and you will never tell me a lie. If you do, it's over. No questions asked. You'll go your way and I'll go mine.'

He promised, and I was his.

I was amazed at the power of the animal lust that we unleashed in each other. I opened myself to him hungrily, feeling no shyness or shame. The spectre of my nephew's assault was laid to rest on that bed.

When I looked down and saw the blood on the sheets my heart leapt with joy. I had given Toshio my most precious possession, and had done so in love. In one way it was the first time for both of us. He told me that he had never deflowered a virgin before. I was filled with indescribable happiness.

That night some of Toshio's fans were throwing a reception for him. He was ready to leave before I was and I told him to go ahead while I took my bath. I still had to put on my make-up and kimono, and I said I would follow in half an hour.

After my little bath, I got out of the tub and went to open the bathroom door. The knob wouldn't turn. It was broken. I pulled and pushed but it wouldn't budge. I started banging on the door. Toshio had already left and there was no one else to hear me. I looked around and, lo and behold, there was a telephone next to the mirror. I picked it up. There was no dial tone. I clicked the hook a few times. Still nothing. I couldn't believe that both the doorknob and the phone were broken, and in the Waldorf-Astoria no less.

I sat inside that bathroom for three hours. I was cold and miserable. Finally I heard a noise inside the room. Toshio knocked on the door.

'Mineko, what are you doing in there?'

At least one of us was calm!

He responded quickly to the hysteria in my voice and found someone to open the door. I was thrilled to see him. But I was too exhausted by the events of the day to go out. Poor Toshio! He had been so distracted at the party that he completely lost track of time. He felt terrible. It was very endearing. He was actually a very considerate man. Apart from this little incident, we spent a glorious four days together in New York City.

I had found what I was looking for. I was madly in love, and the intensity of our passion made a profound difference in my life. More than anything else, it affected my dancing, which attained the expressiveness I had been seeking for so long. Emotion seemed to flow from my heart into every movement, every gesture, making them deeper and more powerful.

Toshio took a conscious, active role in this process. He was a serious critic. Our passion was rooted in our devotion to artistic excellence and that remained its source until the very end. We didn't have the sort of relationship where we sat around cuddling and whispering sweet nothings in each other's ears.

As an actor, Toshio had been exploring the boundaries of

self-expression for more years than I had been a dancer. In this he was very much my senior. Even though our disciplines were different, he was able and willing to offer me specific, pointed advice.

The Inoue style is noted for its ability to express great emotion in spare, delicate gestures. This is the most challenging thing about the form, and Toshio understood how one met that challenge. Whereas Big Mistress was mentoring me from within the paradigm, Toshio was able to guide me from outside of it.

Sometimes, passing a mirror, I would unconsciously do some little movement. Toshio would catch me and say, 'Why don't you do it this way?' His suggestions were often spot on. I'd stop whatever I was doing and, incorporating his idea, rehearse the movement then and there, over and over again.

We were living like a couple but had to keep our affair secret from all but our closest associates. He was still a married man. We never betrayed any intimacy when we were out together in public. This was difficult, so we took trips abroad whenever possible. We never had our photo taken together, even when we were being tourists in some exotic resort – except for the rare one in this book.

In 1973 we took another vacation in New York. This time we stayed at the Hilton Hotel. Mr R. A. gave a party for us, and Toshio introduced me as his fiancée. I was elated, convinced that it was just a matter of time before I became his wife. The press got wind that I was having an affair with a celebrity and the paparazzi hounded me for weeks. The funny thing is, they thought I was seeing somebody else; they got the wrong man. Toshio had a huge home in the suburbs of Kyoto and another one in Tokyo, but he spent every night he could with me. My apartment became our 'love nest'.

Toshio made himself very much at home, and I soon discovered a side of his character that was quite unexpected. He was meticulously neat. Given my housekeeping skills, this was fortunate for both of us. When he had some time off and was home alone he would actually clean the apartment from top to bottom. He wiped down all the surfaces, including the kitchen and the bathroom, with a damp cloth and then a dry one, just like my mother taught me to do, though my housekeeping efforts were usually limited to stabbing the vacuum cleaner around the living-room floor and swishing at the coffee table with a dishrag.

In my defence, I was very busy. My schedule was as full as it had been when I was living at the okiya, but now I had to take care of my living space as well. I went to the okiya every afternoon to get ready for work, but no longer had a contingent of maids picking up after me at home.

Most of the time I managed to keep it all together, but then Toshio would do something that tested my competence, like the time he was shooting a movie at a studio in Kyoto. He started coming home late at night with ten or so of his cronies in tow. I would get in from a full day of work and Toshio would say, 'What have we got for these folks to eat?'

I'd throw whatever ingredients we had in the house into

a big pot and cook them up together. My first attempts weren't so great but they got better over time. Toshio made sure that everyone's glasses were filled. No one ever went home hungry or thirsty. I came to love our impromptu parties.

Toshio was endearingly warm and gregarious. He was great around the house, and spoke lovingly of his children. I couldn't understand why things hadn't gone better for him at home.

Thirty-two

In early May the city of Hakata in Kyushu holds an annual festival known as *Dontaku*. I used to be invited to attend every year, and a group of us would make the trip from Kyoto. I always stayed at the same hotel, ate in the same restaurants, and enjoyed seeing my friends from the local geisha community. I always shared a room with my dear friend Yuriko.

Late one afternoon she and I were talking and the subject of the 'silent pilgrimage' came up. The 'silent pilgrimage' is something that takes place during the Gion Festival, though few people know about it. I had heard a rumour that Yuriko went on the 'secret pilgrimage' and I wanted to know if it was true.

The Gion Festival has taken place in Kyoto for over one thousand years, and is considered one of the three most important festivals in Japan. The festival starts at the end of June and continues until 24 July, and involves a number of Shinto ceremonies and rituals. On 17 July the local gods are invited to come into their sacred palanquins known as *omikoshi* and are taken out into the community for the final week of the festival. They are carried on the shoulders of the bearers from the main residence at Yasaka Shrine, down Shijo Street, to their temporary shrines on Shinkyogoku Avenue. The 'silent pilgrimage' takes place during this one-week period.

'I'd like take part in the pilgrimage, too,' I told her. 'What do I have to do to be included?'

'It's not something you join. It's something you decide to do by yourself and you do it alone, in private. But, still, if you really want your prayer to come true, they say you have to do it for three years in a row,' she answered. 'And you can't tell anybody else that you are doing it. That's part of its power. You have to do it in silence. Keep your eyes lowered. Don't make eye-contact with anyone else. Concentrate completely on whatever is hidden in your heart. Keep your prayer in your mind the entire time, since that is the reason for the pilgrimage.'

I was very moved by her description. Yuriko had very distinct features, unlike an ordinary Japanese face. Her eyes were staggeringly beautiful. They were large, with soft brown centres. She didn't explicitly tell me what I wanted to know, but she offered me a smile that revealed the truth.

I couldn't stop wondering why Yuriko was making the pilgrimage. What was it that she wanted so badly? I kept bringing it up whenever I had the chance, but she always managed to change the subject. Finally, my persistence paid off and she gave up. She started to tell me her story.

This was the first time I had ever heard anything about her childhood.

Yuriko told me that she was born in January 1943 in a town called Suzushi located on the coast of the Japan Sea. Her father's family had been in the fishing business for generations. Her father also ran a successful seafood company. As a young man, he often visited Gion Kobu.

Yuriko's mother died soon after she was born. Before she was weaned, she was sent to live with a succession of relatives. During the war, her father's company was requisitioned by the military and turned into a munitions factory, but he kept on fishing. After the war, he resumed his business and things were going very well. But he didn't send for his daughter. She continued to be passed from relative to relative.

As his fortunes improved, her father began once again to visit Gion Kobu and resumed his friendship with a certain geiko. She married him and became Yuriko's stepmother. At last Yuriko was able to return to her father's side, and soon a little sister joined the family. I imagine this was the first time that she had known the security and warmth of a loving family. However, her happiness did not continue for long. Her father's company went bankrupt. He became desperate and, not knowing where to turn, passed his days in a drunken stupor until he hanged himself in front of the innocent eyes of his young daughter.

Yuriko's stepmother was at a complete loss about what

to do, and farmed Yuriko back out to her dead husband's relatives. The family she was passed to treated her like a beast of burden, not even giving her a pair of shoes to wear. They finally sold her to a 'slave trader' (*zegen*); these men went about the countryside buying girls to sell into the sex trade. (This practice was outlawed with the criminalisation of prostitution in 1959.) Yuriko was sold to an establishment in the Shimabara pleasure quarter of Kyoto.

Shimabara used to be a licensed quarter where women known as *oiran* and *tayu* (courtesans, high-class prostitutes) plied their trade, though they were accomplished in the traditional arts as well. A young oiran also underwent a ritual called a *mizuage* but hers consisted of being ceremoniously deflowered by a patron who had paid handsomely for the privilege. This alternative definition of the word mizuage has been the source of some confusion about what it means to be a geisha. Tayu and oiran worked under contracts of indenture and were confined to the district until their period of servitude was over.

When Yuriko's stepmother found out what had happened to her, she immediately contacted the okasan of the Yokiya in Gion Kobu and begged for her help. The proprietress got in touch with an otokoshi, who skilfully engineered her move from Shimabara into the okiya. Yuriko did not want to return to her stepmother and the okiya agreed to accept her into their care.

This all occurred when Yuriko was twelve years old.

Yuriko was very good-natured and applied herself unflaggingly to her lessons, eventually becoming one of the top geiko in Gion Kobu. Whenever she talked about how much better her life was in Gion Kobu than it had been for the first twelve years, those beautiful big brown eyes of hers filled up with tears.

Two years after she first told me this story, when we were back in Hakata, she finally confided in me her reason for making the 'silent pilgrimage'. She had been in love with a certain man for many years and she wanted to marry him. That is the reason. This is what she prayed for every summer during her silent pilgrimage. Her mind was made up, and even though she received proposals from many other men, she completely ignored them.

Unhappily, for political reasons, her lover ended up marrying someone else, though they continued to maintain a relationship. In May 1980 she was diagnosed with cancer. I don't know if he was the reason she fell sick, but her love for him got even stronger after she became ill. As if in answer to her prayers, he nursed her tenderly as she lay dying. Unfortunately, his efforts were in vain and she met her end on 22 September, 1981 at the young age of thirty-seven. In my mind I believe that her love for him still exists and that it will continue on for a thousand years, or into eternity.

Setsubun falls in the middle of February. It is a holiday that used to mark the beginning of spring in the old, lunar calendar. We celebrate the occasion by scattering beans around the house to drive out evil demons and usher in good luck.

In Gion Kobu we used Setsubun as an excuse to dress up in silly costumes and party. My friends and I always chose costumes that were thematically related to events of the previous year. In 1972 the United States returned Okinawa to Japanese control so that year we dressed up in Okinawan folk costumes.

This group of friends and I were in the habit of using the tips we made during the Setsubun parties to pay for a Hawaiian vacation. We went to almost forty ozashiki, spending as little as three minutes at each one in order to maximise our tips. That night we made over £20,000, enough to travel in style.

It was my turn to be tour director. Besides making the reservations, I was in charge of all our money and passports, which I was carrying with me in my bag when we left Kyoto. We were going to spend the night in Tokyo before leaving for Honolulu the next day.

Unfortunately, I left my bag in a taxi on the way to our hotel. My travel mates were not very sympathetic. They said, 'Oh, Mineko, it's just like you to do something like this.' I was trying very hard to be responsible and was incensed by their reaction.

I had to get us new money and passports by the next afternoon, so I contacted one of my customers and explained my predicament. He kindly agreed to loan me £20,000 in cash. I asked him to bring it to the hotel the following morning. I was deciding which of my government friends to tap for emergency passports when I got a call informing me that a businessman had discovered my bag in the back of the taxi. The taxi driver brought it to a police station where I retrieved it the next morning, in time to make our plane. In the hubbub I forgot to tell my customer that I no longer needed the cash and he came running in with it just as were leaving.

Despite this inauspicious beginning we had a wonderful time. In the end, my friends thanked me for being a great tour leader. One afternoon we took hula lessons on a sunset cruise and the teacher could tell we were dancers. She asked us to perform something for her. It was so much fun that we ended up giving Inoue-style dance lessons on the cruise for the next three days. Many of our customers were well connected in Hawaii and they arranged wonderful dinners for us on Kuai and Oahu.

One day the breeze was gently blowing Miss M's hair. I had never noticed just how pronounced her bald spot was. Then I looked closely at my other two friends. And then at myself.

All four of us had big bald spots right on the top of our crowns. This is a common problem caused by the maiko hairstyles, which start by binding the hair at the crown of the head. The mass is kept in place with a strip of bamboo that places constant stress on the roots of the hair. Our hair stays up for five days at time, and the bamboo irritates the scalp as well. When the scalp itches we often scratch it with the pointed tip of a hair ornament, further breaking the hair at the root. After a number of years the spot eventually becomes bald.

'You know what?' I suggested. 'I think that after we get

back to Japan, when the *Miyako Odori* is finished, we should all check into a hospital together and have our bald spots fixed. What do you think? Shall we make a pact?'

They agreed to think about it.

We went into rehearsal as soon as we returned to Kyoto. I had to prepare a solo piece as well as participate in group rehearsals, plus I was asked to help the younger dancers prepare their parts. We didn't have time to talk about the surgery again until after the *Odori* opened. Miss Y said she was too scared to have it done, but the other three of us decided to go ahead. We left for Tokyo the day the *Odori* closed and checked into a hospital near Benkei Bridge.

The operation consists of snipping the bald skin and pulling the edges together to tighten it, similar to a facelift. My incision was closed with twelve teeny stitches. There are many capillaries in the scalp and the operation was surprisingly bloody, though successful. Except it really hurt to laugh.

Our biggest problem was, we were stuck in the hospital for days. Our Tokyo customers did their best to entertain us. They came by to visit and sent in food from the best restaurants in town. But it was springtime and we were frisky. We got bored and started to bicker, so I made up adventures to amuse us. One afternoon we sneaked out to go shopping. Then we started to sneak out at night to go to our favourite restaurants, even in our bandages. We'd creep back into the hospital in the middle of the night. Another afternoon we line-danced our way to the petrol station down the block.

The head nurse was furious: 'This is not a psychiatric hospital. Stop acting like madwomen. And please stop tying up all our telephone lines.'

After ten days or so the doctor removed our stitches and we were free to go. I think the nursing staff were very happy to see us leave. I wonder if Miss Y still has her bald spot. I bet she does.

Back in Kyoto, I easily slid into my normal routine with Toshio. I had missed him. But all of a sudden, living on my own seemed like more trouble than it was worth. It was a real strain for me to cook meals, clean the house, do the wash, and prepare the bath on top of honouring my professional commitments. There was never enough time. I only slept a few hours a night as it was. I couldn't reduce my nightly engagements, so the only way I could find more time was to shorten the hours I spent rehearsing. It came down to becoming a better dancer or keeping a clean house. There was no contest.

I went to speak to Mama. 'Mama, my cooking isn't getting any better and I don't have enough time to rehearse as much as I need to. What do you think I should do?'

'Have you considered moving back here?'

'I don't know. What do you think?'

'I think it's a good idea.'

So that was that. I moved back into the okiya in June 1972. I had learned that I was capable of being independent, but also that I did not have to be. Besides, Toshio and I had the means to stay at a hotel whenever we wanted, and this we did frequently. I was grown up, a fully-fledged geiko. I knew how to move around in the world. I knew how to handle money and how to shop. And I was in love.

I'm very glad I moved back home when I did because it meant I was there for the last few months of Big John's life. He died on 6 October, 1972.

Thirty-three

On 6 May, 1973 I paid a visit to my parents. It was only the third time I had been back to the house since I left it eighteen years before.

I had heard my father was dying and I wanted to see him once more. When I looked in his eyes I could see that the end was near and that he knew it, too. Instead of offering false words of comfort I spoke to him honestly and openly.

'Dad, I want to thank you for everything you have given me in this life. I am capable and strong and will always remember everything you taught me. Please go freely. There is nothing to worry about here. I will take care of whatever needs to be done.'

Tears streamed down his face.

'Masako, you are the only one of my children who truly listened. You never did let go of your pride, and you have made me very happy. I know how hard you have worked and what it has cost you, and I want to give you something. Open the third drawer of my bureau. Take out the *shibori*

294

obi. Yes, that one. I made it myself and it's my favourite. When you find the man of your dreams, I want you to give it to him.'

'I will, Dad, I promise.'

I took the obi from my father's chest and took it with me. I kept it until I met my husband. I gave it to him. He still wears it.

My father died three days later, on 9 May. He was seventy-six years old. I sat beside his corpse and held his cold hand in mine. 'I promise you, Dad. I will never forget:

The samurai betrays no weakness, even when starving.
Pride above all.'

Even though we only lived together for a few years I had always adored my father and kept him very close to me in my heart. I was immensely saddened by his death.

Mama Masako had given me some money. I took the purple silk wrapper out of my obi and handed it to my mother. I didn't know how much it was, but I imagine quite a bit.

'I'm not sure if this is enough,' I told her, 'but I want you to give Dad the kind of funeral he would have wanted. If you need more, please ask Kuniko or me for the rest.'

'Oh, Ma-chan, thank you so much. I'll do the best that I can. But not everybody around here listens to what I have to say.'

As she spoke, she glanced towards the other room. Yaeko's low, sardonic laugh came drifting in over the sound of clinking mahjong tiles. I felt bad, but there was little else I could do. As an adopted member of the Iwasaki family I was unable to help my mother in any sort of official capacity.

I looked at her with empathy and said, 'Mum, I want you to know that I never stopped loving you, or Dad, and I never will. Thank you so much for giving me this life.'

I bowed then, and left.

When I got home Mama Masako asked me, 'Did you give your mother the money for the funeral?'

'Yes, I handed her whatever was in the purple silk wrapper.'

'Good. It's important that you learn to spend money wisely, to use it at the proper times. It is acceptable to send gifts of congratulations after the fact, but not gifts of bereavement. These should be offered in a timely fashion. This is one occasion when it is important not to be stingy. We wouldn't want to lose face. Now make sure your mother has enough. If she doesn't, I will cover the additional expenses.'

This was very generous of her. And I was glad she was finally teaching me how to use money properly. But when you think about it, the money she gave me to give my mother was money I had earned myself.

Another major event of 1973 was that I received accreditation (*natori*) from the Inoue School, naming me a master dancer. The main advantage in becoming a natori is that one is allowed to learn and perform certain roles that are reserved for the master dancers. For the *Onshukai* that autumn I was assigned the role of Princess Tachibana, one such part.

Big Mistress stood with me behind the curtain as I was about to make my entrance onto the *hanamichi*, the elevated passageway that runs from the rear of the theatre to the stage. She leaned over and whispered in my ear, 'All I am able to do is teach you the form. The dance you dance on stage is yours alone.'

The transmission was done. I was free. The dance was mine.

But being certified did not mean I was allowed to teach. Only teachers trained from the beginning as such were allowed to do that. Nor did it mean I could perform outside of the strictly controlled world of the Inoue School or the Kabukai. I still had to follow their rules. So, while it was nice for my career, the certificate was practically useless. It did not contribute in any way to a state of professional or financial independence.

In midsummer Kyoto celebrates *Obon* (All Souls' Day) by lighting a huge bonfire on a mountainside to guide the souls of our ancestors back to their otherworldly abodes. The fire can be seen from anywhere in the city.

In Gion Kobu we fill black lacquer trays with water and place them on the verandahs of the ochaya to capture the reflection of the flames. People attending an ozashiki that evening take a sip of the water from the tray and say a prayer for good health. This ceremony informally signals the beginning of the summer holiday.

I used to spend a week or so each August in Karuizawa, Japan's premier summer resort. I didn't consider this a vacation. It was more like a business trip. Many government and business leaders have country homes in Karuizawa, along with the aristocracy, who have traditionally retreated to this mountain haven during the steamy hot season. The present Emperor of Japan, Akihito, met Empress Michiko on the tennis court in the middle of town in the 1950s.

I spent my evenings going from one residence to another, entertaining the powerbrokers and their houseguests. Sometimes I would bump into Big Mistress as she was making her own rounds. She was a different person when she was in the country, kinder somehow and not as sombre. She would sit down and we would talk.

She told me what it was like during the war. 'There was so little food. We were all hungry. I went from place to place, spread a mat out on the floor, and danced. People gave me rice and vegetables. That is how I fed my students. It was a hard life. I thought it was never going to end.'

I liked hearing her stories. I could see flashes of the spirit she must have had when she was younger.

The mornings in Karuizawa were my own, and I luxuriated in the relaxation. I got up at 6 a.m. and went for long walks. Then I read until it was time for me to meet Tanigawa Sensei at the Akaneya Café at ten o'clock. Dr Tanigawa and I spent many precious hours together during those long summer days. I was able to ask him anything I wanted. He never seemed to tire of giving me well-thought-out answers.

He loved a good cup of coffee and ordered a different variety every day. Instant geography lesson. He would delight in describing to me the part of the world where the coffee came from. One thing led to another and, before we knew it, it was time for lunch. There was a soba restaurant across the street from the café. We ate there often.

Many of my friends were in Karuizawa at the same time I was. Most of them travelled about on bicycles but I didn't know how to ride. I was too embarrassed to admit it, so I walked around pushing a bicycle by its handlebars. I don't know who I thought I was kidding.

One day I ran into someone I knew.

'Hello there, Mineko. How are you? And what are you doing?'

'What does it look like I'm doing? I'm pushing this bike.'

'Really? Just think, I always thought bicycles were something that one sat on and pedalled. I never knew you were supposed to push them.'

'Very funny. If I knew how to ride this I would.'

'You mean you can't ride?'

'Obviously not.'

'Then why don't you ride about in a horse carriage?'

'Wouldn't that be lovely!'

'Come with me, then. My treat.'

She took me to a nearby hotel and ordered me a horse carriage. I left the bicycle in the drive and spent the afternoon riding around by myself. I must say, I felt like royalty. I was having a grand time.

I passed by one of my friends.

'Mineko,' she called out. 'What are you doing hogging that carriage all to yourself?'

'Watch your language,' I called back. 'Kindly address me politely if you wish to converse with me.'

'Don't be such a twit.'

'Then may I assume you don't wish to join me?'

'You know I do.'

'In that case, please use the right tone of voice. You may begin again.'

'Good afternoon, Sister Mineko. Would you be so *awfully* kind as to permit me to accompany you in the carriage?'

'Certainly, my dear. Delighted to have you.'

Thirty-four

T he Gion Kobu is the only karyukai district in Japan that is allowed to host visitors of state. We are informed of these diplomatic missions months in advance and studiously prepare for them. We read up on the dignitary's country of origin and research his or her personal areas of interest so that we can maintain an intelligent conversation.

I met many heads of state over the years. Each one was so different. There is one evening I remember particularly well. We were entertaining President Ford and Henry Kissinger. President Ford was at an ozashiki in a banquet room downstairs while Dr Kissinger was in one on the floor above. I was asked to entertain at both. I thought the contrast most revealing.

President Ford was pleasant and engaging, but he didn't seem particularly interested in traditional Japanese culture. His ozashiki was rather staid and dull. Secretary of State Kissinger, on the other hand, was curious about everything and kept asking questions. He was very amusing, even mildly risqué. The party became quite boisterous and we all ended up dancing around the room together and singing.

The wonderful thing about the atmosphere of an ozashiki is that when guests get into the spirit of it, as did Dr Kissinger, all distinctions between high and low disappear and everyone is free to relax and have a wonderful time.

And then there are the occasions, like the one in honour of Queen Elizabeth II, where informality of any sort is prohibited. In May 1975 the Queen and her husband Prince Philip made a state visit to Japan. I was invited to attend a banquet for them at the Tsuruya Restaurant.

Even though this was an unofficial dinner, it still had the trappings of a major diplomatic event. I had to show personal identification to the secret service men who were covering the event and it was clear that we were in a restricted zone of specialised security.

We were all in place when the Queen arrived. As we stood to greet her she made a majestic entrance into the room, accompanied by the Duke of Edinburgh. She was wearing a beautiful floor-length dress of pale yellow silk organdy, brushed with a flower pattern suggestive of roses, England's national flower.

We took our seats and the banquet began. The table was laid with elaborate French dinnerware, even though the guests were from Great Britain. The knives, forks and chopsticks were of solid gold and there were large displays of peonies in the middle of the table.

I was seated next to the Queen. In these situations we are not allowed to speak to the dignitary directly. If the visitor asks us a question, we have to ask their attendant if we are permitted to answer face to face. Once granted permission, we still have to converse with them through the official interpreter. It is all quite stilted and cumbersome.

Queen Elizabeth didn't touch anything she was served.

'Doesn't Her Majesty care for anything to eat?'

'Is Her Majesty not feeling well?'

I tried my best, through the interpreter and the attendant, to encourage conversation but the Queen didn't choose to reply. Since I was working, I couldn't enjoy any of the sumptuous feast myself. My mind began to wander. I spent some time studying, as discreetly as possible, the jewellery that the Queen was wearing: her earrings, her necklace, her bracelets.

One of the serving women motioned for me to come outside and led me to the entrance vestibule. The shoe valet, a wonderful old man I had known for years, called me over. He had a mischievous glint in his eye.

'Mineko, there's something here I know you would like to see.'

He took a pair of black satin pumps out of a cedar carrying box. They were the Queen's shoes. Each one was decorated with seven diamonds.

'Can I have one of the diamonds?' I teased. 'What if you take one from each shoe and give it to me? I bet she wouldn't notice.'

'Stop your foolishness,' he chided me. 'I just wanted to show them to you.'

I vented my annoyance. 'Queen Elizabeth hasn't eaten one

morsel of the food that she's been served. Isn't that awful? Everyone worked so hard to prepare this wonderful meal.'

'You don't want to be disrespectful now, Mineko. People in foreign countries eat different things than we do so maybe she can't eat what she's been given.'

'But that doesn't make any sense. You know how these things work. Every little detail is agreed upon beforehand. I don't care if she's a Queen, I still think it's terribly rude.'

I mean, the head chef of the Tsuruya didn't just get up that morning and think, Oh, the Queen is coming today. Whatever shall I cook? I was sure that he had been planning the menu for months and that every item had been sanctioned by the Queen's people. How could she refuse to even sample a meal that had been orchestrated specifically for her enjoyment? I didn't get it.

The old chap tried to humour me. 'Mineko, I understand what you are saying, but please don't make an issue of it. We don't want to provoke an international incident now, do we?'

At his urging, I finally returned to my post. I continued to sit there quietly, forbidden to engage in conversation without permission, waiting for the whole thing to be over.

Shortly afterwards, the translator approached me. 'Miss, the Duke of Edinburgh wishes to speak with you.'

Maybe this would be more interesting. I went over to sit beside him. The Duke gave me permission to speak to him directly and listened intently to my answers to his questions. He appeared to be very interested in the dances of Gion Kobu. He asked me about the Inoue School, about the differences between being a maiko and a geiko, and many other things about our lifestyle. At one point my eyes inadvertently met those of the Queen. There was a steely iciness in her gaze. It brought out the devil in me.

The Queen still hadn't touched a thing on her plate. I continued to chat with her husband and moved ever so slightly closer to him. I feigned an air of intimacy that I imagined would be imperceptible to most but clear to one. I glanced over at her again. She looked out of sorts. It was nice to know that Queens are human too.

The following day I received a call from Tadashi Ishikawa, the head of the Imperial Palace Agency.

'Mine-chan, what in the world did you do yesterday at the ozashiki?'

'What are you talking about?'

'All I know is that the royal couple suddenly decided to sleep in separate chambers last night, and I had to scramble to find the extra security to cover them.'

'And what could that possibly have to do with me?'

'I'm not sure, but you were the only person who spoke directly to the Duke. I assumed you must have done something . . .'

'But the Duke was the one who initiated the conversation and he extended permission for me to speak to him directly. He seemed to enjoy our tête-à-tête immensely.'

'So that's it. That must be what they argued about.'

'But I don't see why. I was only trying to do my job.'

'Of course you were, but . . .'

'Mr Ishikawa, may I ask you something? I have visited

a number of different countries and I always try to eat whatever my host has been kind enough to serve me. To refuse would be discourteous and, if I were a visitor of state, it could even be construed as an affront to the nation, to say nothing of all the people who have worked so hard to prepare the meal. What do you think? Wouldn't you agree?'

'Aha, Mine-chan, I see. It all becomes clear. And I have to hand it to you, you are a little rascal.'

As far as I'm concerned, there is never an excuse for bad behaviour.

Thirty-five

For five years I believed that Toshio was going to divorce his wife and marry me. During this period he lied to me twice. Both lies involved his family. The first time he told me he had to go out of town on business when he was actually spending the night with his wife in Kyoto; she had come down from Tokyo to see him. The second was when we were returning to Tokyo from San Francisco. He said we had to exit the plane separately because he had heard that there were reporters at the gate. Always looking to avoid scandal, I dutifully complied. There weren't any reporters. When I came through customs I saw in the distance that his wife and children had come to the airport to welcome him home.

I know I said in the beginning of our relationship that lying was unacceptable but life is not so simple. Once we became involved I saw that I needed to give Toshio time to work it all out, to take that final step. However, after five years I realised that he wasn't taking it and I had to face facts. We weren't any closer to being a real couple now than we were that night at the Waldorf. I decided to end the relationship and began looking for the right opportunity. He was kind enough to hand it to me.

In March 1976, Toshio lied to me for the third and final time.

I used to travel frequently to Tokyo on business. When I was by myself I stayed on the Ladies Floor of the New Otani Hotel but when I was with Toshio we always stayed in the same suite on the fifth floor of the Tokyo Prince Hotel. I still remember the number of our room.

We had plans to meet in Tokyo one evening so I checked in to our suite when I got to town. I was arranging my cosmetics and toiletries on the vanity unit in the bathroom when the phone rang. It was Toshio.

'I'm in the middle of a production meeting. It looks like it's going to go on for hours. Would you mind making other plans for dinner? I'll catch you later.'

I called a good friend who lived nearby, and luckily, she was free for dinner. We ate and then decided to go out and have some fun. We hit all the in-spots and discos in Roppongi. It had been a while since I had let my hair down and we had a great time. I got back to the hotel around three o'clock in the morning. One of Toshio's attendants was sitting in the lobby when I walked in and he rushed forward to greet me.

'Are you waiting for me?' I asked.

'Yes, Miss, I . . .'

'Is Toshio all right?'

'Yes, yes, he's fine. But he's still in a meeting. He gave me the key and asked me to escort you safely to your room.'

This didn't make a whole lot of sense to me but I was too tired to care. We got in the lift and he pushed the button for the eighth floor.

'I'm sorry, but that's the wrong floor. I'm staying on five,' I told him.

'No, I don't believe so. I was told you are staying on eight.'

This is very odd, I thought as Toshio's assistant unlocked the door to a room I had never seen before. It wasn't a suite. I turned to say something to him but he was hurriedly bowing his way out of the room. He said goodnight and shut the door behind him.

I looked around. There were my bags, exactly where I had left them. And there were my toiletries, lined up in the same order on the vanity unit. I felt as if I had fallen into the grip of a genie. Too tired to worry about what was going on, I took a bath and went to bed.

Toshio phoned at 4 a.m. 'The meeting should be over in a while,' he said, 'but I'm still here.'

In other words, I wouldn't be seeing him any time soon.

'Why the room change?' I asked sleepily.

'Oh that, I'll explain later. There are people here now . . .' He made it sound as if he couldn't talk, but it didn't ring true. He was hiding something.

The next morning I decided to find out what was going on. I told the man at the front desk, who knew me, that I had forgotten my key. He had a bellboy accompany me to the suite and open the door.

No one was in the room but clearly someone had been. The bed was dishevelled. There were used towels on the floor of the bathroom. I opened the cupboard. There was a fur coat hanging in it and a woman's bag on the floor. Needless to say, they weren't mine.

Since this was supposed to be my room, I had no compunction about opening the bag. I looked inside, and there among the clothes was a stack of photographic portraits of Toshio's wife. The pictures were the kind one autographs for fans. Obviously, sometime after I went out last night, Toshio had my things moved so his wife could stay there. I exploded. How could he! I didn't care if she was his wife. This was our room! And I had been there first.

I heard later that Toshio and his wife had had to make a last-minute appearance on a TV show together. But, still, when he found out that she was coming he should have booked another room, not have my things moved from one room to another.

I shuddered with the realisation of what this meant. Here was the truth. His wife came first. She was more important to him than I was. Why else had he gone to such lengths? If he had simply told me that his wife was coming I would have checked out and gone to the New Otani Hotel. I wouldn't have checked into a room on the eighth floor of the Prince, where I stood a good chance of running into her.

It was all too much. I called Housekeeping and asked for a large pair of shears. Then I tore the fur coat off its hanger, took the scissors and shredded the coat into little bits and pieces. Then I turned her bag upside down and dumped it on the bed. I scattered her photographs all over the pile and plunged the scissors into the centre of the heap.

'All right, Toshio. You've made your choice. Now live with it. *Sayonara.*'

I went up to the room on the eighth floor, packed my bags, and sauntered out of the lobby door. I vowed never to return to that suite, or to that hotel, again.

Toshio showed no reaction to what I had done. He continued to treat me as if nothing had happened, never mentioning the incident.

I expected him to confront me about my wanton spree. In my fantasies, I made restitution for the coat and declared my independence. His refusal to bring it up meant we were locked in a weird holding pattern. I began steeling myself to end it outright.

In May Toshio invited me on a family trip to the Yugawara hot-springs resort. We went with his parents, his brother (also a famous actor), and his brother's girlfriend, an actress. It was not considered strange that I was travelling with this artistically accomplished group. His parents valued the cachet that I brought, as a geiko, to the party and were happy to include me in their circle. They approved of my relationship with their son and we were quite fond of each other.

The resort had prepared a seasonal 'iris bath', a traditional spring tonic to revitalise body and mind. Seeking solitude,

I went into the bath alone and thought about what to do. What to say. How to get out of the situation gracefully. I finally reached a decision. I would say nothing. I would break it off, simply by no longer being available.

Toshio loved to drive. He had a gold Lincoln Continental and a hunter green Jaguar and he drove very fast. The next morning he drove me back to Tokyo and dropped me off at the inn where I was scheduled to stay. As soon as he was out of sight, I hailed a taxi and went instead to the New Otani. Toshio suspected something was off. He circled the block and came back to find me. But I was gone.

I checked into the hotel and threw myself down on the bed. I lay there alone for hours, crying my eyes out. I was still trying to rationalise the relationship: Why can't I let things just stay as they are? I asked myself. What difference does it make if he's married? But the fact is, it *did* matter. I refused to be second-best any longer.

When I had no more tears to shed I called a close friend. I was so well-known at that time that I could walk into sumo matches for free. As they say, 'my face was my ticket'. I invited my friend to join me that evening. She wasn't busy and agreed to go.

We were seated in the sand spray seats in the first row, so called because they catch the sand the wrestlers fling off the stage, and had just got ourselves settled when who should come prancing in but the man himself. Flustered, I made a quick exit. I couldn't bear to be around him. I returned home to Kyoto and, observing proper protocol, paid a call on the okasan of the ochaya who was acting as our go-between to inform her of our separation.

Toshio refused to let the matter drop. He tried to see me but I declined. Even his mother got into the act. She came to the okiya a number of times to speak to Mama Masako and me. She beseeched me to reconsider. 'He is broken-hearted about this, Mineko. Won't you please change your mind?' The more she pleaded, the more sure I was that I had done the right thing.

At last they gave up and it was over. And so this is how it ended. This is how I killed the love of my life. In my heart, Toshio was dead. He became, simply, Shintaro Katsu, the actor.

Now that I was on my own I began to think about achieving real independence. I was throughly fed up with the system. I had followed the rules for all these years, but there was no way I could stay and do what I wanted to do. The whole reason that the organisation of Gion Kobu had been systematised in the first place was to ensure the dignity and financial independence of the women who worked there. Yet the strictures of the Inoue School kept us subservient to its authority. There was no room for any sort of autonomy.

Not only were we not allowed to teach, we couldn't even perform what and where we liked. We had to get permission for everything, from our choice of repertoire to which accessories and props we were allowed to use. This arcane system has been in place, unchanged even today, for over 100 years. It contains no procedure for modification, no avenue for improvement or reform. Complaining or resisting is taboo. As noted, I had been trying to initiate changes in the system since I was fifteen years old. To no avail.

Another major problem is that we performers were and are paid almost nothing for our public performances, even for the *Miyako Odori*, with all of its popularity and capacity crowds. A select few (the teachers) are reported to make fortunes from the operation but those of us who actually appear on stage receive very little. This is after we have rehearsed for a solid month and worked selling tickets. The latter is part of our job, by the way. I often asked my best customers to buy blocks of them as giveaways to employees and clients. I sometimes used to sell 2,500 a season. So we support the dance but it does not support us. And we are not mountaintop sages who can live by consuming mist.

I was now twenty-six and facing responsibility for the continuation of the okiya. I began to understand the pressure that Auntie Oima had been under when she found me. I didn't want to do it. Because of my status, I was besieged with younger maiko asking me to become their official Onesan. I gave them all the same answer:

'The Nyokoba may be recognised by the Ministry of Education as a specialised school, but it will not give you a proper accredited diploma. No matter how hard you apply yourself, you will end up where you started: with an incomplete school education. You won't have the academic credentials or qualifications to function in the outside world. Even if you do very well and receive a master certificate from the Inoue School you will not be able to support yourself. I've tried to change things for years but no one has listened. So, I'm sorry, but as long as things remain as they are I don't feel comfortable taking on any Younger Sisters. However, if you'd like, I'd be happy to introduce you to another geiko who might be willing to act as your sponsor.'

Without Younger Sisters there was no way for the business of the okiya to grow. The geiko with us were ageing. Revenues were down. I didn't want to ask any of my customers for additional patronage, though many offered. I had no desire to incur that level of debt or obligation because of the conflict it posed to the ideal of the independent businesswoman that had been instilled in me by all of my mentors. My options were limited. I had to find another way to make money.

Around that time a friend of mine, who was working full-time as a geiko, opened her own nightclub on the side. There was little precedence for this sort of dual role in the Gion, and her innovative behaviour was severely frowned upon, but I thought it was brilliant.

I decided to try the same thing myself. I would renovate the okiya and turn part of it into a nightclub! Once the club was established I could use the income to support my family and I would be free to do what I wanted. Mama Masako could help out in the club when I needed her.

But I was in for a big surprise. It turned out that we didn't own the okiya! Unbeknownst to me, we had been renting it for all these years. And we couldn't renovate something we didn't own. I tried to talk Mama Masako into buying the house, but my reasoning fell on deaf ears. Her solution to our problems was to hoard money, not to spend it. She had no concept of investing in the future. She thought renting was fine.

I disagreed. So I went behind her back. I called the bank and, based on my earnings, was able to secure a mortgage and buy the property with my own money. But then I ran into another roadblock. The house was over 100 years old so was legally ineligible for renovation: we would have to demolish it and start over. I was ready to go ahead but Mama Masako was completely opposed to the idea.

I was determined not to give in. My load was too heavy. I was appearing in eleven different performance programmes every year. I loved the dancing but it didn't pay enough to support the okiya. The only way I could augment the family income was to increase the number of ozashiki I worked but I was already stretched to the limit. And had been for years.

I still wanted to construct a new building on the site of the okiya but realised that it was going to take some time to convince Mama Masako to go along with my plans. But, as always, I couldn't wait. So I went out, located a space to rent, and found backers willing to invest in a club.

I opened my own place in June 1977, and named it Club Hollyhock. I had a partner who oversaw the operation when I wasn't there, but every afternoon, before I went to work, I made sure that everything was in order. And every night, when my ozashiki were finished, I went to the club and stayed until closing.

Thirty-six

Over the next three years I steered a steady course towards retirement. The nightclub was only a temporary measure. My real dream was to create a business that made women more beautiful. I wanted to own a beauty-treatment clinic and I came up with a strategy to make it happen.

First, I had to have a place. I had to convince Mama Masako to let me erect a building. I thought it should have four storeys. I would put the club on the ground floor, a beauty-treatment clinic and hair salon on the first, and divide the upper floors between our living quarters and rental tenants. This should give me enough income to support the household.

Next, I had to sort out the future of all the geiko and employees who were under the care of the okiya. I would mediate engagements for the women who wanted to get married and help the others find new positions or start their own businesses.

Then I could decide how and when to retire. The press was claiming I was the most successful geiko to come along in 100 years, and I wanted to capitalise on this momentum. My retirement would be a huge blow to the system. I was hoping that the shock of my defection and its repercussions would serve as a wake-up call to the conservative leadership that they had to change things. I wanted to make them recognise that the organisation of the Gion Kobu was dangerously out of step with the times and that, if they didn't institute reforms, the Gion Kobu would have no future.

From where I was standing, the demise of the karyukai seemed inevitable. The organisation was so moribund that it was strangling the very treasures it was mandated to preserve. The reality is that, even at that time, the number of okiya and ochaya in Gion Kobu was dwindling. The owners of the ochaya and the okiya were only focused on immediate gain; they lacked a collective vision for the future.

I couldn't sit by and watch Gion Kobu fade away into nothingness. Maybe there was still time for me to make a difference. I made a radical decision. I would retire before I turned thirty. I decided to actively look for ways to subsidise my income.

Keizo Saji, the president of Suntory, happened to phone me around that time.

'Mineko, we are going to be filming a commercial for Suntory Old and I was wondering if you would coach the maiko on their movements? If you're free, could you meet me at the Kyoyamoto Restaurant at four o'clock tomorrow afternoon?'

Mr Saji was a great customer and I was more than happy to oblige.

I wore a light blue early summer silk crepe kimono with a white heron pattern and a five-coloured obi embossed with a gold watermark pattern.

Two maiko were preparing for the shoot when I arrived, which was to take place in one of the private tatami rooms of the traditional-style restaurant. There was a bottle of Suntory Old Whiskey, a bucket of ice, a bottle of mineral water, an old-fashioned glass, a highball glass, and a swizzle stick on a low table by the window. I showed the younger women, step by step, the proper way to mix a drink and they copied each of my actions. The director asked me if I would mind filming a test.

He had me walk down the long corridor of the restaurant, slowing my steps for the sake of the camera. The sun was sinking in the west and Yasaka Pagoda was glowing on the horizon. We shot this scene a number of times, and then they asked me to open the fusuma to the private room. They timed it perfectly so that the bell from Chionin Temple let out a resounding gong just as I was sliding open the panel.

I sat down at the table and began to prepare a drink. Ad-libbing, half in jest, I said to one of the actors, 'Would you like it a little stronger?' When the test was over and they started to film for real I excused myself and left.

Some days later I was in my room getting dressed for the evening. The television was on. I heard the sound of a gong and the line, 'Would you like it a little stronger?' I've heard that somewhere before, I thought, but I wasn't really paying attention.

Later that night I entered an ozashiki and one of my customers said, 'I see you've changed your tune.'

'About what?'

'About being in commercials.'

'No, I haven't. Although Mr Saji did ask me to give some advice to the models in one of his. It was fun.'

'I think he pulled a fast one on you.'

So it *was* me after all!

That old coot, I laughed to myself. I've been hoodwinked! I thought it was strange that he bothered to come on to the shoot . . .

But the fact is, it had been painless and I didn't really mind. *Would you like it a little stronger?* became the catchphrase of the day. And the whole experience was unintentionally freeing. I decided it wouldn't hurt to accept commercial offers and began to appear in photographs, TV commercials, advertisements, and magazines, and on talk shows. I was glad for the additional income and, whenever possible, used the exposure to express my thoughts about the geiko system.

I added the commercial work to my packed schedule and stayed on this treadmill until 18 March, 1980, the day that Mother Sakaguchi died. Her death was a defining moment in my life. It felt as if the brightest light in Gion Kobu had gone dark. Sadly, she was the last in the line of her style of her percussion. The form died with her.

With Mother Sakaguchi gone, I completely lost heart. Any enthusiasm I still had for the Gion Kobu lifestyle evaporated. My body was already exhausted. Now my mind caught up. Mother Sakaguchi bequeathed me a magnificent chalcedony and onyx obi clasp. Whenever I looked at it I felt not only sad but also forlorn, as if my staunchest ally had gone away and left me all alone.

Four months later, on 23 July, I asked Suehiroya to accompany me on a formal visit to the Iemoto. When we entered the studio the Iemoto was on stage by herself. She finished her dance and came to sit facing us. I put my fan down formally in front of myself.

'I have decided to retire from active service as a geiko on 25 July,' I announced.

Big Mistress began to cry.

'Mine-chan, I have raised you like my own daughter. I have seen you through so much, from your illnesses to your successes. Won't you please reconsider your decision?'

A thousand scenes flashed through my mind: her teaching me, rehearsing me, giving me permission to dance this piece or that piece in public. I was moved by her emotion, but she was unable to say the one thing I longed to hear. She couldn't say, 'Whatever you do, Mineko, please don't stop dancing.' The system wouldn't allow it. When I stopped being a geiko I would have to stop dancing.

My mind was made up. I bowed to Big Mistress and, with a steady voice, made my final declaration. 'Thank you so much for the many years of kindness you have shown me. I will never forget how much I owe you. My heart is filled with gratitude.'

I touched my forehead to the floor. The dresser was

speechless. I went home and told Mama Masako and Kuniko. They both burst into tears. I told them to get hold of themselves, because there was so much to do in the next forty-eight hours. We had to prepare parting gifts for everyone in the community.

Big Mistress must have alerted the Kabukai immediately, because the phone started ringing and didn't stop for the next two days. Everyone wanted to know what was going on. The officers of the Kabukai demanded an explanation. They begged me not to leave. But they didn't offer to change anything.

That night I went to my scheduled ozashiki. I pretended that nothing unusual was going on. Everyone asked me what was wrong, why was I leaving. Basically I just said, 'Well, these fifteen years may have seemed short to you but they have been an eternity for me.'

It was well after midnight by the time I got to the Hollyhock. The place was packed. I was suddenly overcome with exhaustion. I took the microphone and announced that I was retiring from the profession. Saying it out loud like that made it seem more real. I asked everyone to please go home and then I closed the place a few hours early.

I was at the Nyokoba by 8.20 next morning for my class. Big Mistress and I worked on the dance *Yashima Island*, one of the dances that may only be learned by those who have received certification. The lesson went on for much longer than usual. When I came down from the stage, she looked me in the eye and let out a big sigh.

There was nothing left to say.

I pulled into myself and bowed, deeply. This is really it, I thought. There is no turning back now. It's over.

I took a second dance lesson from one of the Little Mistresses, as was my custom, then a Noh dance class and a tea ceremony class. I paid my respects to my teachers, bowed goodbye in the *genkan*, and walked out of the door of the Nyokoba for the last time. I was twenty-nine years and eight months old and my life as a geiko of Gion Kobu was over.

As I expected, my retirement sent shock waves through the system – but not in the way I intended. In the three months after I retired, seventy other geiko also left the business. I appreciated the gesture, though it seemed a little late to be showing solidarity with me at that point. And the powers that be didn't change a thing.

Thirty-seven

O n the morning of 25 July I woke up feeling free as a bird. I stretched out luxuriously in my bed and picked up a book. I didn't have to go to class. The other women in the house were all taken care of. I just had to worry about my 'real' dependents, Kuniko and Mama.

Kuniko's dream was to open a restaurant. I promised to carry her for three years and she was busy planning the new enterprise. If the business was a success she could continue; if it was a failure we would close it down. She decided to name the restaurant *Ofukuro no Aji*, or Mother's Home Cooking.

The only person who wasn't getting ready to go out on her own was Mama Masako. I had patiently explained my plans to her over and over again, but she just didn't get it. She was used to being dependent on other people and had no desire to make a life for herself. She basically liked things the way they were. What was I to do? I couldn't kick her out. When I had stood with her in court and proclaimed 'I want to be adopted by the Iwasaki family' I had taken on a serious responsibility. I was honour-bound to take care of her.

Mama Masako and I had slightly different opinions about what it meant to be the atotori. I understood my commitment to Auntie Oima to mean that I was obliged to carry on the name Iwasaki and maintain its artistic integrity. I didn't equate this with a promise to manage the okiya indefinitely. Mama Masako wanted the okiya to continue.

'Mine-chan, you aren't getting any younger. Have you begun to think about who is going to be your atotori?'

It was time to level with her. I spoke in no uncertain terms.

'Mama, please understand. I do not want to manage the okiya. I am tired of this business and want to leave. If it were just up to me I would close down the okiya tomorrow. However, there is another option. If you want to keep it going, I'll give up my position and you can find someone else to be the atotori. I'll give you whatever is in my savings account. You and your next heir can run the okiya and I'll go back to being a Tanaka.'

'What are you talking about? You are my daughter. How could I ever replace you? If you want to close the okiya, then we will close the okiya.'

It wasn't exactly what I was hoping she would say. I was half hoping she would accept my offer and I would be released from my responsibility to her and for the disposition of the okiya. But life is never that easy.

'All right, Mama. I understand. Then let's make a deal. You are welcome to stay with me, but on one condition.

I want you to promise that you won't interfere with my plans. Even if you think I'm making a mistake I need you to let me do things my own way. If you promise, then I will take care of you for the rest of your life.'

She agreed, and finally gave me permission to raze the okiya and build my dream for the future. I didn't feel any guilt over my decision to close the okiya. I had given the Gion Kobu everything I had and it was no longer giving me what I needed. I had no regrets.

I bought a large apartment and we lived there while the new building was under construction. I wrapped up all the precious costumes and objects that the okiya owned and stored them safely in my new home. The building was completed on 15 October, 1980. Due to Mama Masako's suggestions (read interference) I had to change my plans and the building ended up having three storeys instead of four. But it was certainly better than nothing.

I opened a new Club Hollyhock on the ground floor, while Kuniko opened up *Mother's Home Cooking*. We moved into an apartment on the first floor. I still hoped to set up a beauty-treatment clinic on the second, but in the meantime we used the space as guest quarters and for storage.

I was enjoying the relative ease of my new life. On a dare from some of my customers I took up the game of golf. I took private lessons for a few weeks and was soon scoring in the 80s and 90s. No one could believe it, but I think, like with basketball, golf came easily to me because dancing had heightened my sense of balance and given me an unusual degree of fine motor control.

I began to seriously research the business of beauty and to make plans for my clinic. I tested numerous products and met with a variety of experts in the field. One of my customers offered to introduce me to a master hairdresser in Tokyo who might be of help. My customer's wife set up the meeting and agreed to make the introduction. I called Mrs S when I arrived in town to finalise the plans. She asked me to come by for a chat if I wasn't busy, and, having time to kill, I decided to take advantage of her hospitality. Mrs S welcomed me warmly and ushered me into the living room. There on the wall was the most amazing painting I had ever seen. It was an exquisite image of a nine-tailed fox.

'Who painted that picture?' I asked, humming with the intuition that something important was going on.

'Isn't it a wonderful painting? We are keeping it here for the artist. His name is Jinichiro Sato. I'm studying with him. His career is just getting started, but I think he's very talented.'

I was rocked by a sudden realisation. *I'm destined to introduce this artist to the world.* I knew without a doubt that this was what I was meant to do. It was as if someone had given me a mission.

I asked Mrs S all kinds of questions about the painter and soon it was time for me to meet Toshio for dinner. Over the past few years we had salvaged a friendship from the debris of our relationship. Mrs S and I weren't meeting the hairdresser until later that evening.

'I'll see you at the Pub Cardinal in Roppongi at ten-thirty,' I said as I thanked her for her hospitality and left.

Toshio and I had a nice dinner and then he took me back to his office, since he wanted my opinion of something he was working on. We watched a video of the footage and discussed it. Then he insisted on driving me over to Roppongi himself. I was a few minutes late. I saw someone who I thought might be Mrs S (like Kuniko, I am nearsighted) but the woman was sitting with two people, not one, so I assumed I was mistaken. Then they all started waving me over so I smiled my way across the room to them. One of the men was very young and handsome.

Mrs S introduced me to the hairdresser. He wasn't the one. And then she turned to the other man. 'And this is Jinichiro Sato, the artist whose painting you admired earlier.'

'But you're so young!' I blurted out.

'I most certainly am not!' he countered forcefully. He was, in fact, twenty-nine.

'I love that painting,' I told him immediately. 'Is there any way I could buy it from you?'

'Oh, you can have it,' he said. 'Take it. It's yours.'

I was dumbfounded. 'No, no, I couldn't do that,' I said. 'It's much too valuable. Besides, if I don't pay for it I won't feel as if it's mine.'

But he wouldn't hear of it. 'If you like the painting that much I would really like you to have it.' He sounded completely sincere.

Mrs S agreed with him. 'Be gracious, my dear, and take advantage of his kind offer.'

'Well, in that case, I accept the painting gratefully and will return the favour to you somehow in the future.'

I had no idea how prophetic those words would turn out to be. Meanwhile, I spent so little time talking to the hairdresser that we had to reschedule our appointment for the following evening.

I met Jin a few more times over the next week. He seemed to show up whenever I was meeting Mrs S. Then I was invited to a house party at the Ss' home in early November and he was there. He spent a lot of time staring at me but I didn't think anything of it. He was very sharp. Very funny.

On 6 November I got a call from Mrs S. 'Mineko-san, I have something important to talk to you about. Mr Sato has asked me to speak on his behalf. He wants to marry you.'

I thought she was joking, and made some sarcastic reply. But she insisted that he was serious. 'In that case,' I told her, 'please tell him no. I won't even consider it.'

She started phoning me every morning at exactly ten o'clock to repeat his proposal. It was getting annoying. And apparently, she was doing the same thing to him! She was a clever woman. Jin finally telephoned and yelled at me to leave him alone. I yelled back at him that this was none of my doing, and we ended up figuring out what Mrs S was up to. We were both embarrassed. Jin asked if he could come to see me to apologise in person.

Instead of apologising, he proposed. I refused. He wouldn't take no for an answer. He came back a few days later and brought Mrs S with him. He proposed again. I refused. I must admit I was becoming intrigued by his cocky confidence. My refusals didn't seem to phase him. He came again. He proposed again.

In spite of myself, I started to think about it. I hardly knew the man, yet he had the qualities I was looking for. I was searching for some way to keep the polished aesthetic lustre of the Iwasaki name going. Bringing a great artist into the family was one way to accomplish that. And Jin was an extraordinary painter – of that I had no doubt. I believed then, as I do today, that Jin will someday be designated a National Living Treasure. And it wasn't just that he was talented. He had earned a Masters Degree in Art History from the best art school in Japan, Tokyo's Geidai, and had a profound knowledge of the field.

I wasn't getting any younger. I wanted to have children. I wanted to see what it was like to be married. And Jin was so likeable. There wasn't anything objectionable about him.

I decided, once again, to make an entirely fresh start.

The fourth time he proposed I accepted, on one condition. I made him promise that he would divorce me in three months if I wasn't happy.

We got married on 2 December, twenty-three days after we had first met.

Afterword

W hat happened next?

Since I was to become head of the household, Mama Masako adopted Jin into the family and he took the name of Iwasaki.

I applied for and received a licence to be an art dealer. When I spoke to my backers in the club and explained what I wanted to do, everyone gave me his or her blessing. I met with surprisingly little resistance from Mama Masako. It didn't hurt that Jin was such a charmer and so good-looking. Mama soon developed a big soft spot in her heart for him.

I never did open that beauty spa. The instant I saw Jin's painting my carefully laid plan vanished and another took its place. That one painting entirely changed my future.

I sold the new building. I closed the club. Jin and I moved to a house in Yamashina. I got pregnant.

Mama continued to live in Gion Kobu and work as a geiko. Kuniko was not a good businesswoman and hadn't made a success of the restaurant. She gracefully accepted the change in circumstance and moved home with me. She was very excited about the birth of the baby.

My beautiful daughter Kosuke was born in September. Mama continued to work, but came to visit us every week and was very much part of the family.

Jin is not only a great painter, he is also an expert at art restoration. I was fascinated by this aspect of his work, by the deep knowledge of art and technique that it entailed. I asked to study with him and he accepted me as a pupil. Kuniko wanted to learn too, and joined in the lessons after she put the baby down at night. Both of us went on to gain certification.

My mother died in 1987. In 1988 we built a spacious home in Iwakura, a northern suburb of Kyoto, with large studios for all of us to do our work. My daughter thrived and grew into an elegant and graceful dancer.

I think this was the happiest time of Kuniko's life. Sadly, she wasn't around very long to enjoy it. She died in 1996 when she was sixty-three years old.

In the late 1980s Mama Masako's eyes began to bother her and we agreed that she should retire. She was in her mid-sixties and had worked long enough. She too enjoyed her sunset years and died in 1998, when she was seventy-five.

On 21 June, 1997 I was awakened at 5.45 by a searing pain in my throat. A little while later the phone rang.

It was one of Toshio's assistants, calling to tell me that he had died early that morning from throat cancer.

Toshio's last years were not happy ones. They were beset

with bankruptcy, drug problems and illness. I had tried to help him where I could, but he had some serious issues. Mutual friends counselled me not to get involved and I took their advice.

Three months before he died, Toshio had asked me to come and see him. So at least I had the chance to say goodbye. Now he was saying goodbye to me.

Yaeko retired two or three years after I did. She sold her house in Kyoto and gave the money to her son Mamoru to build a house in Kobe so she would have somewhere to live. Instead, he used his wife's money to build a house and spent the money his mother gave him on women. When Yaeko moved into her new home she learned to her chagrin that she was not lady of the manor. Her daughter-in-law gave her a room the size of a cupboard and later threw her out altogether.

In recent years Yaeko developed Alzheimer's Disease and became more impossible than ever. None of my six remaining siblings or I am in communication with her any longer. I'm not even sure where she is living. It's a sad situation, but I can't help feeling that she is merely getting what she deserves.

My own days are unrestrained and unfettered. I am no longer ruled by the dictates of the Inoue School. I dance when I want. I dance how I want. And I dance where I want.

I am grateful for all the blessings and happiness in my life. It has been an extraordinary journey. I am indebted to my father for the pride and integrity that have guided me safely to this peaceful shore. And to Mother Sakaguchi, Auntie Oima, and Mama Masako for teaching me to be independent and free.

I am often invited to return to Gion Kobu. But now I am graciously welcomed as a guest, rather than a performer, and take great delight in the refined pleasure of attending an ozashiki. I feel nostalgic when the young maiko and geiko don't recognise my face, but they definitely know who I am. When I tell them my name is Mineko, they invariably fly into a tizzy and ask, 'Are you the real Mineko? The legend?' It is wonderful to spend time with them.

The karyukai is changing. When I retired, there was no lack of expansive and generous patrons who were well schooled in the aesthetic intricacies of the *métier*. Sadly, this is no longer the case. It is not clear what lies ahead for Japanese society, but it is safe to say that there are not as many truly wealthy individuals as there once were, people with the leisure and the means to support the 'flower and willow world'. I am afraid that the traditional culture of Gion Kobu and the other karyukai will cease to exist in the near future. The thought that little will remain of the glorious tradition beyond its external forms fills me with sorrow.

Scribner

THE GIRL IN THE PICTURE
The Remarkable Story of Vietnam's Most Famous Casualty

Denise Chong

'Masterly . . . reads like the best kind of novel –
both moving and startling'
THE TIMES

On 8 June 1972, nine-year-old Kim Phuc, severely
burned by napalm, ran from her burning village and
into the eye of history. Her photograph, seen around the
world, helped turn public opinion against the Vietnam
War and is one of a handful of images that remain
branded in the public consciousness. Denise Chong has
written a detailed, humanistic account of everyday life in
the wake of the Vietnam War, as well as a meditation on
the aftermath of celebrity, and the power of an image.

'A fascinating account of the life of an
extraordinary human being'
TIME OUT

ISBN 0 7432 0703 3
PRICE £7.99

Scribner

THE LAWS OF EVENING

Mary Yukari Waters

'Every syllable, every sentence, every story has the grace
of a ceremonial gesture'
Sena Jeter Naslund, author of *Ahab's Wife*

At the end of World War Two, a generation of
Japanese women found itself frozen, as if in amber – the
last representatives of an exquisite, ancient culture. In the
past lay the brutality and defeat of World War II. In the
future was the American Century. *The Laws Of Evening*
brings to life these women in the twilight of a civilization.
Through her astonishingly elegant and authentic portraits,
Mary Yukari Waters takes her readers into the human
heart behind the ritual.

'An exquisite debut. In rich, delicate strokes, Waters
masterfully evokes all the beauty and complexity of
post-war Japan, dazzling with her poetry and strange
wisdom' Kate Walbert, author of *The Gardens of Kyoto*

ISBN 0 7432 4816 3
PRICE £10.00

**POCKET
BOOKS**

MRS P'S JOURNEY

The Remarkable Story of the Woman Who
Created the A-Z Map

Sarah Hartley

Disproving the theory that women can't read maps, *Mrs P's
Journey* is the fascinating story of the woman who mapped
London's *A-Z* and created a publishing phenomenon.
Increasingly frustrated at the lack of proper street maps
of London, Phyllis Pearsall threw herself into mapping the
busy, sprawling metropolis – on foot.

'An inspiring story of female tenacity in the face of a
dark and bewildering city'
PETER ACKROYD, *The Times*

'Intriguing and beautifully written'
SUZANNE GLASS, *Financial Times*

'A richly dramatic story and Hartley makes the most of it
. . . a lively and engaging book'
Mail on Sunday

**ISBN 0 7434 0876 4
PRICE £6.99**

POCKET
BOOKS

HAMLET'S DRESSER
Bob Smith

'A masterpiece' Frank McCourt

'An extraordinarily beautiful and moving
memoir' *Daily Express*

Bob Smith had a difficult childhood, with an
unstable, depressive mother, an unsupportive father
and a severely disabled, beautiful sister, who was
largely cared for by Bob. But at the age of ten, he
stumbled upon a line from *The Merchant of Venice* –
'in sooth I know not why I am so sad' – recognized
himself and found a buoy that would keep him
afloat for the rest of his tumultuous life.

Hamlet's Dresser tells the story of Bob's youth,
and how it was changed – and rescued – by
Shakespeare.

'A beautifully written memoir' *The Times*

'Lyrical prose' *Daily Telegraph*

ISBN 0 671 01824 8
PRICE £6.99

POCKET
BOOKS

This book and other **Simon & Schuster UK Ltd** titles are available from your bookshop or can be ordered direct from the publisher.

Please send cheque or postal order for the value of the book, free postage and packing within the UK; OVERSEAS including Republic of Ireland £1 per book.

OR: Please debit this amount from my
VISA/ACCESS/MASTERCARD . . . .
CARD NO: . . . .
EXPIRY DATE . . . .
AMOUNT£ . . . .
NAME . . . .
ADDRESS . . . .
. . . .
SIGNATURE . . . .

Send orders to SIMON & SCHUSTER CASH SALES
PO Box 29, Douglas Isle of Man, IM99 1BQ
Tel: 01624 836000, Fax: 01624 670923
www.bookpost.co.uk
Please allow 14 days for delivery. Prices and availability subject to change without notice